"Valeria Resta's book is a compulsory read for scholars, students, and professionals interested in Arab politics and comparative politics in general. Not only does this book stand out for providing a lucid analysis of the role of political parties in the success of the democratic transition in Tunisia and its failure in Egypt, but it also helps us understand the consolidation of al-Sisi's authoritarian regime after the 2013 military coup and Kaïs Saied's authoritarian turn that has put an end to the only successful democratic experience in the region after the Arab Uprisings."

Inmaculada Szmolka, *Professor of Comparative Politics at the University of Granada, Spain*

Tunisia and Egypt after the Arab Spring

This book examines the processes of transition from authoritarian rule in Tunisia and Egypt between 2011 and 2014, arguing that differences between the two countries can be explained by the conduct of their respective political parties.

Drawing on a new conceptualization of political parties' agency that considers their unique nature as intermediate and intermediary institutions, the book allows for the identification of those factors driving political parties' choices in processes of transition. Moreover, thanks to the employment of quantitative text analysis on the electoral manifestos of the parties involved, this work offers new data for the study of party systems in Tunisia and Egypt. Presenting a new toolkit for analysis, *Tunisia and Egypt after the Arab Spring* ultimately reveals how differing legacies of authoritarian repression across the two countries can help explain why the Tunisian transition culminated with the 2014 democratic constitution, and the Egyptian transition with the 2013 military coup.

Conceptually, the book will appeal to those working in comparative politics and those interested in processes of democratization and authoritarian resilience. Nonetheless, the focus on Tunisia and Egypt makes the book a suitable read for anyone interested in Arab politics and the MENA region generally.

Valeria Resta is research fellow at the University of Milan and Adjunct Professor at the Catholic University of Milan. Her research focuses on the dynamics of authoritarianism and democratization in the Middle East and North Africa. She recently co-edited the *Routledge Handbook on Elections in the Middle East and North Africa*.

Routledge Studies in Middle Eastern Democratization and Government

Edited by Larbi Sadiki
Qatar University

This series examines new ways of understanding democratization and government in the Middle East. The varied and uneven processes of change, occurring in the Middle Eastern region, can no longer be read and interpreted solely through the prism of Euro-American transitology. Seeking to frame critical parameters in light of these new horizons, this series instigates reinterpretations of democracy and propagates formerly 'subaltern,' narratives of democratization. Reinvigorating discussion on how Arab and Middle Eastern peoples and societies seek good government, *Routledge Studies in Middle Eastern Democratization and Government* provides tests and contests of old and new assumptions.

33 **Altered States**
   The Remaking of the Political in the Arab World
   Edited by Sune Haugbolle and Mark LeVine

34 **Narratives of Arab Secularism**
   Politics, Feminism and Religion
   Youssef M. Choueiri

35 **The Role of the Military in the Arab Uprisings**
   The Cases of Tunisia and Libya
   Ali Sarihan

36 **Counter Revolutionary Egypt**
   From the Midan to the Neighbourhood
   Dina Wahba

37 **Tunisia and Egypt after the Arab Spring**
   Party Politics in Transitions from Authoritarian Rule
   Valeria Resta

For more information about this series, please visit: https://www.routledge.com/middleeaststudies/series/RSMEDG

Tunisia and Egypt after the Arab Spring

Party Politics in Transitions from Authoritarian Rule

Valeria Resta

LONDON AND NEW YORK

First published 2024
by Routledge
4 Park Square, Milton Park, Abingdon, Oxon OX14 4RN

and by Routledge
605 Third Avenue, New York, NY 10158

Routledge is an imprint of the Taylor & Francis Group, an informa business

© 2024 Valeria Resta

The right of Valeria Resta to be identified as author of this work has been asserted in accordance with sections 77 and 78 of the Copyright, Designs and Patents Act 1988.

All rights reserved. No part of this book may be reprinted or reproduced or utilised in any form or by any electronic, mechanical, or other means, now known or hereafter invented, including photocopying and recording, or in any information storage or retrieval system, without permission in writing from the publishers.

Trademark notice: Product or corporate names may be trademarks or registered trademarks, and are used only for identification and explanation without intent to infringe.

Library of Congress Cataloging-in-Publication Data
Names: Resta, Valeria, author.
Title: Tunisia and Egypt after the Arab Spring: party politics in transitions from authoritarian rule / Valeria Resta.
Description: Abingdon, Oxon; New York, NY: Routledge, 2024. | Series: Routledge studies in Middle Eastern democratization and government | Includes bibliographical references and index.
Identifiers: LCCN 2023011543 (print) | LCCN 2023011544 (ebook) | ISBN 9781032217161 (hardback) | ISBN 9781032217178 (paperback) | ISBN 9781003269717 (ebook)
Subjects: LCSH: Political parties—Tunisia. | Political parties—Egypt. | Tunisia—Politics and government—2011– | Egypt—Politics and government—2011– | Authoritarianism—Tunisia. | Authoritarianism—Egypt.
Classification: LCC JQ3339.A45 R47 2024 (print) | LCC JQ3339.A45 (ebook) | DDC 324.261109/05—dc23/eng/20230606
LC record available at https://lccn.loc.gov/2023011543
LC ebook record available at https://lccn.loc.gov/2023011544

ISBN: 978-1-032-21716-1 (hbk)
ISBN: 978-1-032-21717-8 (pbk)
ISBN: 978-1-003-26971-7 (ebk)

DOI: 10.4324/9781003269717

Typeset in Times New Roman
by codeMantra

Contents

List of figures   x
List of tables   xi
Acknowledgments   xii

Introduction   1
A true story 1
A set of puzzlements 2
The argument 5
Contributions 9
References 10

1 **Charting different transitions: Tunisia and Egypt compared**   12
Tunisia 12
   The 'Deep State' tries to control the transition 13
   The 'tabula rasa' 15
   Establishing the 'rules of the game': from the ANC to the National Dialogue 16
Egypt 20
   The SCAF controls the transition 20
   Writing the constitution: parliament's dialogue of the deaf 23
   From the intra-parliamentary to the inter-institutional conflict 26
A matter of political parties? 30
Notes 31
References 33

2 **Demand of representation, power resources, and parties' agency: Political parties in transition processes**   35
Locating political parties in transition processes: defining installations 36

viii Contents

    The necessity of installations 36
    Determinants of installations 39
    A model for parties' agency within installations 41
      Pre-existing social divisions 43
      Institutional incentives 44
      Choices parties define 45
    The invisible hand of upgraded autocracies on parties'
      strategies 45
      Previous opportunity structures and transitional party
        advantage 47
      Political learning and transitional party systems'
        polarization 48
    References 49

3 Homogeneous vs. divided societies? Analyzing the demand of representation   55
    2011–2 founding elections: transitional challenges stemming
      from the emergence of two imagined communities 55
      Islamists vs. secularists and the need for pre-constitutional
        consensus 55
      Why does the religious divide matter? Substance vs. form 56
    Hypothesizing the origins of the Islamist/secular divide and its
      consequences for democratic installations 57
      The political sociology approach 57
      Post-independence state building strategies and national
        fractures 58
    Data collection, measures, and methodology 59
    How divided? 63
      Egypt 64
      Tunisia 66
    The importance of organizational intermediaries 71
    Notes 75
    References 75

4 Unfair patterns of competition and transitional parties' power resources   79
    From leftist protests to Islamist dominance: explaining the gap of
      the founding elections 80
    Blame the founding electoral systems? 83
      The Tunisian electoral system 85
      The Egyptian electoral system 86

The double standard: patterns of competition between leftists and
   Islamists before the Arab Spring 87
     Leftist and Islamist oppositions in authoritarian Egypt 89
     Leftist and Islamist oppositions in authoritarian Tunisia 92
Islamists' supremacy after the Arab Spring: organizational
   advantages and reputation 95
     Authoritarian repression and transitional parties'
       organizational advantages 96
     Divided structures of competition and transitional parties'
       reputation 99
Shape and reasons of the 2011 electoral gap awarding Islamist
   parties 100
Notes 102
References 103

5 Authoritarian learning and transitional party systems' politicking   107
    The religious divide and polarization parties work out 107
      The pernicious effects of polarization within installations 107
      Parties as countervailing mechanisms to polarization? 108
    Party systems polarization in 2011 Tunisia and Egypt 110
      Locating parties on a political space 110
      Measuring polarization in 2011/2012 Tunisia and Egypt 112
    A matter of polarization? 117
    Parties' structuring politics: the importance of the past 118
      Formal structures, political learning, and polarization 118
      Beyond mere configurational explanations: political center
        and polarization 120
    Divided they stood, divided they failed 122
      Coalition-building in Tunisia 123
      Coalition-building in Egypt 125
      Common destiny of repression, incentives for joining forces,
        and the resolution of the commitment problem 127
    Notes 129
    References 129

Conclusions   133
    References 141

Appendix   *142*
Index   *145*

Figures

4.1	Perceived priorities in Tunisia and Egypt, 2011	81
4.2	Suitability of a Parliamentary system wherein all parties can contest elections, 2011	82
4.3	Index of secularism, 2011	82
4.4	Support for gender equality, 2011 index	83
5.1	Estimated party positions in 2011 Egypt and Tunisia	115
5.2	Word weights vs. word fixed effects on the Islamist/secular divide in Egypt	116
5.3	Word weights vs. word fixed effects on the Islamist/secular divide in Tunisia	116

Tables

1.1	Results of Tunisian Constituency Assembly, October 23, 2011	17
1.2	Results of Egyptian Parliamentary Elections, November 28, 2011–January 11, 2012	24
2.1	The installation game	40
2.2	Political parties' installation game	43
3.1	Declared vote intention for the elections of the Constituent Assembly/Parliament	60
3.2	Dependent variable coding	61
3.3	Cleavage-dimensions-related multinomial models for vote choice in Egypt	65
3.4	Vote determinants in Egypt	67
3.5	Cleavage-dimensions-related multinomial models for vote choice in Tunisia	68
3.6	Vote determinants in Tunisia	71
3.7	Wald test for independent variables	72
3.8	Wald test for combining outcome categories, Tunisia	73
3.9	Wald test for combining outcome categories, Egypt	73
3.10	Measures of fit for multivariate models	74
3.11	*T*-test results on two independent samples, Egypt	74
3.12	*T*-test results on two independent samples, Tunisia	74
5.1	Stemming process with arabicStemR	115

Acknowledgments

This book has its origins in my PhD thesis, which was completed in late 2017. As such, I would like to first acknowledge Luca Ozzano and Francesco Cavatorta who, as members of the PhD Committee, encouraged me to publish my findings. From that time to these days that see me finalizing the book (late 2022), lot of things have happened. I have accumulated tons of teaching hours and temporary work to make ends meet; I became the mother of an extraordinary girl; I, like everybody else, have tried to adapt to the restrictions induced by the Covid-19 pandemic, and, in the meantime, I have also applied for dozens of jobs without success. All this in some ways was about to curb my enthusiasm about the arguments pushed forth in this book, and I found the courage (and the time) to submit a book proposal only in 2021.

The act of publishing a book, especially if it needs to abide by some basic scientific rules and to meet the standards of academic production might not be considered a lonely enterprise. An academic publication is rather a social production. This is true for a masculine author, and it's even truer when the author is a young mother working in a patriarchal society. As such, the merits for it seeing the light of the day are not entirely mine. Yet, mine – of course – is the responsibility for the possible evils the reader might encounter through these pages.

Among all the people contributing in some ways to this book, the first one I need to thank for me being here writing an acknowledgment page to my first monograph is Francesco Cavatorta. If I just check on my inbox, the number of emails from him is by far greater than that received by anyone else. During these years he has constantly stimulated my curiosity toward the Middle Eastern and North African political landscape through countless talks, wonderful research projects, and precious publications. His has been the intellectual guidance and the material help I chased after during the solitary years of my PhD. I am also grateful to Vittorio Emanuele Parsi, who was the first to believe in my PhD research project and continues to entrust me with the formation of wonderful students enrolling to his master at ASERI. Much of the merit (or the fault, it depends on the perspective) for my venturing into academia goes to Bruna Soravia and Leonardo Morlino, who supervised my MA thesis. They taught me how to conduct research along with the devotion it requires. At the same time, they were also the first to show me how analytical precision can go hand-in-hand with passion. For the same reasons, I wish to thank Francesca

Corrao who sent me to Tunisia in 2011 to study Arabic. In some way, I never came back. Professors like the ones I named thus far are the reason why University, in many ways, is the best place to be in your twenties and the reason why academic research is so engrossing.

I cannot but thank all the people I met in Tunisia during my countless research trips. In particular, I wish to track my gratitude to Imen Ben Mohamed, Ajmi Lourimi, Farida Laabidi, Hafedh Caïd Essebsi, and Moncef Marzouk. A heartfelt thought goes to Maya Jribi. They are not the only ones I interviewed, but for sure the ones I met the most during this research. Of course, I warmly thank all those people who made these meetings possible and all the other people I annoyed with my interviews even in the heat of 50°C.

At the Institute of Arab and Islamic Studies, University of Exeter, I have had one of the liveliest research periods of my life. It is really hard to understand how such few weeks have impacted so much on my work in terms of focus, availability of resources, motivation and, as a result, academic production. For this, I am indebted to Lise Storm, who hosted me in her department and gifted me with precious intellectual exchanges and sisterhood. Lise is not only an example of a top scholar in the discipline worldwide, she's also a model of curiosity, humanity, and grace and I still keep learning so much from her. I wish also to thank all the colleagues I met at IAIS that warmly welcomed me. For their contribution to the various stages of this project, my gratitude goes to Michael Driessen, John Slapin, Rosita Di Peri, Inmaculada Szmolka and Hendrik Kraetzschmar. From them I've learnt a lot. I wish also to thank all the people at the University of Milan for making my PhD years really important for my professional and personal growth. In particular, I wish to thank Fabio Franchino, Luigi Curini, Francesco Zucchini, Marco Giuliani, Maurizio Ferrera and Licia Papavero.

A special word of gratitude goes to the anonymous reviewers and to Larbi Sadiki who gave me the honor of publishing this book in the prestigious *Routledge Studies in Middle Eastern Democratization and Government* book series. Since this book was written in rather troublesome circumstances, I cannot but thank Joe Whiting and Euan Rice-Coates for making the whole publication process smooth. To them goes all my gratitude for their patience and guidance.

A big thank you goes also to my mother and my brothers. They always keep asking me when I will finally find a "true job." This recurrent question constantly reminds me how lucky I am to have the opportunity of doing what I like to do, regardless of the costs. Thank you, Dad, for the curiosity you instilled in me and the analytical spirit that I hope to have inherited from you. I know I never walked alone and I will never do it.

Last but not least, I wish to thank my partner and our wonderful girl for all the love they spread around each and every day. I won't even try to express here how much I love you and I owe you. Words cannot go as far as that and I don't even think this will interest the scholars and students reading this book. Without you both, this book would have seen the light years earlier, but with you my life is beyond anything I dared to hope for.

Introduction

A true story

On August 16, 2013, I found myself in the chaos of Bardo Square, in front of the Tunisian Parliament, being taught how to remove tear gas from my eyes – with a lemon and a wet bandana as it turns out – by a Member of Parliament. A few days earlier, Moustapha Ben Jaafar, the Speaker of the National Constituent Assembly (ANC, from its French acronym), was forced to suspend the works of the ANC in light of the mounting obstructionism from opposition parties against the Troika government, and in particular its leading party, the Islamist Ennahda. In the background was a context of violence and great uncertainty. The assassination of two prominent figures of the leftist Popular Front, Chokri Belaïd (6th February) and Mohamed Brahmi (25th July) fueled the fears and anger of the left and secular opposition. Meanwhile, garbage had started to accumulate in Tunisian streets to symbolize Tunisians' mounting frustration with their living and working conditions, which had not improved after the Jasmine Revolution. In fact, they had worsened. Many of them wondered whether they had not been better off with Ben Ali; some mourned his departure.

In the same period, five weeks earlier to be exact, mounting protests and street demonstrations against the elected President of the Republic Mohamed Morsi had rocked Egypt, which was in the midst of a struggle between the army and the Muslim Brothers for the control of the process of transition. The epilogue of this arm wrestling was Morsi's removal in the 3rd July military coup led by General Abdel Fattah al-Sisi. In light of this precedent, the fear at that time was that even Tunisia was on the verge of a transition failure, as it was facing its own political gridlock. Yet, that midsummer's political crisis was resolved through a National Dialogue among all political forces, first and foremost Ennahda and its main adversary Nida Tounes under the impulse of the "Quartet" (namely the General Union of the Tunisian Workers, the Tunisian Union for the Industry, Commerce and Craftsmanship, the Tunisian League for the Defense of Human Rights and the National Order of Lawyers), which was later awarded the Nobel Peace Prize for its role. The National dialogue designed a new political roadmap, providing for the adoption of the Constitution, the creation of the Independent High Authority for Elections, the adoption of a new electoral law, and, at the end of this constitutive phase, the Ennahda-led government's resignation in favor of a technocratic cabinet. Both the opposition and the parties in government abided by this roadmap, with the former eventually ending their obstructionism and thus collaborating in the constitution-making process. The new Constitution was finally approved on January 26, 2014, along with the institutions and laws to regulate new elections, which took place later that year and led to government turnover. Tunisia thus gained the status of a democratic country, being the first Arab and Muslim country to enjoy this 'label'.

In the summer of 2013, both Egypt and Tunisia were thus confronted with considerable challenges that had to do with the difficulties of appeasing the political differences stemming from the first genuine multiparty political system those countries have ever had. Both had no prior democratic experience available to them to manage the choices and the conduct of the political parties involved. Ultimately, Tunisia succeeded in transiting whereas Egypt failed to do so. This book discusses why this has been the case, and it does so from the perspective of the political parties involved.

A set of puzzlements

In the light of recent Tunisian events, many might wonder whether it still makes sense to compare the two processes of transitions and, in particular, to linger upon the bases of a democratic Tunisia. In fact, even though Tunisia was considered a democratic success story, it looks now at its future with a great dose of apprehension. On July 25, 2021 (on the anniversary of Brahmi's death), in a country exhausted by the consequences of the Covid-19 pandemic, economic restructuring, and foreign debt, President Kaïs Saïed, who had won the presidency in 2019 as an independent and without the support of any party, dismissed the government and froze the parliament, concentrating executive powers in his hands and ruling by decree. Over the following days, several senior officials, governors, and even mayors were purged and restrictions on civil society organizations were implemented. On February 6, 2022 (another significant date, as it is the anniversary of Belaïd's assassination), Saied dissolved the Supreme Judicial Council, giving himself powers over the career of judges. In April 2022, a temporary replacement for the country's top judicial council was set up but there is no indication as to when this state of exception will be over. In December 2021, President Saied announced the launch of a national consultation process that culminated in a successful referendum on constitutional reform on July 25 and scheduled new parliamentary elections for December, 17, 2022, the anniversary of Mohamed Bouazizi's self-immolation. However, there's no guarantee that President Saïed will abide by his own roadmap or respect the outcome of the elections, with many already speaking of a "*coup d'état.*"

Even though the future of Tunisia does not appear as bright as it once was and the causes of recent turmoil have deep roots, the claim that Tunisia is the sole country that managed to achieve a democratic transition after the so-called Arab Spring is still valid because all the elements denoting a completed democratic transition have been there at some point. As per its main definition:

> A democratic transition is complete when sufficient agreement has been reached about political procedures to produce an elected government, when a government comes to power that is the direct result of a free and popular vote, when this government de facto has the authority to generate new policies, and when the executive, legislative and judicial power generated by the new democracy does not have to share power with other bodies de jure.
>
> (Linz and Stepan 1996, 3)

The state of things described above is, with all its limitations and possible inefficiencies, the one inherited by Kais Saied when he was elected President of the Republic in 2019. His populist electoral campaign exploited the deficiencies of the political and the economic system which, in part, were due to the process of reorganization and reconstruction from the previous regime and, in part, had to do with the fact that the socio/economic demands of the 2011 revolutions have been unmet by the political leadership that replaced Ben Ali and its clique (Achcar 2013). Without entering into a discussion upon the causes of the current democratic backsliding, this work will delve into the factors that brought Tunisia to achieve the democratic installation sanctioned with the 2014 Constitution. Even if such a democratic experience has already stop if not come to an end for some, it still remains an empirical fact that deserves attention for the very reason that, at some point in history, it has happened.

Another issue to be discussed is the necessity of another book on the Arab Spring in light of the significant amount of contributions Political Science and Middle East scholarship has produced thus far. By 2014, Brownlee, Masoud, and Reynold had counted already "over a dozen monographs and edited volumes, as well as countless articles" (2015, 7) and, as of April 2022, the key term "Arab Spring" returns over 3.4 thousand results on Google Scholar. However, the problem of theoretical fragmentation about which the three prominent scholars lamented in their 2015 book, persists. Even though a number of contributions – and their *Arab Spring: Pathways of Repression and Reform* is among the best – have tried to fill this gap, the extant literature does not work with portable concepts and theories, remaining largely anchored to country or regional specificities. The reasons for this gap are not only imputable to timing – such events are still too close – but also to the bias of 'exceptionalism' surrounding the study of Middle East and North Africa (hence MENA). For a long time, this region seemed to escape all the theoretical frameworks and the working concepts in use among students of comparative politics. This was for instance the case with the theory of modernization and the paradigm of democratization which were dismissed in the early 2000s, just to name the two most recent and well-known examples. With the passing of time then, students of comparative politics lost interest in the region and students of area studies and Arab politics started to disregard broader comparative politics and political studies altogether. With a few remarkable examples, the understanding of politics in the region has long been entrusted to regional experts with a solid background in its culture, history, and language. These researchers have enhanced our knowledge of the political dynamics of the countries of the region through the production of several significant works, but the latter remain loosely interconnected and very often unable to travel outside the Arab world. This book assists a nascent, but already sound, body of scholarship by refining a theoretical framework able to account for transitions from authoritarian rule where political parties are involved. This is by no means intended to downplay the role of regional and country specificities, but rather to dovetail them within a broader, and portable, theoretical framework.

Another point of discussion, and one of the major ones this project encountered since its embryonal stage, revolves around the usefulness of focusing on political parties. The rationale for doubting how parties could be a 'device' to understand Arab political dynamics is twofold. On the one hand, on a general basis, it is held that political parties in the region have long been empty vessels manipulated by MENA autocrats and therefore cannot genuinely account for any political development in the region. On the other hand, when it comes to the study of the Arab Spring, parties' role within the processes of transition from authoritarian rule has been deemed to be limited and therefore not useful to advance our understanding of these kind of processes throughout the region. However, such doubts are unfounded. First, the claim that political parties throughout the region do no matter can be refuted. Political parties have been active in the region since the 1970s and are key elements for the survival of autocracy and for ongoing processes of democratization. Hence, even though they might not perform the same functions their counterparts carry out in western consolidated democracies, they are nonetheless important for what they can tell us about regional politics (Cavatorta, Storm, and Resta 2021). Second, the affirmation that transitions from authoritarian rule in Tunisia and Egypt didn't see the involvement of political parties is drawn from an understanding of the processes of transition as analytically unique from the crisis of the authoritarian regime to the phase of installation and consolidation. However, the whole process of transition comprises different phases that need to be approached as analytically different sub-processes because they have different goals and hence see the involvement of different actors. The first sub-process is the revolutionary moment that aims at provoking the regime crisis, which, in the best-case scenario, and at least from the perspective of those provoking this crisis, will lead to the fall of the regime, thus marking the inception of the transition properly. As per O'Donnell and Schmitter, this is defined as "the interval between one political regime and another" (1986, 6). After this *pars destruens* follows the *pars construens*. This second sub-process, defined as the phase of installation, is in fact the one within which the rules of the new game are designed, thus setting up the bases for a new political regime supplanting the fallen one. The end of this phase marks the end of the transition altogether and the beginning of consolidation.

In both Tunisia and Egypt, the revolutionary moment begins in late 2010/early 2011 and lasts, at least formally, until Ben Ali's flight (14th January 2011) and Mubarak's resignation (11th February 2011). This phase is followed by the phase of installation which has its highest point in the constitution-making process after the founding elections in late 2011/early 2012. As it happened in the rest of the Arab region throughout the last weeks of 2010 and the first months of 2011, the revolutions in Tunisia and Egypt were animated by spontaneous, unorganized, and de-centralized forms of activated citizenship. Even the Islamist parties, which at that time represented the most powerful opposition to the regime, didn't have any role in their inception and were quite uncertain on the opportunity of joining them. Despite this, asserting that political parties' role was limited during the transition disregards the fact that they were the key players during the phase of installation. As per the transitional roadmaps the two countries were following, after the founding elections, political parties were the sole political actors entrusted with the task of giving their countries a new (and hopefully democratic) constitution along with all other institutions and laws – first and foremost the electoral one – necessary for the design of new political regime. Political parties were certainly poorly institutionalized and had been weakened severely by the previous regime, but this does not obscure the fact that the design of a new political system was up to them and only them. This basic fact suffices here to choose them as units of analysis.

The remaining elephant in the room we need to tackle here before proceeding further is the role of the Egyptian army. The economic power and the political influence of the Army and the Supreme Council of the Armed Forces (SCAF), which has no parallel in Tunisia, is deemed to jeopardize the most similar systems design which this work hinges on, since, according to this research design, the cases under investigation need to only differ in the dependent variable, which consists here in the outcome of the transition. Pushing this argument further, some might even adhere to the body of literature surmising that the Egyptian transition failed precisely because of the centrality of its military forces (Albrecht and Bishara 2011; Said 2012).

There is no doubt that the political role of the Tunisian and Egyptian armed forces is absolutely disproportionate and that the SCAF played a crucial role in the Egyptian transition. Nonetheless, this work is concerned with what happened from the founding elections to, respectively, the military coup in Egypt and the adoption of a democratic constitution in Tunisia. As we have seen above (and as will be discussed in greater depth in the second chapter), this phase has had just one type of key players, namely political parties. During the constitution-making process, the Egyptian army was as peripheral to the process as it was its Tunisian counterpart and, to say it – again – with Brownlee, Masoud, and Reynolds "it could be argued that the men with guns would have been unable to intervene were it not for the conflict among Egypt's political parties" (2014, 194). Yet, while the role of the Egyptian army does not affect the foundations and the validity of this work, it will be argued that it might nonetheless have had a part in disincentivizing parties' efforts to look for a compromise and, at the same time, incentivizing other behaviors that were equally detrimental to the transition process. The last chapter will delve into these mechanics.

The argument

Having cleared the field of potential objections, *Tunisia and Egypt after the Arab Spring* reappraises the processes of transition from authoritarian rule in Tunisia and

6   Introduction

Egypt with a focus on political parties, arguing that the two processes ended up differently precisely because of the differences in the conduct of parties across the two countries. The objective of the book is to illustrate how and explain why it is so.

Extant actor-centric accounts of transitions from authoritarian rule conceive the actions of the actors involved as driven by their power positions vis-à-vis the other actors and their ideological positions. This understanding draws from the experience of earlier transitions in Latin America and Eastern Europe that were 'pacted' among a limited set of actors and only rarely involved also political actors. In order to enlighten how political parties can explain diverging transitional outcomes across Tunisia and Egypt, this work provides a game-theoretical model for parties' agency in processes of transition from authoritarian rule. The model answers the need of accounting for the unique nature of political parties as intermediate and intermediary institutions. Since they are part of the mobilized public and the relevant political elite at the same time, their governing agency (that is the choices they make once in office) is influenced by their representative tasks. Therefore, any attempt at explaining the rationale of parties' conduct during the transition must take into account these two different layers informing their actions.

As every other game-theoretical model of this kind, within the process of transition, political parties are confronted with two choices: either they decide to cooperate with the other political parties to find a compromise (read constitution) or they defect, thus retrenching themselves in their positions unwilling to negotiate on their most preferred issues. Following our conceptualization of parties' agency, this choice is the result of the interplay between (i) the nature and depth of the social divisions that parties represent; (ii) the power resources they have at their disposal, and (iii) the ideological polarization that divides them. Theoretically speaking, the game has different possible solutions that speak to the fact that cooperation among political parties is to be expected when social divisions are not so pronounced and outweighed by the incentives to cooperate, which is the case when parties are not ideologically distant and/or there is no party enjoying much greater power over the others in terms of seats necessary to pass legislation.

The argument of this book is that (a) the different epilogues of the transitions from authoritarian rule in Tunisia and Egypt are to be imputed respectively to the capabilities of Tunisian parties to collaborate to find a compromise and to the unwillingness of Egyptian parties to do so and that (b) these different dispositions owe to differences in the distribution of power among the political parties involved and in the way the public debate was structured in the two countries, which is in turn largely represented in what we can grouped under the notion of authoritarian legacy.

In Tunisia, there was no party able to dictate its agenda due to the seats controlled in the National Constituency Assembly and cooperation turned out to be the only option to govern and manage the transition. In Egypt, on the contrary, the Islamist faction, that is the coalition between the Freedom and Justice party and the Salafi Nour party (a coalition that this book proves to be not as natural as it appeared), commanded the majority of the Parliamentary seats and did not hesitate to seize the opportunity of imposing its preferred options. Moreover, the way the Egyptian political debate had been structured during the transition was of no help. As the quantitative text analyses conducted on the 2011/2012 party manifestos show, Egyptian parties structured the debate around identity issues, while in Tunisia the political competition involved programmatic issues. This latter finding, while proving once again how detrimental identity issues are for any political dialogue, refutes the most popular hypothesis when it comes to the role of political parties in the processes of transition in Tunisia and Egypt, namely that the failure of the Egyptian transition was due to the higher level of political polarization of the Egyptian party system than the Tunisian one. Drawing from Sartori's definition of polarization, this work shows that the problem was not the political distance among the parties involved in the transition, but was rather the content of their discussions and hence the way they structured the political debate.

Despite being deeply entrenched in the contingency of the political process under scrutiny, both these salient dimensions – that is parties' power distribution and the nature of the political debate – speak to the legacy of the previous authoritarian regimes and on the sway the latter can exert on the course of events even after they collapse. With the adoption of some liberal reforms – e.g. the introduction of parliaments, elections, and multipartyism – to provide their autocratic regimes with a semblance of pluralism, which was a necessary condition to receive loans from the International Monetary Fund and the World Bank, autocrats of the MENA region enacted measures to neutralize the effectiveness of such overtures and maintain their hold on power. Both the format and the content of transitional party politics bear the influence of the way political competition was structured under the electoral autocracies in place until the 2011 Uprisings. The variations across Tunisia and Egypt that explain why the two countries managed the process of transition differently are better appraised by looking at the differences in the strategies of repression and co-optation of the oppositions by the previous dictators.

To begin with, the Islamist advantage observed in Egypt after the founding elections has to do with the different structures of opportunity available to political parties according to the way in which political competition was designed during the previous regime. In Egypt, since Islamists were functional in undermining the power of the left-secular opposition, which were really popular when elections were introduced, their proliferation was first encouraged and subsequently kept under control by alternating period of tolerance with others of repression. Before 2011, Egyptian Islamists, in particular those affiliated with the Muslim Brotherhood, thus contested all the elections as independent candidates. This provided them a double advantage when the regime collapsed. First, they could count on a solid and widespread network consolidated through decades. While non-coopted oppositions were banned from political life and were prevented from employing their traditional channels of mobilization (for instance trade unions, universities and professional associations), the Islamists had the chance to build a "parallel Islamic sector" they could count on for the political support. Second, after Mubarak's fall, Islamists enjoyed power reputation inasmuch as, running as independent in authoritarian elections, the name of their party was never affiliated with the previous regime and therefore were perceived by voters as a real alternative to the *status quo ante*. In Tunisia, the success of the Islamist Ennahha was due to its oppositional stance throughout Bourguiba and Ben Ali's era and has little to do with differences in the structure of opportunities available to political parties before 2011. In fact, while Ennahda successfully infiltrated some mosques, charitable, and professional associations, it was banned and repressed just as the most influential leftists and secular parties were. This can explain why the disproportion between the seats controlled by Ghannouchi's party and the others was not as pronounced. Most importantly, this 'common destiny of repression' (Cavatorta and Merone 2013) is at the root of the inclusive and consensual transition Tunisian parties fostered. This calls into question another entangled feature of the previous structure of competition, i.e. its content.

As Brumberg (2013), among others, brilliantly explained, one of the strategies adopted by previous dictators of the region to maintain their power was to play one group against the others through the politicization of identity issues. Thanks to this divide-and-rule strategy, dictators could then present themselves to the various groups as the ultimate brokers of such conflicts and the guarantors of the protection of their vital interests. The choice of focusing on identity issues is due to their variety and their malleability, which guarantee a never-ending source of conflict. All the parties allowed to operate within the previous electoral autocracies had to contend with such politicking. In transitional Egypt, where the share of parties imported from the previous regimes was larger than the Tunisian one, the political debate revolved (again) around identity for the very reason that this was the one political parties had internalized through authoritarian political learning. Even newcomers joining the competition in 2011 were forced to deal with it in order to position themselves on the political space. The fact that Egyptian political parties obstinately refused to negotiate with the others is a further confirmation of the detrimental effects exerted by identity issues on politics in general (as we can now witness in western consolidated democracies) and especially on the constitution-making process. The politicization of identity issues poses a threat to transition processes because they foster mental reservations around the community one is deemed to belong to, thus undermining national unity, which is a background condition for transitions to democracy. To say it with Rustow "[d]emocracy is a system of rule by temporary majorities. In order that rulers and policies may freely change, the boundaries must endure, the composition of the citizenry be continuous" (1970, 351). Differently put, identity issues hamper the resolution of commitment problems necessary for political actors to trust each other and proceed with a compromising agreement (Przeworski 1991) because they call into question different – and perhaps alternative – allegiances. In Tunisia, such problems of commitment had been in large part settled already before the fall of the Ben Ali regime through the cooperation of several opposition parties and movements united by a common destiny of repression. Different from what is held by some scholars (Cavatorta and Merone 2013), this cooperation was not only conducive to the moderation of the Islamist Ennahda, intended as the abandonment of its radical stances and its rapprochement to centrist positions, but also to the inauguration of a new political discourse based on programmatic issues that has also characterized the transitional period, when those parties were finally allowed to participate.

Contributions

These findings speak to possibly the main meta-theoretical contribution of this book, which goes beyond the inter-paradigm debate between democratization and post-democratization studies that animated the academic community when this research project was first conceived. At that time, the political consequences of the Arab Uprisings were appraised either as the inception of new course of regional politics toward democratic governance (democratization studies), or as regimes' ability to pursue their survival strategies despite popular protests (post-democratization studies or the paradigm of the authoritarian resilience). However, both kind of accounts had insurmountable limitations when employed in isolation. On the one hand, democratization studies, while providing a valid tool-kit for analysis consisting through sound working concepts, fell short in accounting for regional dynamics. On the other hand, post-democratization studies had the merit of illuminating important mechanisms behind the strength of regional authoritarianisms, but were hardly apt to provide for punctual explanations to the process of transitions. After all, it was not "the structures" that failed to lead to an agreed upon constitution, but MPs in flesh and blood.

The theoretical model presented here, like other works that in the meantime have seen the light (Nugent 2020; Szmolka 2015), has the merit of combining the insights stemming from the two paradigms to present an explanation for the different transitional outcomes in Tunisia and Egypt that is theoretically sound and empirically precise. Or, at least, a solid compromise between robustness and accuracy.

Beyond its main results illustrated above, this book also contributes to the scholarly debate around the inclusion-moderation hypothesis which is one of the topics that mostly animate the academic debate around Islamist parties in the region. When Islamist parties surfaced in the late 1980s and early 1990s, their presence posed a conundrum inasmuch as it was feared that their political inclusion could pose a threat to the democratic aspirations of those countries but, at the same time, depriving thousands of citizens to be represented by their most preferred parties was equally against the principles of democracy. Drawing from the experience of the Communist parties in western democracies soon after the WWII, the inclusion-moderation argument tackled both concerns by postulating a positive relationship between parties' participation in the political arena and their moderation, thus contributing to the democratization of the whole political system.

In line with other works, this book invites readers to pay attention to the context wherein political parties are included, suggesting that not all polities are apt in triggering moderation with democratizing spillovers. As this book illustrates through the case of Egypt, political parties, through political learning, tend to internalize the basic norms characterizing the political system in which they operate. While communist parties throughout post-WII Europe internalized democratic practices and norms thus contributing to the democratic consolidation of the countries in which they operated, that might not be the case for pre-2011 authoritarian settings where nominally democratic institutions were trumped by the mechanisms that sustained despotic power. Even though Islamist parties have given up on some of their more radical and anti-system claims, like creation of an Islamic state and the implementation of the *Shari'a*, there is little reason to believe that their adaptation to undemocratic systems infused on them pro-democracy attitudes. In this regard, the case of Egypt, where the transitional political debate prompted by the previously included Islamist parties resembled much the one that was in vogue under Mubarak, is emblematic of the necessity of reassessing the inclusion-moderation hypothesis. Counterfactually, contrary to the expectations of the inclusion-moderation argument, democracy saw the light of the day in a party system – the Tunisian one – that appeared more polarized than the one in Egypt.

Other original contributions of this work have to do with the data and techniques of analysis employed. This work is one of the few adopting quantitative methods for political research in the region. While these are now largely used in the study of politics in many parts of the world, their employment in the study of politics across the Middle East and North Africa remains rather limited. The reasons for this gap have to do with the lack of available data and the lack of quantitative training among experts of the region, and the two aspects are often entangled. This is not to say that we do not have data because those studying politics of the region do not have the competencies to produce them. Indeed, many data – think for instance of party manifestos, which saw the light only recently – are not available for the simple reason that they might not exist. However, it also true that there is much more on the ground than we might think. As a matter of fact, the majority of the countries across the Middle East and North Africa qualify as electoral democracies, but no systematic dataset on the electoral results have seen the light yet, nor were these included within extant datasets covering elections around the world. Having said this, I am not upholding the primacy of quantitative methods over the qualitative ones, but just making the case for their employment for what they can offer to the discipline, as the great number of studies drawing from the Arab Barometer surveys indicate. Hoping as well to assist this body of scholarship, this work has collected the party manifestos of the relevant parties in Tunisia and Egypt, thus producing parties' position estimates that contribute to understand the nature and the polarization of the respective party systems. The hope is that the work presented in these pages would be only a first step toward a systematic collection and analysis of data (like, for instance, party manifestos) across the region so as to contribute to a body of scholarship that can assist and be assisted by the broader one of comparative politics.

References

Achcar, Gilbert. 2013. *The People Want: A Radical Exploration of the Arab Uprising*. Oakland, CA: University of California Press.
Albrecht, Holger, and Dina Bishara. 2011. "Back on Horseback: The Military and Political Transformation in Egypt." *Middle East Law and Governance* 3: 13–23.
Brownlee, Jason, Tarek Masoud, and Andrew Reynolds. 2015. *The Arab Spring: Pathways of Repression and Reform*. Oxford: Oxford University Press.

Brumberg, Daniel. 2013. "Transforming the Arab World's Protection-Racket Politics." *Journal of Democracy* 24(3): 88–103. https://muse.jhu.edu/journals/journal_of_democracy/v024/24.3.brumberg.html (January 8, 2016).

Cavatorta, Francesco, and Fabio Merone. 2013. "Moderation through Exclusion? The Journey of the Tunisian Ennahda from Fundamentalist to Conservative Party." *Democratization* 20(5): 857–75. http://www.tandfonline.com/doi/abs/10.1080/13510347.2013.801255 (January 7, 2015).

Cavatorta, Francesco, Lise Storm, and Valeria Resta. 2021. *Routledge Handbook on Political Parties in the Middle East and North Africa*. eds. Francesco Cavatorta, Lise Storm, and Valeria Resta. Abingdon, Oxon: Routledge.

Linz, Juan J., and Alfred C. Stepan. 1996. *Problems of Democratic Transition and Consolidation: Southern Europe, South America and Post-Communist Europe*. Baltimore, MD: Johns Hopkins University Press.

Nugent, Elizabeth R. 2020. *After Repression: How Polarization Derails Democratic Transition*. Princeton and Oxford: Princeton University Press.

O'Donnell, Guillermo, and Philippe C. Schmitter. 1986. "Transition from Authoritarian Rule: Tentative Conclusion about Uncertain Democracies." In *Transitions from Authoritarian Rule: Southern Europe*, eds. Guillermo O'Donnell, Philippe C. Schmitter, and Laurence Withehead. Baltimore: John Hopkins University Press.

Przeworski, Adam. 1991. *Democracy and the Market: Political and Economic Reforms in Eastern Europe and Latin America*. Cambridge: Cambridge University Press.

Rustow, Dankwart A. 1970. "Transition to Democracy: Toward a Dynamic Model." *Comparative Politics* 2(3): 337–63.

Said, Atef. 2012. "The Paradox of Transition to 'Democracy' under Military Rule." *Social Research: An International Quarterly* 79(2): 397–434.

Szmolka, Immaculada. 2015. "Exclusionary and Non-Consensual Transitions Versus Inclusive and Consensual Democratizations: The Cases of Egypt and Tunisia." *Arab Studies Quarterly* 37(1): 73–95.

1 Charting different transitions

Tunisia and Egypt compared

The wave of protests that shook the regimes of the Arab world produced extremely different results, ranging from the civil war to cosmetic government reshuffles to the ousting of incumbent dictators inaugurating a process of transition from authoritarian rule. Tunisia and Egypt are instances of this latter case. In both the countries, the departure of the ruler inaugurated a transition process intended to be toward democracy. Yet, despite some similarities, the development of the transition in the two countries diverged significantly. Tunisia has experienced a somewhat linear transition process controlled by partisan entities within representative institutions, which, in turn, managed to contain political conflicts within the circuit of party politics. In Egypt, by contrast, contentions among the different parties sitting inside the Parliament resulted in a conflict among the different institutions of the state and was intertwined with it, making the transition much more difficult than the Tunisian one. In light of similar premises across Tunisia and Egypt, it can be seen how the role of the Egyptian military, and perhaps also the less emphasized role of the judiciary, is more contingent than hypothesized thus far. The following pages will chart these two different trajectories, thus offering empirical evidence for envisaging a much bigger role of political parties than has been theorized so far.

Tunisia

Despite the turmoil in the summer of 2021, Tunisia still represents by far the best outcome of the so-called Arab Spring. The self-immolation of Mohammed Bouazizi in the inner region of Sidi Bouzid on December 17, 2010, triggered a wave of protests throughout the entire country and provoked the ousting of the incumbent dictator, which occurred also in Libya and Egypt. Yet, contrary to the latter countries, in Tunisia this led to the installation of democracy with the adoption of a new Constitution in January 2014, followed by a change of government with the opposition ruling this time.

After the initial attempt of Ben Ali's entourage to control the transition, 'revolutionaries' managed to take over. The Higher Reform Political Commission formed on January 17, 2011, better known as the 'Ben Achour commission', and composed of civilians, became the main decision-making body and was the place of negotiations and consensus-building among the different components of Tunisian society. This commission crafted the transitional roadmap by providing for the elections of a parliament directly entrusted with writing a constitution, forming a government, and nominating an interim president of the republic. The elections of the National Constituent Assembly (ANC from its French acronym) took place on October 2011. After that, Moncef Marzouki was elected as interim President of the Republic and a new coalition government was formed thus marking the inception of a new course of politics.

In light of this, by 2012, Alfred Stepan looked at the Tunisian experience with great optimism for it displayed all the features identified as crucial in neutralizing authoritarian resilience, namely: a broad agreement on the procedures to produce an elected government; the presence of a government as a direct result of the popular vote; the effectiveness of the government, and the absence of power- sharing with other bodies on the legislative, the executive, and the judicial powers (Linz and Stepan 1996; Stepan 2012). Yet, the hardest moment of the Tunisian transition arrived in the summer 2013 when, amidst the political assassinations of leftist MPs Chokri Belaid and Mohamed Brahmi, the contested legitimacy of the government led to the suspension of the National Constituent Assembly. In those days, and for similar reasons, Egypt was abandoning its path toward democracy. Probably because of this negative example, the major competing parties, the Islamist Ennahda, the biggest government party, and the secular Nidaa Tounes, an extra-parliamentary party founded by Beji Caid Essebsi in 2012 to counterbalance the power of Ennahda, managed to solve the Tunisian crisis by striking a compromise. Even though some observers referred to such agreement as a radical departure from the realization of the revolutionary claims (Achcar 2013; Boubekeur 2016; Merone 2015), this has allowed Tunisia to be, thus far, the only Arab country where democracy has been installed.

The 'Deep State' tries to control the transition

Following Ben Ali's departure on 14th January 2011, its clique within the old regime attempted to appease the protesters while trying to preserve the extant apparatus. In the beginning, doubts were cast upon the irreversibility of Ben Ali's flight. Convinced that this would be only temporary, the Tunisian Prime Minister, Mohamed Ghannouchi, advocated to himself presidential powers waiting for the President to come back in accordance with article 56 of the 1959 Constitution. Yet, the Constitutional Council was indeed of the advice that such leave was permanent and, as provided by article 57 of the Constitution, invested the President of the Chamber of Deputies, Fouad Mebazaa, with the functions of interim president of the Republic. A new government saw the light on January 17th with the aim of pacifying the protesters while making only cosmetic changes. Three members of the country's formal opposition and one activist were included in the new cabinet. Yet, they were reserved only ancillary positions: Ahmad Najib al-Chebbi of the Progressive Democratic Party (hereafter PDP) was appointed as minister of development; Mustafa Ben Jaafar, from the Democratic Forum for Labour and Liberties, obtained the ministry of health; Ahmad Ibrahim (Ettajdid) received the ministry of higher education, while Slim Amamou, the young activist who had been jailed during the uprisings against Ben Ali, had the ministry of youth and sport.[1] At this stage, the core of the authoritarian era was still sound and well.

Confronted with this continuity, and supported by authoritative voices coming from the main opposition parties, such as those of Rachid Gannouchi, the leader of the Islamist party Ennahda, and Moncef Marzouki, leader of the Congress for the Republic party and future interim President of the Republic, a new wave of street protests began. From the inner and poorer areas of Kasserine, Thala, Regueb, and Sidi Bouzid, hundreds of peoples marched toward Tunis in the "liberation caravan"[2] to demand the resignation of Mohamed Gannouchi's government. During the same days, the "14th January Front" saw the light under the impulse of radical leftist parties, in particular the Tunisian Workers' Party (PCOT, form its French acronym). This Front asked for the dismissal of the incumbent government, the dissolution of Ben Ali's party, namely the Democratic Constitutional Rally (RCD), which was the dominant party of the previous electoral authoritarianism, and of all the institutions representing the previous regime – first of all parliament and the political police. In addition, the Front urged the inception of a veritable process of transitional justice and, with it, the improvement of Tunisians' living conditions.[3] On January 23, the "liberation caravan" gathering thousands of protesters travelling from Sidi Bouzid arrived in the Qasbah square of Tunis, residence of the government. Together with the "14th January Front" and other opposition movements, they organized a sit-in asking the immediate dissolution of the government, the RCD, and of the political police. On January 27th, Mohamed Gannnouchi responded to these demands with another government reshuffle which only involved the ministries of National Defense and Foreign Affairs. Civil society continued then to autonomously organize itself and a National Council for the Protection of the Revolution (NCPR) was created including the "14th January Front," the Tunisian General Labour Union (UGTT), the Islamist party Ennahda, and other political and civic associations (Brownlee, Masoud, and Reynolds 2015; Zemni 2014). The goal of this newborn National Council was that of being "the sole depository of popular sovereignty and it asked to be recognized by presidential decree so that it could monitor the work of the transitional government" (Zemni 2014, 5). This led to the creation of the Higher Committee for Political Reform within the government and members of the NCPR were invited to join in. The Higher Committee and the National Council eventually managed to merge into the High Authority for the Achievement of the Revolution Objectives, Political Reform, and Democratic Transition, established by Decree-law n° 2011–6 dated February 18, 2011, with the task of "studying the legislative texts having link with the political organization and proposing the reforms likely to concretize the revolution objectives relating to the democratic process"[4] and to advise the government (art. 2). However, Mohamed Gannouchi's intention to control the transition led to another sit-in on 20th February. Qasbah 2 "called for the prime minister's resignation, the excision of all remnants of Ben Ali's regime from the country's government, and the election of a constituent assembly to write a new constitution" (Brownlee, Masoud, and Reynolds 2015, 128). This new wave of protests was partially successful and Mohamed Gannouchi stepped aside on

February 27th. His successor, Béji Caïd Essebsi, a former Bourguiba's minister and speaker of the parliament under Ben Ali well known for his political prestige, inaugurated a new course of management of the transition.

The 'tabula rasa'

Decree-law n° 2011–4 dated March 23, 2011, related to the provisional organization of the public authorities, dissolved the Parliament and suspended the 1959 Constitution. Formally, provisional legislative and executive powers were entrusted to the interim President of the Republic and the interim government with extremely limited prerogatives, as the bulk of decision-making resided in the High Authority. This was composed by an expert committee of specialists and of a council of

> national political personalities, representatives of the different political parties, authorities, organizations, associations and components of the civil society concerned by the national affairs in the capital and regions, among those who took part in the revolution or supported it and which will be appointed by order of the Prime Minister on proposal from the concerned organizations.
> (art. 2 of Decree-law n° 2011–6 dated 18 February 2011)

This broad composition served the purpose of legitimating the process of "formulating the orientations likely to adapt the legislations relating to the political life so that they meet the requirements of the realization of the democratic transition" (art. 3) with the broader aim of changing the balance of the control of the transition in favor of civil society. Following the demands of protesters, two different commissions were created to investigate cases of corruption and the abuses perpetrated during the uprisings.[5] In addition, the dissolution of the political police[6] and of the RCD,[7] whose members were banned from participating in politics for ten years, was also provided for. Finally, the Higher Independent Electoral Commission (ISIE, from its French acronym) was created to ensure democratic, pluralist, fair, and transparent elections.[8] Its members, chosen by the High Authority among specialized and representative sectors of society were entitled to supervise the entire electoral process, i.e. proposing the division of the electoral constituencies, preparing the electoral calendar, establishing the list of voters, receiving the applications of candidacies, publishing electoral results, and deciding on possible controversies.

As a first step, the ISIE decided to postpone the elections (originally scheduled for July 24, 2011) in order to "meet the administrative, financial, and technical requirements of organizing a free and fair election" (Brownlee, Masoud, and Reynolds 2015, 133). This decision created, unsurprisingly, divisions between larger and smaller parties. The first ones, such as Ennahda, the Congress for Republic (CPR), or the Progressive Democratic Party (PDP), were afraid of losing their competitive advantage and appealed to the urgent need of giving the county a Constituent Assembly. The second ones, such as the Democratic Reform Meeting Movement and the PCOT, welcomed this decision for it offered the opportunity to better organize for the elections.

Another issue of the transitional roadmap that divided the competing factions within society was the mandate of the elected assembly. Ennahda and the parties rallied around the "October 23rd coalition," envisaged a Constituent Assembly with extended prerogatives, as originally stated by the decree law 2011-4. Essebsi, the PDP, and other 50 parties preferred instead an Assembly with the sole objective of writing a constitution within six months and, eventually, to supervise the elected bodies for a further six months.[9] As Brownlee, Masoud, and Reynolds note,

> [t]his disagreement was not merely technical. According to many observers, some non-Islamists feared that Ennahda was poised to capture a majority in the assembly, and therefore these non-Islamists wanted to limit both the assembly's term and its mandate, lest it prove the gateway to Islamist dominion.
> (2015, 136)

In the wake of reciprocal suspicions, an agreement between these two factions was finally reached on September 15, 2011, with the transitional Pact providing for the election of a one-year Constituent Assembly which would have also set the new structure of public authority and elect an interim president. In line with the desire of guaranteeing the widest representation, and to safeguard the smaller parties from the threat of an overwhelming power held by one party, read Ennahda (Lieckefett 2012), the ISIE predisposed that the election of the ANC were to be held according to a system of closed party list proportional representation, also ensuring equal representation between men and women.[10] This encouraged the registration of hundreds of parties, some of which were offshoots of the now banned RCD. The registration of voters, however, did not reflect the enthusiasm of the candidates and the procedures took longer than predicted due to the low turnout at the registration offices.[11]

Establishing the 'rules of the game': from the ANC to the National Dialogue

On October 23, 2011, Tunisian citizens went to the polls to express their political will. As Table 1.1 shows, the Islamist party Ennahda won 89 of 217 seats, followed by the Congress for the Republic, hereafter CPR (29 seats), al-Aridha (26 seats), and the Ettakatol party (20).

In light of these results, Ennahda, CPR, and Ettakatol came to a power-sharing agreement, giving life to what will be known as the Troika. A coalition government among the three led to Hamadi Jebali, Ennahda's MP, becoming prime minister, with CPR's leader, Moncef Marzouki, elected as the interim President of the Republic and Ettakatol's Mustapha Ben Jaafar appointed as the Speaker of the Parliament. Meanwhile, the elected Parliament began to draft the Constitution. The works began on February 2012 with the creation of six commissions, each reflecting the distribution of power inside the ANC, in charge of dealing with specific aspects of the constitution.[12]

This phase of institution-building was characterized by profound disagreement around both procedural aspects and substantive issues concerning the outlook of the future regime. Both confrontations illustrate the power struggle between

Table 1.1 Results of Tunisian Constituency Assembly, October 23, 2011

	Votes	%[a]	Seats	%
Movement Ennahda	1,498,905	34.81	89	41.01
Congress for Republic (CPR)	352,825	8.19	29	13.36
Democratic forum for labour and liberties (Ettkatol)	285,530	6.63	20	922
Popular petition (al-Aridha)[b]	280,382	6.51	26	11.98
Progressive Democratic Party (PDP)	160,692	3.73	16	7.37
Al-Moubadara	129,215	3	5	2.30
Democratic Modernist Pole (PDM)[c]	113,094	2.63	5	2.30
Tunisian Horizon Party (Afek Tounis)	76,643	1.78	4	1.84
Tunisian Workers' Party (PCOT)	60,620	1.41	3	1.38
Free Patriotic Union	51,594	1.2	1	0.46
Movement of Democratic Patriots	32,306	0.75	1	0.46
Popular Movement	31,793	0.74	2	0.92
Movement of Social Democrats (MDS)	22,842	0.53	2	0.92
Sowat al mostakbal[b]	17,340	0.4	1	0.46
Social Democratic Nation Party	15,572	0.36	1	0.46
Neo-Destour Party	15,459	0.36	1	0.46
Maghribi Liberal Party	13,053	0.3	1	0.46
Almostakel[b]	12,172	0.28	1	0.46
al-Wafa[b]	11,578	0.27	1	0.46
al-Amal[b]	10,681	0.25	1	0.46
For a National Tunisian Front[b]	9,923	0.23	1	0.46
Progressive Struggle Party	9,329	0.22	1	0.46
Equity[b]	9,221	0.21	1	0.46
Equality and Equity Party	7,619	0.18	1	0.46
Social Struggle[b]	6,680	0.16	1	0.46
Party of the Cultural Unionist Nation	5,581	0.13	1	0.46
Martyrs' wafa	3,869	0.09	1	0.46
Total	**3,244,518**	**75.35**	**217**	

Sources: ISIE, *Rapport relative au déroulement des élections de L'Assemblée Nationale Constituante*, February 2012.

[a] Percentage of votes by registered voters.
[b] Independent lists.
[c] Coalition list.

competing political forces – inside and outside Parliament – over the control of the transition process to secure a foothold in the political system being set up. Regarding the procedural aspects, the major contention was – again –, the extent of ANC's prerogatives. Despite ANC's time limit sanctioned by the transitional pact, "in December 2011, Ennahda and its coalition partners rejected an attempt within the assembly to impose a timeline on the body or otherwise restrict its powers" (Brownlee, Masoud, and Reynolds 2015, 141). Worried about the absence of an effective balance to the Troika's power and lamenting its autonomous management of the government and the constitution-making process alike, the PDP, the Tunisia Horizon party, and the Republican party joined forces to form the Republican party with the aim of contrasting Ennahda and the Troika. This parliamentary initiative was followed by an extra-parliamentary one. On July 2012 a new party, Caïd

Essebsi's Nidaa Tounes, arose with no other aim, at least in the beginning, than "contrasting Ennahda."[13] Later on, the Popular Front saw the light on October 7, 2012, following the convergence of a dozen of leftist parties including the Movement of Social Democrats (MDS after its French acronym), the People's Movement, the Workers' Party, the Green Party, and the Ba'athist Movement of Tunisia. The rationale behind the creation of this Front was that the more united leftist oppositions were, the greater their bargaining power vis-à-vis Ennahda.

Coming to the substance, profound disagreements emerged in relation to the form of government and the role of Islam in the new regime. As for the former issue, Ennahda was the sole party demanding a parliamentary system, while all the other parties preferred a presidential one or a mixture of the two. Further, several politicians and observers were scared about Ennahda's intention to introduce the *Shari'a* among the sources of law, although such issue had not even been on the party's agenda.[14] Broadly speaking, it was indeed the return of a traditional and Islamic view of society that preoccupied the constitution makers and secular Tunisians (McCarthy 2015; Zeghal 2013). All this crystallized in the form of two draft articles proposed by Ennahda, which had complementarity rather than equality as the cornerstone of the relationship between men and women. In this regard, this period has been referred to as the "reappearance of identity politics" or the struggle of "competing ways of life" (Zeghal 2013). This posed a major challenge to the transition process inasmuch as its success was deeply entangled with the accommodation of the different worldviews tearing Tunisia apart (Stepan and Linz 2013). Linked to this aspect was the broader battle around the legitimation of the governance of the transition. Attacks on Ennahda and the Troika came from both inside and outside the state institutions.

On February 6, 2013, one of the leaders of the leftist opposition, Chockri Belaïd, was assassinated in an ambush that nobody claimed responsibility for. This episode of violence was not alone. Already in October, a Nidaa Tounes activist was killed in a clash with members of the National League for the Protection of the Revolution, which allegedly had hidden ties with Ennahda. Furthermore, already during the summer of 2011 a cinema and an art exhibit had been targeted by radical Islamist groups. Confronted with mounting violence, the opposition front reorganized again. The Republican Party and the Social Democratic Path, both sitting in the ANC, joined forces with the extra parliamentary party Nidaa Tounes of Caïd Essebsi to form the Union for the Sake of Tunisia.[15] Parliamentary and extra-parliamentary oppositions called for the government to resign and blamed in particular the interior ministry for tolerating growing violence, accusing it of being too soft in dealing with the perpetrators. PM Hamadi Jebali, from Ennahda, tried then to form a technocratic government in line with the requests of demonstrators, but his effort proved vain following the reluctance of his own party to take a step back. In disagreement with his party's position, Jebali eventually resigned and was replaced by his party colleague and former minister of interior, Ali Laarayedh. Within the new cabinet, the presence of Ennahda's members was drastically reduced and key ministries were assigned to independent personalities. That spring was also the season of great discontent following the release of the draft constitution alleged to threaten some basic rights and to impose an Islamic view of society.[16] Mass protests lead Moncef Marzouki to call for a National Dialogue., but this was boycotted by the UGTT, the Popular Front and Nidaa Tounes.

New severe tensions arose after the murder of Mohamed Brahmi, the former leader of People's movement on July 25. The following day, the coalitions Union for Tunisia and Popular Front joined forces to set up the National Salvation Front. The Front urged the government, held responsible for the widespread violence, to be replaced by a government of independent technocrats and asked for the dissolution of the ANC and its replacement by a Commission of National Salvation, composed of politicians, leading civil society members, and experts in constitutional law, who would be in charge of writing the Constitution within two months to subsequently submit it to popular referendum. In so doing, the National Salvation Front also incited civil disobedience and promoted a series of general strikes, demonstrations and sit-ins.[17] Bardo's square (where the ANC is located) was besieged by protesters and MPs belonging to the National Front who refused any further discussion inside the ANC and with Ennahda until a new independent government was formed. Social and political turmoil never reached a peak so high within the constitution-making process as in those weeks. Given the political impasse, on August 6, Ben Jaafar, the President of the Parliament, suspended the works of the ANC until a dialogue between the government and opposition was set up.[18] The transition appeared then at great risk with some observers wondering if Ennahda would follow the same fate of the Muslim Brotherhood in Egypt.[19]

Finally, receiving the appeal of President Moncef Marzouki, the General Union of the Tunisian workers (UGTT), the Tunisian Union for the Industry, Commerce and Craftsmanship (UTICA), the Tunisian League for the Defense of Human Rights (LTDH), and the National order of lawyers, set themselves up as brokers of the National Dialogue to overcome the political impasse. This "Quartet" heard the different positions of the political actors involved, especially the governing forces headed by Ennahda and the oppositions led by Nidaa, and drafted the roadmap of the transition. According to its program, the opposition would collaborate with the government for the adoption of the Constitution, the creation of a new ISIE, and the promulgation of the electoral law. In turn, the Troika government would step aside after the achievement of these objectives. Both the opposition and the government abided by the roadmap of the National Dialogue and the transition continued despite some slowdowns as in the case of the composition of the new ISIE. On that occasion, political parties disagreed on the procedure of nomination and the Administrative Court was called to pronounce on this twice. Once again the transition seemed to come to a deadlock "à la Egyptienne." Yet, through negotiations within the ANC, a political solution was found.[20] The Constitution was finally adopted on January 26, 2014, along with the institutions and the laws to regulate new elections. The government of technocrats replaced the Troika government and between October and December 2014 new democratic elections were held to elect a new parliament and choose the new president of the Tunisian Republic.

Egypt

The Egyptian transition, spanning the eighteen months from Mubrak's ousting to Morsi's deposition, did not follow a linear trajectory as the Tunisian one did. When looked at it from the perspective of path dependence, the Egyptian experience is indeed characterized by the continuing emergence of conflicts from one electoral consultation to another, which shaped the transition as a muddled succession of 'bad choices' and 'bad behaviors' that made the democratic breakdown almost inevitable, as Brown notices (2013b). In this regard, the inability of the elected Parliament to find a political solution on the composition of the Constituent Assembly was detrimental in two ways. First, it allowed members of the deep state, namely the judiciary and the Supreme Council of the Armed Forces, to hijack the transition. Second, this situation opened up the scenario wherein the legitimate elected President was forced to wrestle with the army over the control of the transition. This power struggle was characterized by extreme uncertainty. Przeworski clearly shows how incomplete information between incumbents (in our case the remnants of the deep state) and oppositions (here the Islamists and left/secular parties) is a key ingredient in fostering a successful democratic transition (Przeworski 1991). Yet, in the Egyptian case, uncertainty and suspicion marked the mutual relations of the latter front and was crucial for the return of Mubarak's deep state. Fearing the concentration of power in the hands of Mohamed Morsi, which was instrumental to contrast the SCAF and Mubarak's judiciary, the Left, the secular and even some Islamist opposition parties encouraged the SCAF's intervention to depose him. Eventually, such a request was met through the July 3, 2013, military coup that, up to now, has extinguished any democratic ambition for the country.

The SCAF controls the transition

Much like what occurred during the first weeks of the Tunisian transition, Mubarak's resignation of February 11, 2011, was followed by attempts of contending the transition from away the remnants of the deep state. Yet, contrary to the Tunisian case, the deep state, represented by the Supreme Council of the Armed Forces (SCAF), succeeded in maintaining control of the transition. Once Mubarak was ousted,

> power in Egypt was assumed, not by the Speaker of the People's Assembly (as called for by article 84 of the country's constitution), nor by an interim government of national salvation (as called for by many of the protesters), but by the [SCAF], a conclave of twenty senior military officers led by the minister of defense, Muhammad Ḥussayn al-Ṭanṭāwī.
> (Brownlee, Masoud, and Reynolds 2015, 104)

At first, this move drew little attention from Egyptians and international observers alike. On the one hand, the military had always enjoyed the trust of the populace, and its refusal to shoot protesters during the uprising increased this sentiment of confidence, as evidenced by the slogan "The army and the people are one hand" (Ketchley 2013). On the other hand, as Brown simply puts it, "no one else could come up with a timely alternative" (Brown 2013b, 54).

As a first step, on February 13, the SCAF dissolved the parliament and suspended the constitution with the declared aim of creating a favorable environment allowing the building of a new political regime.[21] The timetable presented by the regent authority provided for a term of six months to draft constitutional amendments, submit them to a referendum, and elect a new government. Such a process would have been followed by SCAF's return to the barracks. While leaving in place the Shafiq's government installed by Mubarak on January 29, field Marshal Mohamed Hussayn al-Tantawi, the defence minister, acting as head of state, in accordance with the roadmap, created an eight-member committee to amend the 1971 constitution to render it better suited to the transition. Unlike the Tunisian High Authority, which broadly represented all the components of civil society, this constitutional review committee was very much the expression of the old establishment. It was formed by three members of the Supreme Constitutional Court, three law professors, one member of the Muslim Brotherhood's Freedom and Justice Party (the sole party represented), and one former member of the Council of State with Islamic leanings.[22] The amendments presented on February 16 were approved by popular referendum on March 19, 2011, with 77% of votes, but turnout was as low as 41% signaling mounting dissatisfaction toward SCAF's management of the transition. In stark opposition to the proposed amendments stood the Revolutionary Youth Coalition, which was a coalition formed on February 1, 2011, as the stakeholder of the young revolutionaries. It included the 6 April Youth movement, Justice and Freedom, Muslim Brotherhood youth, ElBaradei's campaign, The Popular Democratic Movement for Change (HASHD), the Democratic Front, and the administrators of the renown Khaled Saeed Facebook group.[23] The Revolutionary Youth Coalition, but also the National Progressive Unionist Party (NPUP), the New Wafd party, and other left/secular parties looked at the total dismantling of the old regime as a precondition for the founding elections. SCAF's partial assent to some of their demands, like Shafiq's ousting and the dissolution of the State Security Agency, were simply considered not enough. In contrast, the two major factions of the country, namely the Muslim Brotherhood and Moubarak's National Democratic Party (NDC), supported the amendments. The Muslim Brotherhood saw in them a clear way to parliamentary control and the NDC was at ease with the soft transition the military forces seemed to have charted.

However, what followed the popular consultation was not the reinstitution of the 1971 Constitution as modified by the referendum, but a new Constitutional declaration unilaterally adopted on March 30 by the SCAF. This document was intended to be a fundamental law providing a move toward civilian rule: it guaranteed democratic rights (art. 3–23) while indicating the timing and procedures of the transition (art. 24–62). Controversially, in envisaging the developments of the transition, the SCAF arrogated to itself legislative and executive powers to "deal[..] with the administration of the affairs of the country" (art. 56) "until a time at which the People's Assembly and the Shura Council assume their responsibilities and the president of the republic is elected and assumes his/her position" (art. 61). To counterbalance all this, the SCAF convened a National Accord Conference with representatives of all political parties to reach a non-binding accord over the basic outline of a new constitution. Yet, neither the Muslim Brotherhood's newborn Freedom and Justice party (FJP), nor the youth revolutionary groups joined the conference in sign of protest against SCAF's ambivalent behavior.[24] At first, the National Accord Conference opted for drafting a constitution before parliamentary and presidential elections.[25] However, the two major opposing groups, the FJP and the Revolutionary Youth Coalition, strongly rejected this proposal and elections were finally scheduled for November.[26]

Amidst growing suspicions, each faction approached the elections trying to safeguard its prerogatives by undermining its rivals. At that time, two trends common to almost all political parties emerged. On the one hand, they cherished SCAF's benevolence in order to count on a strong ally (De Smet 2014). On the other hand, they started to organize in broad electoral coalitions against what they saw as their worthiest rival. The FJP gathered with other parties such as the Dignity Party and Tomorrow Revolution to prevent the return of Mubarak's clique. In turn, the Egyptian Bloc gathered left and secular parties, such as the Social Democratic Party, the Free Egyptians Party, and the National Progressive Union Party (NPUP, also known as Tagammu), to counterbalance the power of Islamists parties, in particular that of the FJP. Finally, in line with a trend emerging in post Arab Spring elections, Salafist parties under Nour's aegis broke with their tradition of political quietism and joined in the electoral competition united in the Islamist bloc to challenge the plethora of secular parties while, at the same time, contesting the FJP's monopoly on political Islam in Egypt.

Sharing anti-Islamists parties' preoccupations, the SCAF's cabinet declared its intention to settle super-constitutional principles in order to bind and limit Islamists' prerogatives within the constitution-making process. Again, opposition against this measure was vibrant and culminated in a meeting on September 19, between the SCAF and the representatives of 36 among Egyptian political parties and movements to agree upon a new roadmap. The new agreement was formalized in the SCAF's decree of September 27 calling for national elections. Nonetheless, a new attempt at controlling the work of the Constituent Assembly arrived on November 1 with the Draft Declaration of the Fundamental Principles for the New Egyptian State, also known as the "Al-Salmi's bill" after the Deputy Prime Minister who presented it.[27] This document settled super constitutional principles as well as the criteria for the election of the Constituent Assembly. This time more attention was devoted to assuaging the concerns of the major competing factions involved in the transition. Secular factions would be reassured from religious attempts at establishing an Islamic state by the first fundamental principle, namely that "The Arab Republic of Egypt is a democratic civil state which is based on citizenship and on the rule of law" (art. 1). In return, Islamists would be appeased by the acknowledgment that "Islam is the religion of state, and the Arab language is the official language of state. Islamic jurisprudence (shari'a) is the principal source of legislation" (art. 2). How these two principles would be reconciled in practice is difficult to guess. In addition, the SCAF tried to insulate itself from civilian interference with the provision that

> the Supreme Council for the Armed Forces is solely responsible for all matters concerning the armed forces, and for discussing its budget, which should be incorporated as a single figure in the annual state budget. The Supreme Council for the Armed Forces is also exclusively competent to approve all bills relating to the armed forces before they come into effect.
>
> (art. 9)

Finally, the SCAF, here labelled as the defender of the "constitutional legitimacy," envisaged a 100 members Constituent Assembly composed of "eighty members, who are not members of the People's Assembly and of the Shura Council, and who represent all segments of Egyptian society including political forces, political parties, trade unions, professional and religious groups" and twenty "chosen from among the representatives of parties and independents, according to the proportion represented by the People's Assembly and Shura Council" (art. 1 of the Criteria for the formation of the Constituent Assembly to develop a new constitution for the country). Unsurprisingly, this document encountered the massive opposition of the Muslim Brotherhood and the Revolutionary Youth Coalition. The first decried the imposition of supra-constitutional principles and the disempowerment of the Parliament at the eve of their certain victory at the elections. The second saw in the document a further attempt at hijacking the transition they provoked. Either because "the military preferred no supra-constitutional principles to a document that would consolidate liberal principles and ultimately sanction the supremacy of civilians in the political system" (Awad 2013) or because the SCAF did not want to confront the mobilizing potential of both the Brotherhood and the Revolutionary Youth Coalition (Brownlee, Masoud, and Reynolds 2015), the document was withdrawn and a new government, without al-Salmi, saw the light.

Writing the constitution: parliament's dialogue of the deaf

By modifying some provisions of Law No. 38 of 1972 on the People's Assembly and Law No. 120 of 1980 on the Shura Council, SCAF's decree 199 of September 27, 2011, constitutes the backbone of the legal framework regulating the elections of the two chambers of Parliament.[28] As will be detailed in the fourth chapter, the electoral system envisaged was a mixed one: two-thirds of the members of each chamber would be elected through a closed party list system with a national threshold of 0.5%, and the remnant third through the individual-candidate voting system (art. 2 and 3). In continuity with the Nasserist tradition, it was provided that half seats in Parliament were to be reserved to workers and farmers (art. 2). Members of the People's Assembly – now 498 (art. 1) – would be elected in three stages, with the first stage starting on November 28, 201,1 and the run-off for the third stage ending on January 10, 2012, while members of the Shura Council were to be voted in other three stages from 29 January to 11 March 2011 (art. 6).

24 *Charting different transitions: Tunisia and Egypt compared*

Table 1.2 Results of Egyptian Parliamentary Elections, November 28, 2011–January 11, 2012

	Votes[a]	%[a]	Seats	%
Democratic Alliance	10,138,134	37.5	235	46.2
Freedom and Justice Party			213	41.9
Dignity Party (al-Karama)			6	
Tomorrow Revolution (Ghad al-Thawra)			2	
Civilization Party			2	
Islamic Labor Party			1	
Egyptian Arab Socialist			1	
Egyptian Reform			1	
Affiliated Independents			9	
Islamic Alliance	7,534,266	27.8	123	24.2
Al Nour			107	21.1
Building and Development Party			13	
Authenticity Party			1	
Egyptian Bloc	2,402,238	8.9	35	6.9
Socialist Democratic Party			16	
Free Egyptians			15	
Progressive Unionists (MPUP)			4	
New Wafd Party	2,480,391	9.2	39	7.5
al-Wasat	989,003	3.7	10	2.0
Reform and Development	604,415	2.2	9	1.8
Revolution Continues	754,863	2.8	7	1.4
National Party of Egypt	425,021	1.6	5	1.0
Freedom Party	514,029	1.9	4	0.8
Egyptian Citizen Party	235,359	0.9	4	0.8
Union Party	141,382	0.5	2	0.4
Conservative Party	272,910	1.0	1	0.2
Democratic Peace Party	248,281	0.9	1	0.2
Justice Party	184,553	0.7	1	0.2
Arab Egyptian Unity Party	149,253	0.6	1	0.2
Independents			21	4.1
Total	**27,065,134**		**498**	

Source: Brownlee, Masoud, and Reynolds (2015).

[a] PR votes.

The expected victory of the Islamists was nevertheless surprising for its scale. As shown in Table 1.2, the Freedom and Justice party, leader of the Democratic Alliance rallying other minor parties like the Dignity Party, al-Hadara, and affiliated independents, gained 218 out of the 498 seats at the People's Assembly and 105 out of the 180 elected seats in the Shura Council. Further, the Salafist Nour party, head of the electoral coalition Islamist Alliance, gained 108 seats in the lower chamber and 45 in the upper one. Conversely, the results of secular parties were disappointing. The New Wafd Party obtained 39 seats in the People's Assembly and 14 in the Shura Council. The Egyptian Bloc, an electoral alliance created in August 2011 to counterbalance the Muslim Brotherhood, gained 35 and 8 seats respectively in the two chambers. Among its founding parties, the Egyptian Social

Democratic Party, founded by Mohamed Abou El-Ghar, gained 15 seats at the People's Assembly. The same poor figure applies also to the Free Egyptians Party established by the magnate of telecommunications Naguib Sawiris, while the oldest leftist opposition party, the National Progressive Unionist Party, gained only three seats in the People's Assembly. NDP's offshoots, that had reorganized despite the ban, contested elections divided in seven different parties achieving poor gains: the National Party of Egypt, created thanks to the NDP's former chairman Talaat Sadat in order to reorganize the party, secured only five seats while the Union Party gained only three seats. Overall, NDP's affiliated presence in the People Assembly did not exceed the two dozen, while in the Shura Council only the Freedom Party managed to elect three of its representatives.

As stated by the modified Law No. 38 of 1972, the People's Assembly convened on March 17, 2012, while the Shura Council on March 24, 2012. Instead of being the site of compromise to give the country a democratic constitution, the Parliament soon turned to be the arena of relentless conflict among the different political currents. Following the withdrawal of the Draft Declaration of the Fundamental Principles for the New Egyptian State, MPs were left with no guidance in determining the composition of the Constituent Assembly. This led to profound disagreements between Islamists and Seculars. For the former, the composition of the assembly had to reflect the balance of power in the elected Parliament. For the latter, the Constituent Assembly had to be the expression of the different political persuasions present in the country, regardless of their electoral performances.

During the first session of the People's Assembly, it was established that the Constituent Assembly would be composed of 50 MPs and 50 members from outside Parliament.[29] Despite the fact that such decision was voted by Parliament, lawyers and activists appealed the administrative court alleging that the parliament-appointed panel did not reflected the diversity of Egyptian society and violated article 60 of the March Constitutional Declaration related to the procedures for selecting the Constituent Assembly.[30]

On March 22, amidst street protests,[31] political parties and MPs announced their nominations for the Constituent Assembly, which were finally voted by parliament two days later. The Constituent Assembly would then be made up of 25 FJP's MPs, 11 Nour's MPs, and other 14 MPs chosen among secular and leftist independents as far as the MPs' quota was concerned (35 of them from the People's Assembly and 15 from the Shura Council). The remaining 50 non-MPs members included 25 figures from the unions and an equal amount of public Egyptian figures. In light of the overwhelming presence of Islamists within the Constituent Assembly, left and secular parties led by the Egyptian bloc decided to withdraw from it.[32] Such an act turned out to be superfluous. On April 10, the Supreme Administrative Court declared the panel of constitution-makers unconstitutional on the ground that this was composed also by self-appointed parliamentarians[33] and the Constituent Assembly was finally dissolved. After confrontations among all parties and the SCAF,[34] a new constitution drafting assembly saw the light on June 12,[35] and, again, its composition was challenged in the courts. This time the Supreme Constitutional Court did not disband only the Constituent Assembly, but the whole elected Parliament due to the unconstitutionality of the electoral law. According to the SCC, the electoral system used for the founding elections discriminated between independent candidates and party members insofar as the former were granted access only to one-third of seats allocated through the first-past-the-post electoral formula while the latter had instead access to both the individual candidature and the closed party list seats, thus enjoying a much greater advantage.

While it has been argued that the SCC, entirely formed by judges appointed by Mubarak, had probably gone beyond its prerogatives with this decision (Brown 2013a), its intervention provoked by the elected MPs is surely indicative of "the persistent resort to adjudication to decide on essentially political conflicts" (Awad 2013, 287) due to the dialogue of the deaf political parties were having inside Parliament.

From the intra-parliamentary to the inter-institutional conflict

The decision of the Supreme Constitutional Court arrived at an extremely delicate moment of the Egyptian transition, namely on the eve of the Presidential elections that took place between 23/24 May (first round) and 16/17 June (runoff). In this regard, the many interventions of Mubarak's courts impacted on both the electoral race and the political prerogatives of the highest office. On the one hand, already in April, the High Judicial Election Commission disqualified MB's first candidate, al-Shatir, from the presidential race. In absolute legal continuity with the Mubarak era, as Brownlee et al. note, the electoral commission argued that al-Shatir could not yet enjoy its political rights following the 2008 convictions issued by a military court for membership of a banned organization (Brownlee, Masoud, and Reynolds 2015, 117). On the other hand, SCC's decision to outlaw the Parliament had the consequence, intentional or not, of placing the elected president in open confrontation with the SCAF over governing powers and the control of the transition.

Following the disbandment of the Parliament by the SCC, the SCAF issued another constitutional declaration on June 17, the exact day of the runoff between the MB's candidate, Mohamed Morsi, and Ahmad Shafiq, a member of Mubarak's clique. Through this constitutional declaration, the SCAF entrusted to itself legislative power "until a new parliament is elected" (art. 56 B) with the declared aim of fulfilling the legal void created by SCC's sentence. The SCAF assumed therefore the prerogative of forming a new constituent assembly "if the constituent assembly encounters an obstacle that would prevent it from completing its work" (art. 60 B) and of intervening in the process of constitution making if "the new constitution contains an article or more which conflict with the revolution's goals and its main principles or which conflict with any principle agreed upon in all of Egypt's former constitutions" (art. 60 B1). More than that, it established its veto power over presidential decisions on national security (art. 53/1 and 53/2). Finally, and again, the SCAF secured its autonomy from civilian oversight (art. 53)

Thus, when Morsi won the presidential race, he found himself fighting on two fronts. On the one hand he had to confront the fact that "the coalition undergirding the Mubarak regime had begun to regroup" (Brownlee, Masoud, and Reynolds

2015, 118), as emerged clearly from its modest advantage (51.7%) over Ahmed Shafik in the runoff. On the other hand, following the constitutional declaration of June 17, Morsi entered in competition with the SCAF for guiding the transition with confidence in its popular legitimacy, even if he eventually found himself with tied hands vis-à-vis the SCAF. To confront both challenges, Morsi tried to gather the support of the left and secular camps by

> inviting dozens of national leaders from across Egypt's political spectrum to a June 21 summit at Cairo's Fairmont hotel, to 'discuss developments and changes in the political scene and the steps to be taken in the face of current challenges'.
> (Brownlee, Masoud, and Reynolds 2015, 119)

Eventually, the "Fairmont Accord" succeeded in securing the support of several opposition groups due to Morsi's promises to form a national unity government led by an independent figure and to balance the composition of the Constituent Assembly in order to make it more representative of the different political persuasions present in the country. Yet, such promises were quickly disregarded.

As a first step in his role of President, Mohamed Morsi tried to reinstate the Parliament that had been elected in 2011/2012 and to convene new parliamentary elections two months after the approval by referendum of the country's new constitution and the adoption of a new law regulating parliament.[36] Unsurprisingly, such a move not only alarmed the judiciary and the military, who held meetings to figure out their next moves,[37] but also provoked harsh reactions from the political oppositions. Rifat al-Said, leader of the NPUP, condemned Morsi's decision asserting that "in any decent and democratic country, a president cannot disrespect the judiciary"[38] and called for both the boycott of the parliamentary session and street protests. In addition, al-Baradei tweeted that "the executive decision to overrule the Constitutional Court is turning Egypt from a government of law into a government of men."[39] Eventually, the Supreme Constitutional Court overturned Morsi's decree, and he found himself politically isolated. To overcome his isolation, the newly elected President formed a cabinet of technocrats and left the ministries of defense, foreign affairs, and the interior in the hands of the professional bureaucracies that had controlled them in the Mubarak era (Brownlee, Masoud, and Reynolds 2015, 120). However, the composition of Morsi's government was not the expression of his decision to acquiesce with the *status quo ante*. It was just the last tribute to political cohesion before the launch of a series of attacks aimed at dismantling the deep state, or at least to prevent it from controlling the transition. With the pretext of the Sinai's disorders,[40] Morsi started to openly challenge the military. First, he removed the two most important figures of the SCAF, namely Field Marshall Tantawi, replaced by al-Sisi, and the Chief of the General Staff Sami Annan, replaced by Sidki Sobhi. Further, and most importantly, he cancelled SCAF's constitutional amendments of June 17 and amended the constitutional declaration issued by SCAF on March 30, 2011. By so doing he granted himself all powers, including full executive and legislative authority, and the prerogative to decide on all public policies in Egypt and to sign international treaties.[41] In the absence of SCAF's retaliation, Morsi then turned to Mubarak's judicial apparatus. He named Mahmud Makki, a former judge of the Court of Cassation and activist for judicial independence under Mubarak, as his vice president. With the twofold aim of obtaining again the support of the political oppositions and to shake the judiciary, Morsi attempted to remove the general attorney, Abdel Meguid Mahmoud, who was accused of being too soft on the prosecution of those responsible for a violent episode on February 2 during the Egyptian uprisings, by naming him ambassador to the Vatican.[42] Yet, the judiciary got the better of the elected executive, Mahmoud refused to be reassigned, and Morsi had to rescind his decree.

Confronted with the obstructiveness of Mubarak's judiciary and with no political support from outside his party, Morsi shifted from a firm-handed to a "heavy handed" approach (Moustafa 2012). On November 22, he issued a new Constitutional Declaration aimed at seizing power from SCAF's hands while securing it from judicial interferences by stating that

> previous constitutional declarations, laws, and decrees made by the President since he took office on 30 June 2012, until the constitution is approved and a new People's Assembly is elected, are final and binding and cannot be appealed by any way or to any entity. Nor shall they be suspended or canceled, and all lawsuits related to them and brought before any judicial body against these decisions are annulled.
>
> (art. 2)

Such 'untouchability' was also granted to the Shura Council by preventing its dissolution from courts' rulings as happened with the People's Assembly (art. 5). Moreover, Morsi extended the Constituent Assembly's time limits and attempted to start controlling the judiciary by appointing the prosecutor-general (art. 3). Finally, the declaration provided the president with the power of taking "the necessary actions and measures to protect the country and the goals of the revolution" (art. 6).

Even though Morsi justified this move on the grounds of bringing the power back from the deep state to the newly elected bodies, "the effect was to further heighten opposition to the president, providing a focal point around which previously scattered liberals, leftists, and Mubarak supporters could coalesce" (Brownlee, Masoud, and Reynolds 2015, 122). The first signal of Morsi's ability at unifying his enemies arrived two days after the Constitutional Declaration when the National Salvation Front was set up. This was a coalition among a wide range of liberal, secular, and leftist groups, such as the Egyptian Popular Current, the Constitution Party (al-Dustour), the NPUP, the Free Egyptians, the New Wafd, the Democratic Front, the Egyptian Social Democratic Party, Nasserist Democratic Party, and the Conference Party.[43] Together, they were led by prominent political figures with extremely different, if not opposite, backgrounds such as diplomat Nobel laureate ElBaradei; Amr Moussa, who had served as minister of foreign affairs with Mubarak and was president of the Arab League, and Hamdeen Sabahi, historical opposition figure to the authoritarian rule since the 1970s, founder of the Dignity Party and candidate in the 2011 Presidential race as an exponent of the Left.[44] The National Salvation Front asked Morsi to rescind the Constitutional Declaration, to form a new and more plural Constituent Assembly, to implement the measures of transitional justice, and to form a new government of national salvation in line with the Fairmont Accord. Confronted with this organized protest, Morsi tried to appease the tensions through a national dialogue and to ensure the approval of the Islamist-led constituent assembly's draft constitution through a popular referendum, but in vain. On December 8, he withdrew the controversial decree, but confirmed the constitutional referendum to be held on December 15.[45] This was only a partial concession to the requests of the National Salvation Front, and protests continued. Eventually, the draft constitution was approved in a two-step election with 64% of votes in favor, but the effect of the mobilization of the opposition was evident in the very low turnout, at 33%.[46]

In line with the transitional roadmap, the approval of the Constitution was followed by the attempts to organize new Parliamentary elections that would have put Egypt on the track of democratic stability. This entailed the draft and the approval of the Parliamentary law and of the electoral law. Yet, considerable uneasiness over unchecked presidential powers was stirring. In April, *Tamarrod*, a new grassroots protest movement saw the light and launched a petition to ask Morsi to step down and allow for presidential elections to be held. Here, again, the initiative enjoyed the support of many and diverse social organizations and political parties. Among them there were the Kefaya Movement, the April 6 Youth Movement and Shayfeencom (three civil society organizations established in mid-2000s to protest against Mubarak's authoritarianism), the National Salvation Front, but also members of Mubarak's ruling party as well as religious groups ranging from the Jihadists to the moderate Strong Egypt Party. Possibly with the help of the Interior Ministry,[47] Tamarrod's organizers announced that the petition had reached 22 million signatures by the end of June[48] and the mass demonstrations they organized for June 30 proved to be a colossal showdown. Millions of people took the streets of the major cities demanding Morsi's resignation and, if necessary, the intervention of the military to depose him.[49] The day after, on 1st July, the Defense Minister General Abdel Fattah al-Sisi launched an ultimatum to the incumbent president by giving him 48 hours to "respond people's demands" or prepare for SCAF's intervention "due to its national and historic duties, out of respect for the demands of the great Egyptian people, to announce a roadmap and measures for the future."[50] The following day, on a televised speech, Morsi rejected the ultimatum by insisting that "legitimacy is the only way to protect [the] country and prevent bloodshed, to move to a new phase."[51] In the meantime, the pro-Morsi National Alliance to Support Legitimacy called its supporters "to rally in defense of legitimacy and reject any attempt to overturn it."[52] On July 3rd al-Sisi announced the deposition of the elected president, suspended the Constitution, and appointed an interim government presided over by a senior jurist.[53] The two pillars of the authoritarian deep state, i.e., the military and the judges, finally came "back on horseback" (Albrecht and Bishara 2011), thus shattering any hope of a successful transition to democracy.

A matter of political parties?

The different outcomes of two processes of transition from authoritarian rule described here have been explained by pointing to the structures and the mechanisms that characterized the previous authoritarian regimes (Brownlee, Masoud and Reynolds 2015; De Smet 2014; Hinnebusch 2015; Stacher 2015); to differences in how these processes have been designed and managed (Brown 2013b; Moustafa 2012); to the differences in the socio-economic structures across the two countries (Brownlee, Masoud, and Reynolds 2015); and to the role of the actors involved in the transition. In this latter regard, much attention has been devoted to the role of the military in the Egyptian political arena which has no parallel on the Tunisian one (Bou Nassif 2017; Makara 2013; Taylor 2014). Yet, the focus on another set of political actors, that is the political parties involved in the transition, can unveil how SCAF's centrality in the Egyptian transition is largely a consequence of political parties' inability to manage the transition when they were given the opportunity to do so through the founding elections. In fact, since the first mass protests, the two countries followed a similar transitional path up to the moment when political parties took control of it. In Tunisia, albeit not without turmoil, they managed to agree on a set of procedural and substantive rules supporting the establishment of a new democratic regime. In Egypt, parties' inability to settle their divergences through political means led to the political activation of elements within the deep state, first the judiciary and then the military, thus aborting the transition.

Long overlooked, the role of political parties within the processes of transition in Tunisia and Egypt is not only empirically grounded, as we have seen, but, as will be shown in the following pages, is also analytically suited to combine structurally driven explanations with more contingent accounts. It is so because during the constitution-making or the installation phase, political parties in Tunisia and Egypt were the only key players and their agency determined the outcome of the transition. Yet, for their very essence, political parties are also the result of the social and institutional contexts in which they operate. Such a structural luggage, which in the cases of the transition processes in Tunisia and Egypt was imported from the previous electoral authoritarianism, not only impact on the format of the two-party systems, but also on parties' power resources and on the way political parties structure politics during the installation phase.

More than that, choosing political parties as units of analysis has the merit of binding together the paradigm of democratization studies with that of authoritarian resilience. On the one hand, the choice to focus on political parties and their agency draws from the mainstream literature on democratization studies and transitology. Even if deemed to be too tautological, this understanding has nonetheless the merit of pointing out immediately observable analytical dimensions. On the other hand, the insights on the functioning of electoral authoritarianism regimes furnished by studies on authoritarian resilience have the merit of highlighting the reasons behind transitional parties' agency and, with it, the outcome of the two transition processes scrutinized here. Differently put, while democratization studies indicate what to look at, authoritarian resilience studies suggest what to search for. Integrated in a fine-grained model for parties' agency within installations, as this work ventures to do, these two streams of literature, far from being mutually exclusive, are complementary in the construction of mid-range theories which allow students to "undertake the challenge of synthesis" (Bryen et al. 2012) thus going beyond the inter-paradigm debate and, more importantly, to exit the particularism of Arab studies (Valbjørn 2015).

Notes

1 See: "Tunisia's Mohammed Ghannouchi defends new government" on the BBC website. Available at http://www.bbc.com/news/world-africa-12213284 (last access: March 1, 2017).
2 See: "'Liberation caravan' reaches Tunis" on al Jazeera. Available at: http://www.aljazeera.com/news/africa/2011/01/2011123124352723753.html (last access: March 1, 2017).
3 See: "Communiqué de fondation du Front du 14 janvier", 20 January 2011. Available at: http://www.europe-solidaire.org/spip.php?article26968 (last access: March 1, 2017).
4 Full English text available at http://www.legislation.tn/sites/default/files/journal-officiel/2011/2011G/Jg0132011.pdf (last access: March 1, 2017).
5 See: Decree-law n° 2011–7 dated 18 February 2011 and Decree-law no. 2011–8 dated 18 February 2011.
6 See: http://www.bbc.com/news/world-africa-12669461 (last access: March 2, 2017).
7 See: Decree-law n° 2011–35 dated 10 May 2011.
8 See: Decree-law n° 2011–27 dated 18 April 2011.
9 Interview with Hafedh Caïd Essebsi. Tunis, July 2012.
10 See: Decree-law 35–2011 dated 10 May 2011.
11 See: https://www.tunisienumerique.com/prorogation-jusquau-14-aout-2011-des-delais-dinscription-sur-les-listes-electorales/62093.
12 See: http://majles.marsad.tn/assemblee/commissions (last access: March 2, 2017).
13 Personal interview with Hafed Caïd Essebsi, July 2012.
14 Personal interview with Ajmi Lourimi, Ennahda's MP, and member of its Shura Council, the decisional body of the party, and Imen Ben Mohammed, Ennahda's MP, July 2012.
15 See: "Union for Tunisia – Jebali's Initiative 'Step Forward On Right Path'", 12 February 2013. Tunis Afrique Press (TAP).
16 See: "Tunisia's Theocratic Temptation", 3 May 2013. *The New York Times*.
17 See: http://front-populaire.org/?p=2414 (last access: March 2, 2017). Moreover, personal interview with Hamma Hammami. Tunis, August 2013.
18 See: http://www.bbc.com/news/world-africa-23596640 (last access: March 2, 2017).
19 See: http://english.alarabiya.net/en/perspective/analysis/2013/07/27/Islamists-fall-from-grace-Will-Tunisia-s-Ennahdha-follow-the-Brotherhood.html (last access: March 2, 2017).
20 Personal interview with Oussama Al Saghir, Ennhdha's MP and member of the commission for the elections. Tunis, October 2013.
21 Mai Shams El-Din, "Armed Forces suspend constitution, dissolve parliament", 13 February 2011, *Daily News Egypt*. Available at http://www.dailynewsegypt.com/2011/02/13/armed-forces-suspends-constitution-dissolves-parliament/ (last access: March 9, 2017).
22 See: "In Egypt, a Panel of Jurists Is Given the Task of Revising the Country's Constitution", 15 February 2011, *The New York Times*.
23 See: "Egypt revolution youth form national coalition", 9 February 2011, Ahram on line available at http://english.ahram.org.eg/~/NewsContent/1/64/5257/Egypt/Politics-/Coalition-of-The-Revolutions-Youth-assembled.aspx (last access: March 3, 2017).

24 See: "Deputy PM alleges attempts to spoil accord on constitution", 26 May 2011, *Egypt Independent*.
25 See: "National Accord Conference calls for constitution before elections", 21 June 2011, *Egypt Independent*.
26 See: "Egyptian Parliamentary Election Date Set for November", 25 July 2011, IHS Global Insight.
27 Full text available at: http://www.constitutionnet.org/sites/default/files/2011.11_-_constitutional_principles_document_english_0.pdf. Ali al-Salmi, Sharaf's deputy PM, was appointed by the SCAF to the interim government as "minister of democratic transition", see: Mona el-Ghobashy, "Egyptian Politics Upended", MERIP, 20 August 2012.
28 The other decrees regulating the elections of the Parliament are Decree 123 dated October 3, 2011, modifying disposition of Decree 120 dated September 26, 2011, thus finally allowing political party members to contest individual candidacy seats, and Decree 130 dated November 19, 2011, setting the rules for voting abroad.
29 See: "Egypt Parliament opens nominations for constituent assembly", 18 March 2012, *Al-Ahram online*.
30 "Legal experts challenge decision to stock constituent assembly with sitting MPs", 19 March 2012, *Al-Ahram*.
31 "Protesters rally against Islamists dominating Constituent Assembly", 23 March 2012, *Daily News Egypt*.
32 "Egyptian secular parties withdraw from Constituent Assembly", 27 March 2012, *Xinhua General News Service*.
33 Egyptian Court Suspends Constitutional Assembly", 10 April 2012, *RTT News*.
34 "SCAF, political parties agree to 6 criteria for forming constituent assembly", 28 April 2012, *Al-Ahram*.
35 "Official: The 100 members of Egypt's revamped Constituent Assembly", 12 June 2012, *Al-Ahram*.
36 "Egypt's reinstated parliament to convene Tuesday", 9 July 2012, *Agence France Presse*.
37 "Egypt's ruling generals warn Morsi to respect the constitution", 9 July 2012, *The Guardian*.
38 "Egypt's reinstated parliament to convene Tuesday", 9 July 2012, *Agence France Presse*.
39 "Morsi orders Parliament to return", 7 July 2012, St. Paul Pioneer Press (Minnesota).
40 "Egypt says 7 suspected militants killed in Sinai", 12 August 2012, *Associated Press*.
41 "Egypt's President Morsi cancels SCAF's constitutional amendments", 13 August 2012, *Intellinews - MENA Today*.
42 "Egypt prosecutor-general to remain in office", 13 October 2012, *Al-Jazeera*. Available at http://www.aljazeera.com/news/middleeast/2012/10/20121013135626371129.html (last access: March 8, 2017).
43 "Profile: Egypt's National Salvation Front", 10 December 2012, *BBC News*.
44 "Egypt's opposition coalition: the key players", 6 December 2012, *The Guardian*.
45 Matt Bradley, "Egypt's Morsi Partially Annuls Decree Expanding His Powers", 8 December 2012, *The Wall Street Journal*.
46 "Egypt votes in second phase of constitution referendum", 22 December 2012. Available at https://www.theguardian.com/world/2012/dec/22/egypt-votes-second-constitution-referendum (last access: April 22, 2017).
47 Asma Alsharif and Yasmine Saleh, "Special Report – The real force behind Egypt's 'revolution of the state'", 10 October 2013, *Reuters*.
48 "Profile: Egypt's Tamarod protest movement", 1 July 2012, *BBC News*.
49 David D. Kirkpatrick, Kareem Fahim and Ben Hubbard, "By the Millions, Egyptians Seek Morsi's Ouster", 30 June 2012, *The New York Times*.
50 Full text of SCAF's ultimatum pronounced by al-Sisi available at https://www.theguardian.com/world/middle-east-live/2013/jul/01/egypt-stanoff-millions-protest#block-51d1e142e4b042dd8f04a137 (last access: March 9, 2017).

51 David D. Kirkpatrick, Kareem Fahim and Ben Hubbard, "Morsi Defies Egypt Army's Ultimatum to Bend to Protest", 2 June 2012, *The New York Times*.
52 "Egypt protests: Muslim Brotherhood reject army ultimatum; The Brotherhood and its Islamist allies in government reject an army ultimatum for President Morsi to negotiate with protesters, as demonstrations continue in Cairo's Tahrir Square and across the country", 2 July 2012, *The Telegraph*.
53 David D. Kirkpatrick, "Army Ousts Egypt's President; Morsi Is Taken into Military Custody", 3 July 2012, *The New York Times*.

References

Achcar, Gilbert. 2013. *The People Want: A Radical Exploration of the Arab Uprising*. Oakland, CA: University of California Press.
Awad, Ibrahim. 2013. "Breaking out of Authoritarianism: 18 Months of Political Transition in Egypt." *Constellations* 20 (2): 275–92.
Bou Nassif, Hicham. 2017. "Coups and Nascent Democracies: The Military and Egypt's Failed Consolidation." *Democratization* 24 (1): 157–74. https://doi.org/10.1080/13510347.2016.1142533.
Boubekeur, Amel. 2016. "Islamists, Secularists and Old Regime Elites in Tunisia: Bargained Competition." *Mediterranean Politics* 21 (1): 1–21. https://doi.org/10.1080/13629395.2015.1081449.
Brown, Nathan J. 2013a. "Egypt: A Constitutional Court in an Unconstitutional Setting." In *Political and Constitutional Transitions in North Africa: Actors and Factors*, 1–20. New York.
———. 2013b. "Egypt's Failed Transition." *Journal of Democracy* 24 (4): 45–58.
Brownlee, Jason, Tarek Masoud, and Andrew Reynolds. 2015. *The Arab Spring: Pathways of Repression and Reform*. Oxford: Oxford University Press.
Brynen, R., Moore, P. W., Salloukh, B. F., & Zahar, M. J. (2012). *Beyond the Arab spring: authoritarianism & democratization in the Arab world* (Vol. 4). Boulder: Lynne Rienner Publishers.
Hinnebusch, Raymond. 2015. "Globalization, Democratization, and the Arab Uprising: The International Factor in MENA's Failed Democratization." *Democratization* 22 (2): 335–57. https://doi.org/10.1080/13510347.2015.1010814.
Ketchley, Neil. 2013. *"The Army and the People Are One Hand!" Fraternization and the 25th January Egyptian Revolution. Comparative Studies in Society and History*. Vol. 56. https://doi.org/10.1017/S0010417513000650.
Lieckefett, Michael. 2012. "La Haute Istance et Les Élections En Tunisie: Du Consensus Au 'Pacte Politique'?" *Confluences Méditerranée* 82 (3): 133–44. https://doi.org/10.3917/come.082.0133.
Linz, Juan J., and Alfred C. Stepan. 1996. *Problems of Democratic Transition and Consolidation: Southern Europe, South America and Post-Communist Europe*. Baltimore: Johns Hopkins University Press.
Makara, Michael. 2013. "Coup-Proofing, Military Defection, and the Arab Spring." *Democracy and Security* 9 (4): 334–59. https://doi.org/10.1080/17419166.2013.802983.
McCarthy, Rory. 2015. "Protecting the Sacred: Tunisia's Islamist Movement Ennahdha and the Challenge of Free Speech." *British Journal of Middle Eastern Studies* 0194 (January): 1–18. https://doi.org/10.1080/13530194.2015.1005055.
Merone, Fabio. 2015. "Enduring Class Struggle in Tunisia: The Fight for Identity beyond Political Islam." *British Journal of Middle Eastern Studies* 42 (1): 74–87.

Tamir Moustafa, 'Drafting Egypt's Constitution: Can a New Legal Framework Revive a Flawed Transition? (Brooking Doha Center, Paper Series, 1 March 2012)

Przeworski, Adam. 1991. *Democracy and the Market: Political and Economic Reforms in Eastern Europe and Latin America*. Cambridge: Cambridge University Press.

Smet, Brecht De. 2014. "Revolution and Counter-Revolution in Egypt." *Science and Society* 78 (1): 11–40.

Stacher, Joshua. 2015. "Fragmenting States, New Regimes: Militarized State Violence and Transition in the Middle East." *Democratization* 22 (2): 259–75. https://doi.org/10.1080/13510347.2015.1010810.

Stepan, Alfred C. 2012. "Tunisia's Transition and the Twin Tolerations." *Journal of Democracy* 23 (2): 89–103. http://muse.jhu.edu/journals/journal_of_democracy/v023/23.2.stepan.html.

Stepan, Alfred, and Juan J. Linz. 2013. "Democratization Theory and the 'Arab Spring.'" *Journal of Democracy* 24 (2): 15–30.

Taylor, William C. 2014. *Military Responses to the Arab Uprisings and the Future of Civil-Military Relations in the Middle East: Analysis from Egypt, Tunisia, Libya, and Syria*. New York: Palgrave Macmillan.

Valbjørn, Morten. 2015. Reflections on self-reflections–On framing the analytical implications of the Arab uprisings for the study of Arab politics. *Democratization*, 22(2), 218–238.

Zeghal, Malika. 2013. "Competing Ways of Life: Islamism, Secularism, and Public Order in the Tunisian Transition." *Constellations* 20 (2): 254–74. https://doi.org/10.1111/cons.12038.

Zemni, Sami. 2014. "The Extraordinary Politics of the Tunisian Revolution: The Process of Constitution Making." *Mediterranean Politics*, no. June: 1–17. https://doi.org/10.1080/13629395.2013.874108.

2 Demand of representation, power resources, and parties' agency

Political parties in transition processes

As we have seen, despite the different patterns undertaken by the transition in Tunisia and Egypt, the process of constitution-making – or installation – following the founding elections, constitutes itself as a crossroad, with Tunisia taking the road of democratic installation and Egypt going down an authoritarian comeback. Hence, the search for possible explanations for these different outcomes cannot but start from here. The phase of installation is the sub-phase of the broader process of transition where the "devolution of power from a group of people to a set of rules" (Przeworski 1991, 14) occurs. In the cases of Tunisia and Egypt, such a phase was dominated by political parties, which makes the case for a reappraisal of the concept of agency in order to better suit their complex nature and the institutional setting that conditions their very existence and their choices.

Very often, the concept of agency is indeed put at the center of analyses on installation processes, with prominent contributions coming from game-theory readings. However, the actors from which the agency originates are always conceptualized as single actors with externally given preferences. This modeling might create some problem in case of collective actors like political parties characterized for being 'intermediate institutions' between the governing apparatus and citizens and, also, crucially interconnected with the institutional setting they have been operating from. In fact, political parties are at once the decision makers on the more salient issues regulating the exercise of power and the life of people, and also the incubator of the political demands stemming from civil society. In this regard, their functions are usually divided between those of governing and representation and both influence each other. Hence, when analyzing transitional parties' agency in the fulfillment of their governing functions – like those they are called to perform during installations –, their representative role should be taken into account as informing it. Simply put, the way political parties structure the political space, by politicizing pre-existing social divisions, determines what they can or cannot do once elected. It follows that the choice to cooperate or not with other parties to find a 'compromise' during the phase of installation is the result of the interplay between (i) pre-existing social divisions; (ii) their resources, and (iii) their ideological positions.

Out of a conceptualization of agency so defined, the role of the structures and mechanisms in place during the previous authoritarian regimes – enlightened by

DOI: 10.4324/9781003269717-3

the body of scholarship of the authoritarian resilience that poses itself as alternative to the one of democratization studies – are relevant for at least two reasons. On the one hand, the previous authoritarian regimes represent the context within which the political learning of parties active in 2011–3 occurred, determining their ideological position. On the other hand, they constituted the opportunity structures available to parties that act as determinants for their power resources. This is not to say that previous regimes do not have any role in casting the other key element of our conceptualization of agency, namely the social divisions the parties have to deal with once they collapse. Quite on the contrary. Yet, for the sake of regime transitions, what ultimately counts is how these are politicized at the time of the founding elections, which is in large part a function of parties' political learning.

The conceptualization of parties' agency during processes of transitions sketched out in the following pages contributes to the extant literature in at least two possible ways. To begin with, it expands the extant definition of agency thus allowing for a working concept that suits the nature of political parties. It is important to note that the conceptualization and the game theory model presented here do not arrive at drastically different conclusions from those we would have arrived without it. The difference in the disproportion of parties' power resources (that is the number of seats they control) emerges here as one of the determinant factors as it would have emerged under a simple conceptualization. Yet, and crucially, what this model allows is making more intelligible the reasons of this disproportion and other factors that emerge perhaps as equally important in explaining the processes of transition in Tunisia and Egypt. These factors, as will be detailed in the following chapters, have rather to do with the structures of power and the institutions in which those parties grew. By so doing, this conceptualization of parties' agency connects two important traditions of literature, thus supporting the wider discipline of comparative politics.

Locating political parties in transition processes: defining installations

The necessity of installations

In mainstream scholarly understanding, the broad process of democratization is treated as the result of three distinct processes having different objectives and responding to diverse underlying mechanisms: transition, installation, and consolidation. The first refers to the interval between one political regime and another, the second denotes the introduction of democratic institutions and procedures, and the third is the process by which these are internalized and become unchallenged. According to this conceptualization, installation only refers to the turning-point moment between the two other phases. The rare appearance of this term in the main treaties of democratization, with scholars preferring to speak of 'regime completion', 'democratization', or 'constitution' instead (Linz and Stepan 1996; O'Donnell and Schmitter 1986; Przeworski 1991), testifies the lack of analytical distinctiveness and autonomy imputed to installation. This was the result of an (really successful) attempt of theory-building stemming from the empirics of transitions from authoritarian rule in Southern Europe and Latin America, where "installation [was] short ad very difficult to distinguish from transition" (Morlino 2015, 18). Even following findings stemming from democratization processes in Eastern Europe, where the installation phase was longer and the constitution-making caught the attention of prominent scholars (Elster 1995; Geddes 1998; Reynolds 2002), did not alter this reading. In contrast, a different reappraising of the notion of installation is among the major analytical implications stemming from the more recent processes of transitions in the Arab world. Already in 2010, with Capoccia and Ziblatt expressed the need "to systematically analyze *the historical episodes in which democratic institutions were created or substantially reshaped*" (2010, 934; emphasis is in original). In their work, the lexicon of historical institutionalism – e.g. path dependence, sequencing, and critical juncture – enters in the study of democratization. The stemming methodology, informed by Arab transitions' empirics, is more attentive to the unfolding of the different sub-processes and their direction of causality (Ahmed and Capoccia 2014). Along the same lines, Morlino has proposed to conceive of installation as a "different, alternative or possibly subsequent process with respect to liberalization," i.e. the initial moment of transition (Morlino 2011, 86).

While the very definition of transition expands temporally and analytically from the fall of the previous regime, thus departing from its crises, to the settlement of a new one, the installation phase only refers to the process concerned with building the new regime's structures, therefore relying on different actors and mechanisms from the ones involved in the other phases of democratization (Morlino 2011, 2015; Przeworski 1991). More precisely, for Morlino (2011, 86), installation

> involves the complete expansion and genuine recognition of civil and political rights; where necessary, the full civilianizing of society; the emergence of a number of parties and a party system, but also of collective interests' groups such as unions and other organizations; and the drawing up and adoption of the principal democratic procedure and institutions that will characterize the regime.

However, for others (Elster 1995; Landau 2012; Merkel 1998), installation only coincides with the constitution-making process, or some sort of institutional arrangement of a similar kind, with the acknowledgment that the establishment of the structures and institutions characterizing the new regime has been often arranged among a small, and in some case un-elected, political elite while nonetheless bringing to successful democratizations, as the Latin-American and the European cases show. Indeed, while the complete expansion of full-fledged political and civil liberties, the organization of collective interests and the emergence of parties and party systems can be attained also within the subsequent phase of democratic consolidation, as many studies showed (Mainwaring and Scully 1995; Merkel 1998), the establishment of the 'rules of the game', through the drawing up and adoption of the principal democratic procedures and institutions that will characterize the new regime, is a *sine qua non* condition for the installation to be achieved and a new regime to come about (Linz and Stepan 1996; Merkel 1998; O'Donnell and Schmitter 1986; Przeworski 1991). The concomitant restructuring of civil and political society is hence relevant in accounting for the contextual factors within which the institutional settlement occurs, or the quality of the transitional process overall (Kitschelt et al. 1999; O'Donnell and Schmitter 1986; Rustow 1970). From this understanding, it can not only be seen that installations can be regarded as *processes*, but also that their accomplishment is *necessary* (even though not sufficient) for a new (and hopefully democratic) regime to come about.

Installation processes, defined as "the devolution of power from a group of people to a set of rules" (Przeworski 1991, 14), can occur in a variety of ways. They can be the result of trial and error over a long span of time and with the involvement of the military, as happened in 1975–82 Portugal; they can stem from a rapid bargaining process among a restricted political elite as happened in Spain; or they can coincide with the making of a new constitution followed by elections, as happened in Eastern Europe and Tunisia. Despite the different configurations installations processes can display (Morlino 2011, 85–91), political elites' negotiations emerge as the ultimate constant and distinctive feature of these processes. In all cases of regimes change, or attempted ones, the introduction of new institutions stems from the arrangements of the at-that-moment relevant political elite (Perthes 2004). Both this process and the resulting institutional arrangements might vary depending on cases, as the variety of transitions from authoritarian rule and democracies shows. However, the very content of pacts leading to democratic installation is invariably related to the establishment of institutions (i) providing individuals with equal rights and freedoms and (ii) perceived by the majority of people as legitimate (Morlino 2011; Przeworski 1991; Weingast 1997). The first aspect comes from the very definition of democracy (Dahl 1971; Morlino 2011; Sartori 1987), the second relates to its stability (Przeworski 1991, 2006). To arrive at such an outcome, the institutions set up during installation have to display two features. On the one hand, they need to impose limits on the governing power since this is the only way individuals are granted their freedoms and rights (Morlino 2011; Weingast 1997). On the other hand, in order to endure and become the only 'game in town', the agreed-upon institutions must be self-enforcing, in the sense that compliance with the institutional framework so defined shall "constitute the equilibrium of the decentralized strategies of all the relevant political forces" (Przeworski 1991, 26). These two features are deemed to follow the resolution of coordination problems within both the political elite and the citizenry in that the settled institutions represent focal points able to trigger citizens and elite reactions vis-à-vis possible violations of individual and collective rights and freedoms by whoever has the power to govern (Weingast 1997).

Institutions so defined require that (i) the political elite involved in the installation bargain arrive at an agreement through pacts, defined

> as [...] explicit, but not always publicly explicated or justified, agreement[s] among a select set of actors which seek to define (or better, redefine) rules

governing the exercise of power on the basis of mutual guarantees for the 'vital interests' of those entering into it.

(O'Donnell and Schmitter 1986, 42)

and that (ii) these pacts find mass support through a process of attitudinal adaptation (Linz and Stepan 1996; Merkel 1998). While this latter aspect relates to the consolidation of democracy, the first constitutes precisely the core of the installation process. Here the relevant political elite is required to arrive at a shared consensus about the rules and the codes of political conduct (O'Donnell and Schmitter 1986; Przeworski 1991; Rustow 1970). Historically this can be the result of adaptation, whereby anti-system factions gradually abandon their radical ideological stances in order to compete for office following the rules established by ruling factions, or can be the result of 'elite settlement' following traumatic events such as the ousting of dictators, as in Tunisia and Egypt (Higley and Burton 1989). In this latter case, "warring elite factions suddenly and deliberately reorganize their relations by negotiating compromises on their most basic disagreements, thereby achieving consensual unity and laying the basis for a stable democratic regime" (Higley and Burton 1989, 21). The experience of transition from authoritarian rule in Tunisia and Egypt differs precisely because the Tunisian experience instantiates a case of 'elite settlement', while in the Egyptian case the warring factions fell short in finding a shared set of rules and institutions to regulate the exercise of governing power. Because of the centrality of the actors within installation processes, the focus on the determinants of installation prompted by agency-based approaches appears as particularly suitable to understand the varying success of democratic installations.

Determinants of installations

Elite settlement within installation processes can be thought of as a substitute for violent revolution, as a catalyst for social integration, and as incubators for the management of the reform agenda (Yeh and Chang 2009). In this regard then, because the institutions that result from the elite settlement influence the "distribution of economic, political and ideological resources" (Przeworski 1991, 81), they are reflective of actors' power relationships (real or perceived), and their ideology at the moment of installation.

Przeworski (1991) has been one of the first to be concerned with how power-relationships among actors affect the phase of installation. In his account, there is no power distribution among actors really conducive to democracy in situations of complete information. In cases of uneven distribution of power, the dominant faction will surely profit from installation to consolidate its power advantage thus falling short in bringing about a legitimate and self-enforcing democratic setup. Alternatively, if the distribution of power is balanced, 'anything can happen' because all the factions involved will not have particular incentives in negotiating their priorities with the other, nor to do the contrary. For Przeworski, the only installation process conducive to democracy is the one in which all the actors involved do not actually know their relative power resources. Only in such a way, he argues, the actors will agree on the establishment of checks and balances. They do so by "counteract[ing] increasing return to power [while] provid[ing] insurances to the eventual losers" (ibid. 88). This hypothesis perfectly suits the understanding of democracy as a limited form of government, or as 'institutionalized uncertainty'. Yet, it nonetheless leaves unexplained a wide range of cases wherein knowledge over power distribution did not prevent actors to reach an enduring and democratic agreement.

In this regard, several scholars tend to focus on the role of actors' normative orientations to explain both the prospects and the outcome of the installation bargaining processes (Ginsburg, Elkins, and Blount 2009; Landau 2012; Negretto 1999). Consider for instance the cases of known and even relation of forces, that is when the actors involved in the game have the same bargaining power, and this aspect is known to all of them. As Przeworski notes, this is a typical case of coordination problem, that can nonetheless be solved through focal points, i.e. "solutions that are readily available and are not seen as self-serving" (1991, 85) provided not only by traditions and/or foreign examples, as the author reports, but also by political learning. In a similar vein Elster (1995) notes that not only the content of "motivations and motivational assumptions" matters in cases of known and even power relationships among the actors involved by serving as focal points, but their configuration among the deciding political elite is also important. In such cases, as long as probable political cleavages do not concentrate along the same dimension across all issues, the actors can coordinate on cooperative outcomes through bargain processes (Colomer 1995; Raiffa 1982). Departing from a cooperative understanding of installation processes, in situations of uneven power balance democracy becomes a viable and stable solution if the dominant faction is normatively "committed to the democratic project" (McFaul 2002, 225).

Drawing from this actor-centric understanding of processes of installations, it then emerges that the actors' strategies are influenced by both their power resources and their normative orientation. In game-theoretical terms, it can simply be expressed by the following model (Table 2.1).

In this game, the utility function of both the actors is represented by c, that is the expected benefits coming from collaboration and p, that stands for the expected gains deriving from a unilateral imposition. The first argument represents, for instance, the gains derived from the avoidance of protracted conflict that can be detrimental for players' survival, or the acknowledgment that collaborating is

Table 2.1 The installation game

		Player B	
		Cooperate	Defect
Player A	Cooperate	c-p; c-p	c-p; p-c
	Defect	p-c; c-p	p-c; p-c

per se a value in that it infuses the installation process with the required legitimacy. This can be conceived as a function of a given actor's perceived ideological distance from the other player(s) in that the more different the normative orientation or the policy preferences of actors, the lesser the expected gains from cooperation (Lust-Okar 2005; Tsebelis 2002). The second argument, by contrast, can instead be conceived as a function of actors' power position, in that the greater one's power advantage over the other(s), the greater the expected payoff from defection strategies (Przeworski 1991). Each and every player's profile depends on the combination of *c* and *p*. From the game it emerges that whenever *c* outweighs *p* the dominant strategy for both players is to cooperate. In line with the different contributions outlined above, this entails that either both actors share a common understanding about the nature of the future state (or are equally frightened by the prospect of a protracted stalemate), or that no party has huge positional advantages within the bargain process and cooperation imposes itself in order to avoid (and/or exit) the gridlock. Recent contributions aimed at grasping the differences between Tunisia and Egypt are consistent with this understanding in that they explain the different outcomes by alternatively pinpointing to different degrees of polarization (Cross and Sorens 2016; Lesch 2014) and the different power relationship across the two party systems (Brownlee, Masoud, and Reynolds 2015; Carey 2014; Tavana 2012). Yet, when the agent involved in the bargain process are political parties, such strategy profiles are to be reappraised in order to account of their unique nature as intermediate and intermediary institutions.

A model for parties' agency within installations

The actors involved in the installation phase vary. They can be non-elected members of the civil society and the ruling elite, or can be technocrats appointed by selected commissions (Ginsburg, Elkins, and Blount 2009). Nonetheless, when founding elections are held to form a constituent assembly, political parties become the key players of this sub process. Interestingly enough, the role of political parties in democratization studies has been analyzed, receiving a great deal of attention, only within the process of democratic consolidation, when the rules are already established (for a remarkable exception see Bermeo 1990). In this regard, the functioning of newborn democracies is deemed to be enhanced at the pace of party systems' institutionalization. Democracy, as we know it, is representative democracy, wherein parties fulfil a set of vital functions for its working. They provide interests articulation and aggregation; they lower citizens' costs of information, allowing them to take part in public discourse; they guarantee popular control of the government through the recruitment and selection of candidates; finally, they fulfil the task of organizing parliaments and governments. Due to this, the interest of extant research is actually oriented toward the *institutionalization* of party systems, for only such an entrenchment within the polity enables democracy to consolidate and function (Huntington 1968, 397–461; Kuenzi and Lambright 2001, 2005; Mainwaring and Scully 1995; Morlino 1995; Randall 2001; Randall and Svåsand 2002a,b; Yardimci-Geyikci 2015). In contrast, the role of parties in contributing to the installation of democratic rules has been often overlooked. There are two reasons for this gap. First, this gap is attributable to the aforementioned bias that has built the theoretical framework, and therefore the research agenda, on the experience of Southern European countries where transition and installation were perceived as a single process. Second, this is due to the concept of *'tabula rasa'*, according to which political parties are understood to be the product of political liberalization that comes with the process of transition from the authoritarian rule (Dahl 1971; Mainwaring 1998; Morlino 1995): how can they form and organize when there is no freedom of speech or association, as it is the case in authoritarian regimes? In principle, this claim is certainly true. However, transitions do not always occur between perfectly typified and binary categories of authoritarianism and democracy. Indeed, the empirical reality has shown us a great variety of hybrid regimes where elections – although often sham – are not rare, for they serve a variety of goals, all attributable to regime survival, even in the context of authoritarian rule (Cavatorta, Storm, and Resta 2021; Diamond 2002; Gandhi and Lust-Okar 2009; Geddes 2006; Schedler 2002). As consequence, political parties, even though weak and poorly organized, are already present when undemocratic regimes collapse and/or organize in view of the founding elections. This is precisely what happened in Tunisia and Egypt. Here, the political parties active and well-known even before the downfall of the authoritarian regime were the same who played a significant role during the process of installation (Hamid 2014; Storm 2014). Hence, understanding how they might have contributed to the different outcomes observed is of paramount importance.

Differently from any other kind of actors, political parties are "central intermediate and intermediary structure[s] between society and the government" (Sartori 1976, ix). Paralleling this view, in democratization processes, political parties are deemed to be 'anchors of democracy' in that they hook and bind society to governmental institutions, being at once part of the mobilized public and of the political relevant elite (Asseburg and Wimmen 2016; Morlino 2011; Perthes 2004). According to their dual nature, political parties' functions are commonly distinguished between governing and representative functions (Mair 2002). The first set refers to actions and decisions performed by political parties in their in-office capacity, such as organizing parliaments and governments, or – as in the cases under investigation – deciding on "ground rules within which day-to-day legislation and government are to be conducted" (Elster, Offe, and Preuss 1998, 64). The second, by contrast, refers to all those functions fulfilled by parties in organizing the political participation of citizens (Huntington 1968) such as aggregating dispersed interests and formulating policy options. Consolidated democracies display a great interplay between the two functions meaning that the governing activity of political parties determines the dividing lines of the electoral competition and vice versa (Deegan-Krause and Enyedi 2010). In contrast, in the aftermath of founding elections in emerging democracies – lacking any previous parties' governmental commitment – it might be plausible to think of the governing agency as a function of the representative one. This means that parties' strategies in the exercise of their ruling functions, that in the case of democratic installations are cooperation

Table 2.2 Political parties' installation game

		Party B	
		Cooperate	Defect
Party A	Cooperate	(PO-SD)-*P*; (PO-SD)-*P*	(PO-SD)-*P*; *P*-(PO-SD)
	Defect	*P*-(SD-PO); (PO-SD)-*P*	*P*-(PO-SD); *P*-(PO-SD)

or defection with their counterparts in searching for a compromise, are the result of (i) pre-existing social divides; (ii) the decision parties take when aggregating them in their electoral offer; and, of course (iii) their power position in term of seats within the representative institutions. Thus, specifying the actor-centric model, party's governing agency – so as influenced by their representative agency – within processes of installations appears as follow (Table 2.2).

Very much like the previous model, in this case as well the actors involved are confronted with the incentives and costs of cooperation stemming from their power positions, P, and normative orientation. Yet, unlike in the previous case, political parties' normative orientation is the compounded result of given social divisions, SD, which is the "raw material political entrepreneurs work with" (Enyedi 2005, 700) and the decisions taken by political entrepreneurs when formulating their political offer, PO. The fist parameter, that is SD, increases at pace of the number and/or depth of pre-existent social divisions. The latter can also be expressed as $1/(|P_A - P_B|)$ where P_A and P_B represent the positioning of parties A and B within the political space. PO, which is clearly the inverse of political polarization, can therefore be thought of as an index of the centripetal drives present within the party system. Clearly, these three factors are not independent. More than often, they are correlated. For instance, deeply divided societies induce ideological polarization. Yet, attesting the primacy of one or the other factor in the determination of party systems' outlook is an open debate. In purely formal terms, the resolution of the present game allows for different Nash equilibria, but suggests that cooperation is the dominant strategy under three different scenarios, each emphasizing one of the features alternatively pinpointed by scholars as responsible for party systems' configuration, and – in turn – for the transitional outcomes.

Pre-existing social divisions

One possible formulation for solving the transition game (SD < PO – P) could be that cooperation is the dominant strategy when social divisions are not very pronounced, so they act as parties' power advantage, and are easily outweighed by the incentives parties have in cooperation. In this case, the attention falls on the attributes society presents, and to which many scholars have devoted their works. Drawing from the political sociology tradition, according to which party systems reflect and 'freeze' pre-existing social cleavages (Lipset and Rokkan 1967), many scholars attribute the quality of parties' governing process – and in particular the feasibility of the bargaining process – to social traits. Even though in consolidated democracies the paradigm of cleavage politics appears to be under revision (Franklin 1992), in emerging democracies, this aspect is deemed to be more relevant where

> democratic elections create feedback loops of accountability and responsiveness that foster a certain convergence between the preferences of constituencies, as democratic principles, and their representatives, as legislative agents, and reward or punish the latter for their contribution to the governance of the polity.
>
> (Kitschelt et al. 1999, 77)

Newborn or reorganized parties tend indeed to secure their survival by acting as 'satisfiers' of the demands of their constituencies (Frye 2010). It follows that the presence of intense social divisions in transitional settings is regarded as a threat to the consensual politics needed to set up new democratic institutions. This concern was already expressed by Rustow when he treated national unity as the background condition to democratic transition meaning that "the vast majority of citizens in a democracy-to-be must have no doubt or mental reservations as to which political community they belong to" (1970, 350). In this respect, the presence of identity or religious cleavages in divided societies makes the feasibility of democracy quite uncertain (Horowitz 1993). Transitions from the authoritarian rule in the MENA region display both kind of social divisions. Yet, while there is a widely shared agreement that tribal divisions are at the heart of the Libyan failure (Heydemann 2016; Shehata 2014), it is not clear how the religious divide can account for the different transitional outcomes across Tunisia and Egypt. Chapter 3 will shed light on the nature and depth of such a cleavage through a multinomial modeling of the vote choice in the founding elections to ascertain whether Tunisian success and the concomitant Egyptian failure are to be attributed to different social divides that are expressed by transitional political parties.

Institutional incentives

Transitional societies might be divided along different and multiple fractures but such divisions are not always conducive to a polarized party system. What matters in this regard is how they are translated into the governing party system. In this regard, the specific format and degree of polarization displayed by a given party system has been explained by pinpointing the role of state institutions in converting social divisions in political divisions. The second scenario conducive to cooperation ($P < PO - SD$) occurs when no party (or faction) enjoys great power advantage, in the absence of problems related to the excessive polarization of the party system. In this case, as a number of scholars have noticed, the predominance of one faction over the its rivals contributes to explain why certain transitions fail while others succeed. Central to these considerations is the role of the electoral systems in emphasizing or smoothing parties' electoral strength inside representative institutions (Carey 2014; Masoud 2014) and the consequences electoral systems have on both the format (Duverger 1954) and the polarization (Sartori 1976) of party systems and the decision-making process overall. Yet, as it will be shown in Chapter 4, the opportunity structures characterizing previous regimes can also account for explaining the distribution of power resources among the parties of a given party system.

Choices parties define

A third scenario occurs when the incentives toward moderation outweigh parties' power advantage and the degree of societal divisions (PO > P + SD). This is the case wherein political parties successfully manage to act as "countervailing mechanisms" to social polarization described by the inclusion moderation hypothesis (Driessen 2014; Tepe 2013) and whenever problems of credible commitment are settled (Kalyvas 2000; Ly Netterstrøm 2015). Indeed, sociological and institutional accounts alone cannot fully explain the cleavages' structure and the degree of polarization of a party system. On the one hand, political sociology falls short in explaining the sinusoidal relevance for the vote choice of certain divides that do not reflect the actual socio/demographic composition of society, such as for instance the relevance of religion in modernized and secularized societies (Elff 2009; Evans and De Graaf 2013; Thomassen 2005). On the other hand, while the institutional structure, such as the electoral system and the form of government, can account for the format of the party system, it cannot predict the dividing lines or the degree polarization of the emerging party system, which owes a lot to political parties' entrepreneurship. In this sense the concept of agency refers to "significant elite actions in which the actors face a relatively high degree of choice" (Deegan-Krause and Enyedi 2010, 695). Here the focus is on political entrepreneurs' choices when aggregating and articulating social demands for the formulation of public policy options. When doing so, political parties' elites actually decide to what issues they devote their attention, thus emphasizing issues' salience; how to position with regard these issues; and how to combine them on programmatic platforms. This is part of the wider representative agency functions described by Mair (2002). From this, the presence or absence of political polarization is in large part attributable to political entrepreneurs' choices concerning the salience some issues should have and their party's positioning vis-à-vis them. Nonetheless, more attention should be devoted to investigating how such decisions are taken, which is exactly what will be done in the Chapter 5.

The invisible hand of upgraded autocracies on parties' strategies

As described above, parties' decisions to cooperate in establishing the rules of game are the result of pre-existing social divisions, their agency, and their power position inside elected bodies. Because the parties entitled to take crucial decisions within the installation process are the same that operated also under the previous authoritarian regime, it might be the case that the structuring of competition under non-democratic rules has a role in transitional parties' strategies, which, in turn, have a role in the success or failure of a transition.

Several contributions in post-democratization studies rightly pinpoint to the role of structures (Albrecht and Schlumberger 2004; Carothers 2002; Valbjørn 2012). Yet, while being extremely enlightening, such accounts largely fail to contextualize the role of structures within the transition. In particular, these accounts fall short in explaining when and how such structures might have come into play. After all, both countries experienced the same kind of transition from the fall of authoritarianism up to the moment elected political parties became central in the decision-making process. In light of this, the crucial question is how authoritarian structures can account for parties' behavior.

Scholars engaged in understanding why Arab authoritarianisms appeared so resilient before the uprisings of 2011 – and also after the revolts, considering the "modest harvest" of the Arab Spring – showed that this was in large part to be attributed to the then incumbents' deliberate strategies aimed at undermining patterns of democratization following the partial and cosmetic overture of those regimes to democratic procedures (Albrecht 2010; Heydemann 2007; Lust-Okar 2005). Beginning in the mid-1970s, Arab autocracies underwent a process of economic liberalization led by the International Monetary Found (IMF) and the World Bank to recover from the failures of their socialist economic planning. To align with democratic standards, these economic openings were also accompanied by measures of political liberalization. These novelties led to a major adjustment in the strategies and the structures incumbents needed to maintain power, shifting from allocative to inclusionary co-optation (Albrecht 2005; Albrecht and Schlumberger 2004). In addition to the introduction of nominal democratic procedures, such as the reopening of national parliaments and the calling of elections, incumbent dictators relied on a complex mix of formal and informal tools to secure their power. On the one hand, as Lust showed, they created uneven structures of competition allowing some opposition parties to compete for elections while banning others (Lust-Okar 2005). On the other hand, they arbitrarily employed more implicit forms of co-optation, frauds, and repressive means which often entailed a certain degree of violence (Gandhi and Lust-Okar 2009; Kraetzschmar and Cavatorta 2010; Schedler 2002). In this way, the dictators of the region could manipulate the political space by directly intervening on inclusion and competition with tremendous effects for the proliferation of party-like formations and their mutual relations (Abdelrahman 2009; Albrecht 2010; Gandhi and Przeworski 2007; Kraetzschmar 2011; Resta 2018).

All the political entrepreneurs involved in the processes of transition in Tunisia and Egypt developed their political learning within authoritarian regimes. By the same token, almost all the relevant political parties – like Ennahda, the FJP, Ettakatol, Wasat and CPR – which handled power after the downfall of the previous regimes and were called to give their country a democratic constitution, started their process of institutionalization within the uneven structural setup just described. Therefore, it is plausible to think that while, prior to 2011, these structures served their purpose in that they altered the development of genuine patterns of competition and participation, they nonetheless are also at the root of differences in parties' power resources and ideological polarization of the transitional party system once the dictator is gone.

Previous opportunity structures and transitional party advantage

Divisions between legal and illegal oppositions in upgraded authoritarian regimes created different opportunities structures for the partisan factions active during the autocratic era with consequences as far as the installation phase after the fall of the regime is concerned. Before the uprisings, legalized oppositions could run for elections and they eventually joined the ruling party inside representative institutions. With the passing of the time, they ended up colluding with the authoritarian regime, mostly because of the spoils system employed by the regime to reward loyal oppositions. Illegal oppositions, for their part, were all prevented from joining the electoral race, but the channels of mobilization available to them varied from one party, or movement, to another. Across the Arab region, the illegal oppositions included both previously strong leftist parties and Islamists movements. Even though all the illegal oppositions relied on the same (il)legal plan, authoritarian repression did not damage them equally for reasons related to dictators' strategic calculations and to the structural organization of the targeted group. The harsh repression against leftist groups started in the late 1970s as a consequence of the popular support they enjoyed in denouncing regime's economic deficiencies. Suppressing them was indeed a somewhat easy task for dictators because these formations relied all on well-known and traditional channels of leftist mobilization, such as workers and students' associations or networks inside factories and poorer areas, which the state apparatus eventually infiltrated or crushed (Bianchi 1989; Hinnebusch 1981, 2005; Perkins 2004). In so doing, the regime propagandistically recurred to arguments related to the preservation of national unity, to the stability needed to achieve economic and social development, and, crucially, to the defense of the values of religion from atheism. In contrast, when dealing with Islamic movements in mid-1980s, the regime used a double strategy. On the one hand, as for leftist formations, political formations inspired by Islam were violently repressed whenever proved to be too strong to be cooptated. On the other hand, the presence and the proliferation of Islamic associations was tolerated for fear of being regarded as offenders of religion and due to the conviction that Islamists were easily controllable and innocuous (Bianchi 1989; Lust 2011; Wickham 2002).

Following from this, some parties already enjoyed a mobilization advantage with the advent of the first free, fair, and democratic elections in 2011 and 2012 (Resta 2018). As far as the front of previous legal oppositions is concerned, these, as expected, achieved only poor electoral showings. They were perceived as part of the previous authoritarian regimes and by relying for their survival on regime's benevolence they dismissed their partisan infrastructure, rendering them both unpopular and unprepared for genuine electoral politics. Previous illegal oppositions were expected to be welcomed by the electorate for their real opposition to the previous regime, but leftist parties found themselves without any kind of linkage with their potential constituencies because the regime had dismantled them. Islamist formations instead could rely instead on the extant religious networks which they had exploited and used also during authoritarian rule (Masoud 2014). It then follows that the P parameter in our model, which measures a given party's power position through the number of a party's seats in the elected parliament, is indeed much more influenced by previous patterns of uneven competition than thinking of it as a parameter of the effect of the electoral system, or as an index of parties' real support, would allow. Possibly, as Chapter 4 will show, Islamist dominance at the ballot box, far from proving that Arab citizens want an Islamist rule, simply confirms that authoritarian regime's structures continues to exert their influence also after its collapse, and that, for this reason, the development of a genuine party system takes time (Capoccia and Ziblatt 2010; Kitschelt 1992; Mainwaring and Scully 1995; Pierson 2004).

Political learning and transitional party systems' polarization

The way dictators shaped competition in the Arab region does not only affect parties' power resources once they have been ousted. It is equally important that they have a role in shaping the nature and the degree of the ideological polarization emerging in the process of transition. It is so because parties' politicking is a "signaling game" among the competing parties whereby past experiences of political learning determine the salience parties' entrepreneurs will accord to specific issues and their positioning on them (Kitschelt 1995, 456). Hence, the way political competition and political participation were structured might account also in this case for the different outcome of the transition observed in Tunisia and Egypt, but under a different light.

Writing before the Arab Spring, Lust noticed that prolonged economic crises hitting the Arab countries were not conducive to the rise of popular protests or political reforms, as students of democratization expected, due to the way political participation was structured by incumbent dictators. More precisely, oppositions' inability to organize a united front against the regimes was due to the arbitrary division of oppositions between legal and illegal, which ended up in magnifying the differences between the two camps by altering actors' cost of cooperation. It is so because under structures of competition so designed, and given the reasons to voice against the status quo, excluded groups would necessarily face higher costs in case of failure when confronting the regime, including harsh repression, imprisonment, and the like, and therefore will tend to exploit possible mobilization initiatives prompted by legal oppositions. Yet, at the same time, legal oppositions are discouraged from confronting the regime in that they face the risk of losing the privileges they acquired and, if their initiatives are successfully exploited by illegal oppositions, they can also be victims of repression. Therefore, the status quo is hardly challenged. From the perspective of our investigation on the role of parties in transitional settings, the interesting consequence of this kind of institutional arrangement is its tendency to polarize opposition actors: the excluded groups continue to capitalize on popular discontent by increasing the saliency of critical issues; the included actors will perceive the former as a threat to their power position and will tend to align with the regime in opposing them.

When the division between included and excluded groups overlaps with the division between secularist and Islamist oppositions, and when the authoritarian regimes are secular in their institutional foundations and ideology, then the ideological evolution of those groups is subject to a centrifugal pushing around the religious divide. Islamist illegal oppositions tend to radicalize their claims, sometimes recurring to violence, while legal secularist oppositions, uncertain over the real strength of the illegal opposition and their true intentions, will tend to adopt anti-Islamist stance to preserve their privileges for they see them at risk in case of Islamists' success (Lust 2011). In contrast, if Islamists oppositions are included into the electoral competition, then the ideological alignment of both groups is subject to centripetal pushes following what Somer predicted with his inclusion-moderation hypothesis (2014). On the one hand, the electoral competition will force Islamists parties to reduce the salience and moderate their positioning about religious issues – gradually moving away from the implementation of shari'a, diminishing references to jihad, recognizing the rights of religious minorities and acknowledging women's rights – to maximize their votes for entering state institutions (Kurzman and Naqvi 2010). On the other hand, secular opposition parties, facing such moderation, will reduce their anti-Islamist stances and tend to compete with religious formations on other issues such as the economic ones.

Tunisia and Egypt, since late 1970s, have been both regarded as secular regimes characterized by divided structures of competition exhibiting the cleavage between secular opposition, included in political competition, and Islamists who are instead excluded from it (Lust 2011; 2005). Even though, in both countries, excluded groups included also left/secular parties that had proved to be strong in the mid-1970s. Nonetheless, beyond this broad description, important differences are given across Tunisia and Egypt insofar while in Tunisia Islamist formations were excluded from political competition and occasionally repressed in all spheres of society, in Egypt they were tolerated as associational organizations and, even though formally excluded from political competition, they were allowed to field independent candidates in parliamentary elections. In addition to the effects of the formal structures of competition, it is also plausible to think that the way dictators informally intervened in the party system has observable repercussions as well on polarization at the time of installation.

Drawing from this, it is then plausible to expect that the choices political parties define in shaping their electoral offer when aggregating dispersed interests, that is our model parameter *PO*, will reflect different patterns of political learning due to different formal structures of competition and informal means of manipulation more or less conducive to political polarization. This aspect is discussed in depth throughout the fifth chapter.

References

Abdelrahman, Maha. 2009. "'With the Islamists?—Sometimes. With the State?—Never!' Cooperation between the Left and Islamists in Egypt." *British Journal of Middle Eastern Studies* 36 (1): 37–54. https://doi.org/10.1080/13530190902749556.

Ahmed, Amel, and Giovanni Capoccia. 2014. "The Study of Democratization and the Arab Spring." *Middle East Law and Governance* 6: 1–31. https://doi.org/10.1163/18763375-00601002.

Albrecht, Holger. 2005. "How Can Opposition Support Authoritarianism? Lessons from Egypt." *Democratization* 12 (3): 378–97. https://doi.org/10.1080/13510340500126798.

———. 2010. *Contentious Politics in the Middle East : Political Opposition under Authoritarianism*. Gainesville: University of Florida Press.

Albrecht, Holger, and Oliver Schlumberger. 2004. "'Waiting for Godot': Regime Change without Democratization in the Middle East." *International Political Science Review* 25 (4): 371–92.

Asseburg, Muriel, and Heiko Wimmen. 2016. "Dynamics of Transformation, Elite Change and New Social Mobilization in the Arab World." *Mediterranean Politics* 21 (1): 1–22. https://doi.org/10.1080/13629395.2015.1081448.

Bermeo, Nancy. 1990. "Rethinking Regime Change." *Comparative Politics* 22 (3): 359–77.

Bianchi, Robert. 1989. *Unruly Corporativism: Associational Life in Twentieth-Century Egypt*. New York: Oxford University Press.

Brownlee, Jason, Tarek Masoud, and Andrew Reynolds. 2015. *The Arab Spring: Pathways of Repression and Reform*. Oxford: Oxford University Press.

Capoccia, G., and D. Ziblatt. 2010. *The Historical Turn in Democratization Studies: A New Research Agenda for Europe and Beyond. Comparative Political Studies*. Vol. 43. https://doi.org/10.1177/0010414010370431.

Carey, John M. 2014. "Party Systems and the Choice Sets Voters Confront in Transitions to Democracy." In *Workshop on Democracy and Regime Change*, 1–31. Istanbul: Sabanci University.

Carothers, Thomas. 2002. "The End of the Transition Paradigm." *Journal of Democracy* 13 (1): 5–21. https://doi.org/10.1353/jod.2002.0003.

Cavatorta, Francesco, Lise Storm, and Valeria Resta. 2021. *Routledge Handbook on Political Parties in the Middle East and North Africa*. Edited by Francesco Cavatorta, Lise Storm, and Valeria Resta. Abingdon, Oxon: Routledge.

Colomer, Joseph M. 1995. *Game Theory and the Transition to Democracy: The Spanish Model*. Aldershot Hants: Edward Elgar.

Cross, Ester, and Jason Sorens. 2016. "Arab Spring Constitution-Making: Polarization, Exclusion, and Constraints." *Democratization* 23 (7): 1292–1312. https://doi.org/10.1080/13510347.2015.1107719.

Dahl, Robert A. 1971. *Polyarchy: Participation and Opposition*. New Haven and London: Yale University Press.

Deegan-Krause, Kevin, and Zsolt Enyedi. 2010. "Agency and the Structure of Party Competition: Alignment, Stability and the Role of Political Elites." *West European Politics* 33 (3): 686–710. https://doi.org/10.1080/01402381003654742.

Diamond, Larry Jay. 2002. "Thinking about Hybrid Regimes." *Journal of Democracy* 13 (2): 21–35. https://doi.org/10.1353/jod.2002.0025.

Driessen, Michael D. 2014. *Religion and Democratization: Framing Religious and Political Identities in Muslim and Catholic Societies*. New York: Oxford University Press.

Duverger, Maurice. 1954. *Political Parties*. London: Methuen.

Elff, Martin. 2009. "Social Divisions, Party Positions, and Electoral Behaviour." *Electoral Studies* 28 (2): 297–308. https://doi.org/10.1016/j.electstud.2009.02.002.

Elster, Jon. 1995. "Forces and Mechanisms in the Constitution-Making Process." *Duke Law Journal* 45 (2): 364–96.

Elster, Jon, Claus Offe, and Ulrich K. Preuss. 1998. *Institutional Design in Post-Communist Societies: Rebuilding the Ship at Sea*. New York: Cambridge University Press.

Enyedi, Zsolt. 2005. "The Role of Agency in Cleavage Formation." *European Journal of Political Research* 44 (5): 697–720. https://doi.org/10.1111/j.1475-6765.2005.00244.x.

Evans, Geoffrey, and Nan Dirk De Graaf. 2013. *Political Choice Matters: Explaining the Strength of Class and Religious Cleavages in Cross-National Perspective*. Oxford: Oxford University Press.

Franklin, Mark N. 1992. "The Decline of Cleavage Politics." In *Electoral Change: Responses to Evolving Social and Attitudinal Structures in Western Countries*, edited by Mark N. Franklin, Thomas T. Mackie, and Henry Valen, Cambridge: Cambridge University Press 1992:383–405.

Frye, Timothy. 2010. *Building States and Markets After Communism: The Perils of Polarized Democracy*. New York: Cambridge University Press.

Gandhi, Jennifer, and Ellen Lust-Okar. 2009. "Elections Under Authoritarianism." *Annual Review of Political Science* 12 (1): 403–22. https://doi.org/10.1146/annurev.polisci.11.060106.095434.

Gandhi, Jennifer, and Adam Przeworski. 2007. "Authoritarian Institutions and the Survival of Autocrats." *Comparative Political Studies* 40 (11): 1279–1301.

Geddes, Barbara. 1998. "A Comparative Perspective on the Leninist Legacy in Eastern Europe." *Comparative Political Studies* 28 (2): 239–74.

———. 2006. "Why Parties and Elections in Authoritarian Regimes?" Los Angeles, paper presented at the Annual meeting of the American Political Science Association. CA.

Ginsburg, Tom, Zachary Elkins, and Justin Blount. 2009. "Does the Process of Constitution-Making Matter?" *Annual Review of Law and Social Science* 5: 201–23. https://doi.org/10.1146/annurev.lawsocsci.4.110707.172247.

Hamid, Shadi. 2014. "Political Party Development Before and After the Arab Spring." In *Beyond the Arab Spring: The Evolving Ruling Bargain in the Middle East*, edited by Mehran Kamrava, 131–50. Oxford: Oxford University Press.

Heydemann, Steven. 2007. "Upgrading Authoritarianism in the Arab World." *The Saban Center for Middle East Policy at the Brooking Institution*. Vol. 13: 1–40.

———. 2016. "Explaining the Arab Uprisings: Transformations in Comparative Perspective." *Mediterranean Politics* 21 (1): 1–13. https://doi.org/10.1080/13629395.2015.1081450.

Higley, John, and Michael G. Burton. 1989. "The Elite Variable in Democratic Transitions and Breakdowns." *American Sociological Review* 54 (1): 17–32. https://repositories.lib.utexas.edu/handle/2152/10296.

Hinnebusch, Raymond. 1981. "The National Progressive Unionist Party : The Nationalist-Left Opposition in Post-Populist Egypt." *Arab Law Quarterly* 3 (4): 325–51.

———. 2005. "Political Parties and Trade Unions." In *A Companion to the History of the Middle East*, 334–54. Malden, Oxford and Carlton: Blackwell Publishing Ltd.

Horowitz, Donald L. 1993. "Democracy in Divided Societies." *Journal of Democracy* 4 (4): 18–38. https://doi.org/10.1353/jod.1993.0054.

Huntington, Samuel P. 1968. *Political Order in Changing Societies*. New Haven and London: Yale University Press.

Kalyvas, Stathis N. 2000. "Commitment Problems in Emerging Democracies: The Case of Religious Parties." *Comparative Politics* 32 (4): 379–98. http://www.jstor.org/stable/422385.

Kitschelt, Herbert. 1992. "Political Regime Change: Structure and Process-Driven Explanations?" *American Political Science Review* 86 (4): 1028–34.

———. 1995. "Formation of Party Cleavages in Post-Communist Democracies: Theoretical Propositions." *Party Politics* 1(4):447–72. https://doi.org/10.1177/1354068895001004002.

Kitschelt, Herbert, Zdenka Mansfeldova, Radoslaw Markowski, and Gábor Tóka. 1999. *Post-Communist Party Systems: Competition, Representation and Inter-Party Cooperation*. New York: Cambridge University Press. http://www.amazon.com/dp/052165890X.

Kraetzschmar, Hendrik. 2011. "Mapping Opposition Cooperation in the Arab World: From Single-Issue Coalitions to Transnational Networks." *British Journal of Middle Eastern Studies* 38 (3): 287–302. https://doi.org/10.1080/13530194.2011.621687\r(null).

Kraetzschmar, Hendrik, and Francesco Cavatorta. 2010. "Bullets over Ballots : Islamist Groups, the State and Electoral Violence in Egypt and Morocco." *Democratization* 17 (2): 326–49. https://doi.org/10.1080/13510341003588757.

Kuenzi, Michelle, and Gina Lambright. 2001. "Party Systems and Democratic Consolidation in Africa's Electoral Regimes." *Party Politics* 11 (4): 423–46. https://doi.org/10.1177/1354068805053211.

———. 2005. "Party System Institutionalization in 30 African Countries." *Party Politics* 7 (4): 437–68. http://ppq.sagepub.com.pros.lib.unimi.it/content/7/4/437.full.pdf.

Kurzman, Charles, and Ijlal Naqvi. 2010. "Do Muslims Vote Islamic?" *Journal of Democracy* 21 (2): 50–63.

Landau, David. 2012. "The Importance of Constitution-Making." *Denver University Law Review* 89 (2): 1–23.

Lesch, Ann M. 2014. "Troubled Political Transitions: Tunisia, Egypt and Libya." *Middle East Policy* 21 (1): 62–74.

Linz, Juan J., and Alfred C. Stepan. 1996. *Problems of Democratic Transition and Consolidation: Southern Europe, South America and Post-Communist Europe*. Baltimore: Johns Hopkins University Press.

Lipset, Seymour Martin, and Stein Rokkan. 1967. *Party Systems and Voter Alignments: Cross-National Perspectives*. New York: Free Press.

Lust, Ellen. 2011. "Missing the Third Wave: Islam, Institutions, and Democracy in the Middle East." *Studies in Comparative International Development* 46 (2): 163–90. https://doi.org/10.1007/s12116-011-9086-z.

Lust-Okar, Ellen. 2005. *Structuring Conflict in the Arab World: Incumbents, Opponents, and Institutions*. Cambridge: Cambridge University Press.

Ly Netterstrøm, Kasper. 2015. "The IslamIsts' Compromise in Tunisia." *Journal of Democracy* 26 (4): 110–24. https://doi.org/10.1353/jod.2015.0055.

Mainwaring, Scott. 1998. "Party Systems in the Third Wave." *Journal of Democracy* 9 (3): 67–81.

Mainwaring, Scott, and Timothy R. Scully. 1995. *Biulding Democratic Institutions: Party Systems in Latin America*. Stanford: Stanford University Press.

Mair, Peter. 2002. "Populist Democracy vs. Party Democracy." In *Democracies and the Populist Challenge*, edited by Yves Mény and Yves Suret, 81–98. Basingstoke UK: Palgrave.

Masoud, Tarek. 2014. *Counting Islam: Religion, Class and Elections in Egypt*. New York: Cambridge University Press.

McFaul, Michael. 2002. "The Fourth Wave of Democracy and Dictatorship: Noncooperative Transitions in ThePostcommunist World." *World Politics* 54 (2): 212–44.

Merkel, Wolfgang. 1998. "The Consolidation of Post Autocratic Democracies : A Multi Level Model." *Democratization* 3 (3): 37–41.

Morlino, Leonardo. 1995. "Political Parties and Democratic Consolidation in Southern Europe." In *The Politics of Democratic Consolidation: Southern Europe in Comparative Perspective*, 315–88. Baltimore: Johns Hopkins University Press.

———. 2011. *Changes for Democracy: Actors, Structures, Processes*. New York: Oxford University Press.

———. 2015. "Transition to Democracy: What Theory to Grasp Complexity?" *Historien* 15: 13–31.

Negretto, Gabriel L. 1999. "Constitution-Making and Institutional Design. The Transformation Presidentialism in Argentina." *European Journal of Sociology* 40 (2): 1–33. https://doi.org/10.1017/S0003975600007451.

O'Donnell, Guillermo, and Philippe C. Schmitter. 1986. "Transition from Authoritarian Rule: Tentative Conclusion about Uncertain Democracies." In *Transitions from Authoritarian Rule: Southern Europe*, edited by Guillermo O'Donnell, Philippe C. Schmitter, and Laurence Withehead, 1st ed. Baltimore: John Hopkins University Press.

Perkins, Kenneth J. 2004. *A History of Modern Tunisia*. Cambridge: Cambridge University Press.

Perthes, Volker. 2004. *Arab Elites: Negotiating the Politics of Change*. Boulder, CO: Lynne Rienner Publishers.

Pierson, Paul. 2004. *Politics in Time: History, Institutions and Social Analysis*. Princeton: Princeton University Press.

Przeworski, Adam. 1991. *Democracy and the Market: Political and Economic Reforms in Eastern Europe and Latin America*. Cambridge: Cambridge University Press.

———. 2006. "Self-Enforcing Democracy." *The Oxford Handbook of Political Economy*, 1–21.

Raiffa, Howard. 1982. *The Art and Science of Negotiation*. Cambridge, MA: Cambridge University Press.

Randall, V., and L. Svasand. 2002. "Party Institutionalization in New Democracies." *Party Politics* 8 (1): 5–29. https://doi.org/10.1177/1354068802008001001.

Randall, V., and L. Svåsand. 2002. "Introduction: The Contribution of Parties to Democracy and Democratic Consolidation." *Democratization* 9 (3): 1–10. https://doi.org/10.1080/714000270.

Randall, Vicky. 2001. "Party System and Voter Alignments in the New Democracies of the Third World." In *Party System and Voter Alignment Revisited*, edited by Lauri Karvonen and Stein Kuhnle, 238–60. London and New York: Routledge.

Resta, Valeria. 2018. "Leftist Parties in the Arab Region before and after the Arab Uprisings: Unrequited Love?" In *Political Parties in the Arab World: Continuity and Change*, edited by Francesco Cavatorta and Lise Storm, 23–48. Edinburgh: Edinburgh University Press.

Reynolds, Andrew. 2002. *The Architecture of Democracy: Constitutional Design, Conflict Management, and Democracy*. Edited by Andrew Reynolds. New York: Oxford University Press.

Rustow, Dankwart A. 1970. "Transition to Democracy: Toward a Dynamic Model." *Comparative Politics* 2 (3): 337–63.

Sartori, Giovanni. 1976. *Parties and Party Systems. A Framework for Analysis*. Cambridge: Cambridge University Press. https://tinyurl.com/ycyudw97

———. 1987. *A Theory of Democracy Revisited*. Chatham, N.J.: Chatham House.

Schedler, Andreas. 2002. "The Menu of Manipulation." *Journal of Democracy* 13 (2): 36–50. https://doi.org/10.1353/jod.2002.0031.

Shehata, Dina. 2014. "The Arab Uprisings and the Prospects for Building Shared Societies." *Development* 57 (1): 84–95. https://doi.org/10.1057/dev.2014.29.

Somer, Murat. 2014. "Moderation of Religious and Secular Politics, a Country's 'Centre' and Democratization." *Democratization* 21 (2): 244–67. https://doi.org/10.1080/13510347.2012.732069.

Storm, Lise. 2014. *Party Politics and the Prospects for Democracy in North Africa*. Boulder, CO: Lynne Rienner.

Tavana, Daniel L. 2012. Consensus after conflict: Electoral system choice in revolutionary Egypt. John F. Kennedy School of Government.

Tepe, Sultan. 2013. "The Perils of Polarization and Religious Parties: The Democratic Challenges of Political Fragmentation in Israel and Turkey." *Democratization* 20 (5): 831–56. https://doi.org/10.1080/13510347.2013.801254.

Thomassen, Jacques. 2005. "Modernization or Politics?" *The European Voter: A Comparative Study of Modern Democracies*. Edited by Thomassen Jacques. Oxford: Oxford University Press: 254–265.

Tsebelis, George. 2002. *Veto Players: How Political Institutions Work.* Princeton: Princeton University Press.

Valbjørn, Morten. 2012. "Upgrading Post-Democratization Studies: Examining a Re-Politicized Arab World in a Transition to Somewhere." *Middle East Critique* 21 (1): 25–35. https://doi.org/10.1080/19436149.2012.658496.

Weingast, Barry R. 1997. "The Political Foundations of Democracy and the Rule of Law." *The American Political Science Review* 91 (2): 245–63. https://doi.org/10.2307/2952354.

Wickham, Carrie Rosefsky. 2002. *Mobilizing Islam: Religion, Activism, and Political Change in Egypt*. Columbia University Press.

Yardimci-Geyikci, Sebnem. 2015. "Party Institutionalization and Democratic Consolidation: Turkey and Southern Europe in Comparative Perspective." *Party Politics* 21 (4): 527–38. https://doi.org/10.1177/1354068813487110.

Yeh, Jiunn-rong, and Wen-chen Chang. 2009. "The Changing Landscape of Modern Constitutionalism : Transitional Perspective." *National Taiwan University Law Review* 4 (1): 145–84.

3 Homogeneous vs. divided societies? Analyzing the demand of representation

2011–2 founding elections: transitional challenges stemming from the emergence of two imagined communities

Islamists vs. secularists and the need for pre-constitutional consensus

In 2009 Nader Hashemi wrote that "in societies where religion is a marker of identity, the road to liberal democracy, whatever other twists and turns it makes, cannot avoid passing through the gates of religious politics" (2009, 9). What happened after the 2011 uprisings seems to confirm his claim. In the two cases when the 2011 mass protests led to free, fair, and competitive elections, Islamist parties appeared in both cases as the leading political force even though the protests were led by young, leftist, and secularized people. As illustrated in the first chapter, the results of the founding elections, which saw the victory of Islamist factions, not only seemed to reinvigorate the conventional wisdom according to which Muslim populations are inherently imbued with religion (Huntington 1996; Kedourie 1992), they also presented the picture of two polarized publics, a potential danger for the process of installation. As outlined in the previous chapter, this process refers to the establishment of the rules of the game behind the functioning of the polity. Yet, in order to do so, it presupposes the definition of the political community for which such rules are designed, and, in this respect, the presence of two inherently opposed 'imagined communities' can represent a major obstacle for a compromise to see the light. It is a fact that constitutions always "identify and formalize the most fundamental beliefs, norms, values and aspirations of the political collectivity" (Lerner 2011, 26). This entails "the need for pre-constitutional societal consensus regarding shared norms and values that underpin the state" (ibid., 27). In the literature, this has been referred to as, alternatively, national unity (Rustow 1970), a set of shared beliefs (Elster 1995; Higley and Burton 1989), or a shared political culture (Lipset 1959; Weingast 1997). Viewed in this way, the fact that in Tunisia and Egypt the public appeared divided as far as both identity and preferred political regime were concerned, leads to questions about the existence of such pre-constitutional consensus.

DOI: 10.4324/9781003269717-4

Analyzing the demand of representation

Why does the religious divide matter? Substance vs. form

While the religious divide is unanimously considered as a threat to democratic consensus, the reasons underpinning this position range from substance to form-related accounts. First, the religious divide is particularly puzzling for the installation of a democratic polity (Bâli and Lerner 2017; Driessen 2014; Stepan 2000) in that religion is at once an "infungible identity" (Hashemi 2009) and a system of rules whose obedience often contrasts with the respect of rules in a democratic polity (Huntington 1996; Kedourie 1994; Strauss 1938). The second order of explanations considers the religious divide like any other kind of social division. In this regard, what matters is not the content of the divide but rather its ability to provoke the emergence of two divided societies, i.e. those societies characterized by "intense internal disagreements over the vision of the state" (Lerner 2011, 29). Regardless, the emergence of some forms of "closure of social relationships" that prevents the possibility for cross-cutting alliances, represents a problem for democratic installation because it hampers the democratic compromise (Driessen 2014; Landau 2012; Negretto 1999), leading to a zero-sum bargaining process that undermines the legitimation of the incipient regime (Gunther and Mughan 1993; Negretto 1999). From this it follows that the focus shifts from the nature to the depth and the compositions of the observed divide (Chandra 2005; Chandra and Boulet 2003; Gunther and Mughan 1993; Horowitz 1993).

Paralleling these ontological differences, some scholars have recently accounted for the outcomes observed in Tunisia and Egypt by pointing to the need for a conceptual refinement aimed at capturing the fact that such kind of transition processes are qualitatively different from the ones known thus far (and that hence inform the body of scholarship of democratization studies) because of the prominent role of the disagreement over the role of religion (Blaydes and Lo 2012; Brown 2017; Driessen 2014; Parolin 2013; Stepan and Linz 2013). Other students, by contrast, account for the different patterns of transition in the two countries by investigating the depth and the composition of the religious divide. Within this latter camp, a variety of positions have emerged. For some, the religious divide is confined to a limited set of social issues linked to the role of women and is more likely to be circumscribed to the middle class (Wegner and Cavatorta 2018; Merone 2015; Pellicer and Wegner 2014). For others, the religious divide expresses a socio/economic differentiation between wealthier people included into the social and economic system – voting for secular parties – and the deprived strata of the society – voting for Islamist parties instead (Van Hamme, Gana, and Maher 2014; Elsayyad and Hanafy 2014). In a similar vein, marginalized people are reported to vote for Islamist parties on the basis of either their perceived priorities expressed through defined policy preferences (Berman and Nugent 2015; Garcia-Rivero and Kotze 2007) or because of the material benefits that might come with such kind of vote choice (Clark 2004a,b; Lisa 2010; Lust 2009). In contraposition with this reading, some studies have found a positive correlation between low-income strata and the choice to vote for secular regime parties in reason of vote-buying and other patronage strategies adopted by such parties to secure votes in the poorer area (Corstange 2018). Finally, another reading conceives the religious divide as a function of the channels of socialization available to citizens, and explains the Islamists' dominance in terms of greater opportunities they enjoy to get in touch with potential voters (Masoud 2014).

All these accounts, while shedding light on the determinants of voting behaviour for Islamists parties, do not allow for a comprehensive understanding of the nature and the depth of the religious divide that characterized the 2011–2 elections in Tunisia and Egypt. Several of these accounts are based on district levels data, others are only interested in finding the determinants of the vote choice for Islamist parties (for a remarkable exception see: Wegner and Cavatorta 2018). In what do the constituencies of the major competing parties differ? Is religious commitment relevant for the vote choice? Does it overlap with other socio-economic features? Is it really driven by different organizational opportunities? Does the 'religious vote' express an anti-democratic posture *per se*, or is it rather the depth of the cleavage which undermines cross-cutting bargaining alliances? Such questions can be better answered through vote choice modeling, relying on the political sociology approach. On the one hand, the employment of vote choice modeling on the basis of surveys' answers allows to highlight the characteristics of the voters of a specific party, thus infusing more precision in the findings. On the other hand, structuring such models on the political sociology approach, which is centred on the concept of cleavage, enables to assess the depth of the divide.

Hypothesizing the origins of the Islamist/secular divide and its consequences for democratic installations

The political sociology approach

The political sociological approach revolves around the idea that critical junctures shaping the history of nations produce several divisions within society that are subsequently politicized by political parties. This leads to the generation of political cleavages that structure the party system and political competition. Despite the fact that the majority of scholars refer to the apparent polarization along the Islamist/secular axis with the term of *cleavage*, Bartolini and Mair's well-known definition makes clear that a cleavage is not simply a division at the ideological *or* social level. Indeed, a cleavage encompasses the two of them, passing through a set of values and beliefs that provide individuals with a sense of belonging to their social group and drive their political choices. For analytical purposes,

> the concept of cleavage can be seen to incorporate three levels: an empirical element, which identifies the empirical referent of the concept, and which we can define in social-structural terms; a normative element, that is the set of values and beliefs which yields a sense of identity and role to the empirical element, and which reflects the self-consciousness of the social group(s) involved; and an organizational/behavioural element, that is the set

of individual interactions, institutions, and organizations, such as political parties, which develop as part of the cleavage.

(Bartolini and Mair 1990, 215)

Hence, either the three elements overlap, or it is better to speak of divisions or differences instead (Deegan-Krause 2006). In Whitefield's words, to properly refer to a cleavage "it is necessary to show that social differentiation exists, that it has intelligible consequences for citizens' ideological perspectives, and that these consequences are important in shaping vote choice" (2002, 186).[1] This precision is required not only for the sake of theoretical meticulousness but, more importantly, for the consequences that such competing "form[s] of closure of social relationships" (Bartolini and Mair 1990, 216) might have on the constitution-making process.

According to the approach by Lipset and Rokkan, the divisions within society that will subsequently be politicized to form a cleavage derive from critical junctures, defined as moments in which the placement of "institutional arrangements on paths or trajectories, which are then very difficult to alter" occurs (Pierson 2004). In their model, the processes of creation of nation states and the subsequent Industrial Revolution created dividing lines within European societies that were politicized with the advent of universal suffrage and democratization and that were eventually frozen in the structure of the party systems (Lipset and Rokkan 1967).

Post-independence state building strategies and national fractures

Lipset and Rokkan's study is based upon the experiences of Western European countries and is extremely specific to this reality. Hence, applications of this model outside this context might be problematic. Yet, as Randall (2001) points out, it still represents a useful analytical framework to investigate how divisions within society translate, or not, into the party systems allowing also for cross-countries comparisons (Randall 2001). In her seminal article, the author warns that the nature and the sequence of the occurrence of the critical junctures across Third World countries won't necessarily fall under the predictions of Lipset and Rokkan's model and raises the question of the influence played by colonial experiences in fashioning political cleavages. The fight for independence, which availed itself of the nationalist ideology, prevented indeed the politicization of other social divisions (ibid.). However, new cleavages, be them identarian or functional, might appear as a consequence of post-independent strategies aimed at the formation and the consolidation of the new states. As Migdal illustrates, states' ability to survive largely relies on a series of factors among which mobilization emerges as the most important. Yet, at its origins, the state is just an organization among many others, sometimes in competition with them. To gain compliance, if not legitimation, state leaders must offer individuals a series of attractive incentives.

> Such packaging rests, of course, on the bedrock of material needs, but it also lends meaning to people's behaviour as they meet those needs. A consciousness about social behaviour aims to tie actions together in some meaningful

or purposeful way, to transcend through action the specific act itself. These systems of meaning or symbolic configurations, whether ideology or beliefs or anything else, make manageable a universe, which could otherwise seem overwhelmingly threatening and impenetrable.

(ibid. 26)

Post-independence Tunisia and Egypt exemplify this dynamic. Following the enfranchisement from foreign domination – which in Tunisia was embodied in the French protectorate while in Egypt in the influence exerted by the English crown through the Egyptian royal family even after the official end of colonisation –, Habib Bourguiba and Gamal Abdel Nasser embarked on the construction of a "viable, prosperous and modern state" (Perkins 2004, 130). The economic and social reforms put in place since the mid-50s constitute the policy packages to substantiate the newly acquired independence to attract the allegiance of the people while creating a unified nation, inexistent up to that moment (Gelvin 2004). On the one hand, a series of state-driven economic plans of socialist inspiration were implemented to fight against underdevelopment. On the other hand, the transformation of civil society was pursued through a series of policies aimed at undermining of the role of Islam in the public sphere, as it was supposed to hinder the new, and modern, *esprit* of those countries. It can thus be argued that Tunisia and Egypt, like many others third world countries and differently from western experiences, have only had one critical juncture – that is national independence – that has created two fractures: an identitarian and a functional one. The first opposes those embracing secular and modern values against those nostalgic of the Islamic roots of the Tunisian and Egyptian cultures. The second has created a division between those who benefited from state economic policies (in terms of e.g., infrastructures and work opportunities) and those marginalized, if not exploited, by them. These two lines of divisions are apt to create two different kinds of publics both at the empirical level, that is in individuals' socio/economic conditions, and at the normative level of the cleavage, namely in peoples' values, beliefs, and political convictions. Only if there is covariance between these two levels and the organizational one, can the Islamist/secular divide be properly defined as a cleavage.

Data collection, measures, and methodology

The analysis conducted to investigate the nature and the depth of the divisions that emerged in occasion of the 2011/2012 elections avails itself of the data collected by the Arab Barometer project (hereafter AB). This is a survey dataset that gathers individuals' positions on a series of social, cultural, and religious topics, opinions about institutions and political attitudes along with demographic information that replaces the lack of data at the individual level in the MENA region. At the time of writing (early 2022), AB has conducted six waves of surveys, progressively increasing the number of countries covered, and tracking the change of citizens' attitudes and beliefs over time. For the purposes of the present research, only the Second Wave will be used (hereinafter ABII). This Wave has been conducted during

60 *Analyzing the demand of representation*

the years 2010 and 2011. In Egypt, face-to-face interviews have been conducted from June 16th to July 3rd, while in Tunisia from September 30th to October 15th, 2011. This make these data more reliable as far as the questions about vote intention are concerned for the Tunisian elections, which took place on October 23th, but a bit less for the Egyptian case, where elections started on November 28th, 2011, and concluded on January 11th 2012. The dataset counts as many as 1219 observations in Egypt and 1196 in Tunisia. This latter sample has been subsequently self-weighted for the probability of selection, moreover, post-stratification weights have been used in the present analysis to correct imbalances based on age and gender.

In ascertaining the presence of a cleavage behind the results of 2011/2012 elections, multinomial logistic models have been used to detect possible correlation between the attributes of individuals and the vote choice. The dependent variable is the declared intention of vote defined here as a nominal variable with three categories: vote for Islamists, vote for secular parties, and vote for other parties. By so doing, it will be possible to grasp the differences in the determinants of vote choice between the two major electoral blocs emerging from the electoral contest, holding respondents that voted for other parties as the reference category. However, as Table 3.1 shows, the stemming sample is really small for the low rate of respondents declaring to vote for a political party, 446 in Tunisia and 129 in Egypt, due to indecisiveness (as is the case for Tunisia) or preference for an independent candidate instead (as is the case or Egypt).

Moreover, except for the case of Ennahda, placing individual parties into broader political categories, like what I termed here as "right" and "left", has been necessary to overcome problems of excessive disproportion among categories due to too small size of the cells. Table 3.2 reports the coding procedure. In Tunisia, Ennahda has been contrasted with leftist secular parties, namely the Progressive Democratic Party (PDP), the Democratic Form for Labour and Liberties (Ettakatol), the Congress for Republic (CPR), the Tunisian Workers Party (PTT), Ettajdid, the Socialist Party (PS), and the Tunisian Workers' Communist Party (PCOT). All these parties have been gathered together in light of their leftist roots, programs, and self-definition. Hence, the dependent variable assumes value 1 if the vote choice is for Ennahda, 2 it the vote choice falls on one of the aforementioned leftist parties and 0

Table 3.1 Declared vote intention for the elections of the Constituent Assembly/Parliament

	Tunisia	*Egypt*
Political party	466	129
Independent candidates	102	822
Don't know	585	189
Declined to answer	42	1
Do not participate/will see	1	78
	1,196	1,219

Source: ABII questions EG307 and T307.

Analyzing the demand of representation 61

Table 3.2 Dependent variable coding

	Vote Islamist parties	Vote Liberal/Secular	Vote other parties
Tunisia	240	75	151
Parties included	Ennahda (240)	PDP (30)	
		Ettakatol (15)	
		CPR (18)	
		PTT (2)	
		Ettajdid (2)	
		PS (1)	
		PCOT (7)	
Egypt	40	37	52
Parties included	FJP (33)	Free Egyptians (26)	
	Nour (3)	Wafd (10)	
	Virtue Party (1)	Democratic Front (1)	
	BD (1)		
	Wasat (2)		
DV Value	1	2	0

Note: Numbers in parenthesis indicate the amount of respondents declaring to vote for that specific party.

if respondents declared to vote for other parties. In Egypt, the Freedom and Justice Party (FJP), Nour, the Virtue Party, the Building and Development Party (BD), and Wasat have been considered as belonging to the same category of Islamist parties, with value 1 in the dependent variable, and contrasted against the Right/secular front made up of the Free Egyptians, Wafd party, and the Democratic front, for which the dependent variable assumes the value of 2. Also in this case, when respondents declare to vote for other parties than the ones listed above, the dependent variable assumes the value of 0. In light of the small size of the working sample, tests of representativeness will be presented at the end of the chapter to complement, and add further insights to, the analyses.

The independent variables are designed to account for each level of the cleavage. As far as socio-economic characteristics of individuals are concerned, these are here expressed as self-reported house income, years of schooling, and place of residence and are aimed at capturing patterns of exclusion both at the national and at the regional level to test whether 'material explanations' hold. Self-reported house income is an ordinal variable ranging from 1 to 4 where higher values indicate higher levels of respondents' perceived wealth. Education is also an ordinal variable constructed in accordance with UNESCO's parameters.[2] Following them, each level of completed cycle of studies is here indicated in terms of school years, the minimum values is 0 denoting illiteracy while the maximum is 18 thus indicating at least the achievement of a master degree. The exploration of individuals' material conditions takes here into account also where people live. In order to have a measure of deprivation[3] (Berman and Nugent 2015), a new variable has been created: it assumes value 1 if respondents simultaneously live in rural and marginalized areas, 0 in all the other cases. Marginalized areas have been coded according to the regional pro capita consumption and unemployment rate of respondents' governorate (Boughzala and Hamdi 2014).[4]

The normative level dimension is differentiated here among values and beliefs regarding identity and political attitudes toward policy issues that emerged as salient during the transition. As far as identity issues are concerned, these are measured through self-definition of religiosity and cultural conservatism. The first is a categorical variable assuming three values: not religious (1), somewhat religious (2), and religious (3). The other identity variable – cultural conservatism – is measured through an index reporting individuals' positioning on gender issues. Since some members of religious parties question gender equality through a conservative reading of religious texts and thus invoke the return to a traditional and patriarchal society, it might be probable that individual positioning on such issues will discriminate between Islamists and seculars voters (Zeghal 2013). Because the items included are ordinal categorical variables, this index has been constructed through an exploratory factor analysis on the polychoric correlation matrix of the items included (Choi, Peters, and Mueller 2010; Vermunt and Magidson 2005). This procedure is particularly useful in that it allows for the identification of latent dimensions when working with ordinal variables by assuming that these are obtained by categorizing normally distributed unobserved variables and estimating the maximum likelihood of their product moment correlation. In line with Kostenko et al. (2016), two latent factors emerge: one attributable to the public sphere and the other to the private one. Nonetheless, both need to be considered; therefore, a simple composite index has been created taking into account both spheres. The Cronbach's alpha coefficient for a test scale based on the aforementioned items is 0.775 for Egypt and 0.804 for Tunisia, meaning that the resulting indexes have internal consistency and can be considered reliable measures of individuals' standing on gender issues, both in the public and in the private sphere. The variable so derived is a continuous one assuming values from 1 to 4, where higher values denote increasing opposition to gender equality.

Individuals' regime preferences have been operationalized as: perceived suitability of democracy; preferred kind of regime; preferred source of law and trust toward 'deep state' institutions. Perceived suitability of democracy is a continuous variable ranging from 0 to 10 where higher values stand for respondents' positive evaluation regarding the suitability of democracy for their country. State preference is a dummy variable indicating either support for a religious or a civil state. Two ordinal variables (ranging from 1 to 4) are indeed required for the preferred source of law, indicating increasing support for either the enforcement of laws according to Shari'a or according to popular will. While most studies approach the religious divide in terms of preferences for more religious people in public offices (Garcia-Rivero and Kotze 2007), or just preferences over Shari'a (Berman and Nugent 2015), in this analysis both variables concerning the preferred source of law are included because these are weakly correlated (0.19) meaning that for most of the surveyed people Shari'a and popular will are not mutually exclusive (Jamal and Tessler 2008; Tessler 2015; Tessler and Gao 2005). Keeping both variables is then aimed at accounting for pro or anti-democratic attitudes behind the vote choice that otherwise would be overlooked. Trust toward deep state institutions is also taken into account because many contributions suggest that the vote for Islamist parties is largely attributable to the desire of a radical change with the past (Garcia-Rivero and Kotze 2007; Hashemi 2009). For the case of Egypt, an additive index has been created to account for trust toward the military and the judiciary while for the case of Tunisia, the index is deemed to measure confidence toward the police and the judiciary. Finally, mosque attendance and trade union membership are included to describe whether the link between possible social groups and their normative orientation is mediated by some sort of organizational/environmental component, thus creating a cleavage that is expressed politically through the vote choice. For some authors this organizational dimension alone is sufficient to explain individuals' vote choice (Gunther et al. 2016; Masoud 2014), regardless other forms of divisions. For instance, Pellicer and Wegner found that "in countries with large Islamist networks it is clear that Islamists do not differ demographically from voters of other parties" (Pellicer and Wegner 2015, 5) meaning that what makes the difference in the vote choice is not the socio/economic characterization of voters, but rather how they are politically socialized by the networks they are in. Given the low rate of respondents belonging to a charitable association, only mosque attendance is considered here because of the associational networks that avail themselves of the mosques to exist and develop, and that transcend worshipping functions (Masoud 2014).

All these variables are controlled for (mean centred) age and sex. On the one hand, many studies suggest that older constituencies are less inclined to vote for an Islamist party than are the younger ones (Başlevent, Kirmanoğlu, and Şenatalar 2005; Elsayyad and Hanafy 2014). On the other hand, women are reportedly less inclined to vote for an Islamist party because of their opposition to gender equality (Wegner and Cavatorta 2018).

How divided?

To reconstruct the presence of a cleavage behind voting behaviour, I first analyze each level separately though different multinomial models. This procedure allows to detect which factors are statistically significant within each level thus avoiding the risk of multicollinearity, that is the association between two (or more) explanatory variables. When this happens, only one of the involved variables appears as impacting significantly on the outcome variable. In our case, it might be possible then that by including all the independent variables at once in the model only normative variables appear to have a significant effect on vote choice, even though individual political orientation might stem from predefined socio-economic conditions or organizational intermediaries. This circumstance is also to be expected because ideological perspectives might be thought as an intervening variable between social differentiation and vote choice, as per Whitefield's refinement of the definition of cleavage.

Egypt

By contrasting the different categories of the dependent nominal variable within each level of the cleavage considered individually, few statistically significant differences emerge between those voting for Islamist parties and those voting for their major competing faction. As shown in Table 3.3, at the empirical level only house income emerges as significant. This is positively correlated with the vote choice for an Islamist party and its log odds coefficient of 0.48 indicates that, keeping the other variables constant, for a unit increase in individuals' perceived wealth the probabilities to vote for an Islamist party than to vote for the parties in the reference category increases by 62%. However, the coefficients of the house income variable are not significantly different when contrasting the probabilities of voting for an Islamist party rather than one in the reference category against those of voting a Right/secular party rather than those in the base outcome. This means that while house income significantly discriminates with Islamist voters against those voting for parties in the reference category, it does not discriminate between Islamist and Right/secular voters. The other variables of the empirical level do not seem to play a statistically significant role in discriminating Egyptians' vote choices. Surprisingly, this applies also for the sex variable inasmuch as women, contrary to received wisdom, are as less likely to vote for an Islamist party as they are to vote for a Right/secular party with respect to the reference category.

As far as the normative level (see the second column in Table 3.3) is concerned, cultural conservativism is significantly correlated positively with the electoral preference for Islamist parties rather than those in the reference category in that a unitary increase in the index of cultural conservatism more than doubles the probabilities to vote them. However, the impact of this variable in determining this choice does not statistically differ from that behind the vote choice for secular parties (whose log odds coefficient is of 0.407). Similarly, the belief that popular will should be the basis for legislation is negatively correlated with the religious vote. Yet, its coefficients (–0.494 and –0.225) are not statistically different across religious and secular voters vis-à-vis the other ones. By the same token, a unit increase in the agreement with the statement that the Shari'a should be among the sources of law more than doubles the relative probability of voting for an Islamist party instead of one of those in the reference category and diminishes by 23% the probability of voting a Right/secular party instead of one in the reference category. Moreover, as expected, the two coefficients are statistically different across the two groups. Unsurprisingly (and cautioning from referring to political Islam and democracy in either/or terms), the belief that democracy is suitable for Egypt is significantly and positively correlated with both the vote choice for Islamist and Right/secular parties rather than others. Both kinds of voters indeed share the belief that democracy is suitable for Egypt and, in so doing, they distinguish themselves from the voters of parties in the reference category. In total contradiction with other studies (Garcia-Rivero and Kotze 2007), trust toward institutions is significantly and positively correlated with religious vote but negatively (even though not significantly) correlated with the Right/secular vote, and such difference is statistically relevant.

Analyzing the demand of representation 65

Table 3.3 Cleavage-dimensions-related multinomial models for vote choice in Egypt

	Socio/economic level		Normative level		Organizational level	
	Islamists	Right/Secular	Islamist	Right/Secular	Islamist	Right/Secular
Age	0.00563	−0.0107				
	(0.0159)	(0.0176)				
Female	−0.238	−0.349				
	(0.481)	(0.495)				
Deprived areas	−0.290	0.0925				
	(0.478)	(0.489)				
School years	−0.00145	0.0512				
	(0.0404)	(0.0444)				
House income	0.484*	0.289				
	(0.261)	(0.271)				
Religiosity			0.354	−0.163		
			(0.461)	(0.426)		
Cultural conservativism			1.181**	0.407		
			(0.590)	(0.472)		
Shari'a			0.804**	−0.228		
			(0.404)	(0.290)		
Popular will			−0.494*	−0.255		
			(0.276)	(0.258)		
Suitability of Democracy			0.226**	0.196*		
			(0.113)	(0.106)		
Religious state			0.796	0.0558		
			(0.682)	(0.749)		
Trust in institutions			0.717*	−0.132		
			(0.399)	(0.298)		
Trade union membership					−0.561	0.235
					(0.654)	(0.572)
Mosque Attendance					0.221	−0.126
					(0.212)	(0.184)
Constant	−1.017	−1.423*	−9.397***	−0.229	−0.908	0.0464
	(0.786)	(0.844)	(3.010)	(2.170)	(0.787)	(0.654)
Observations	126	126	120	120	127	127
Pseudo R^2	0.0348		0.1326		0.0153	
Prob > Chi^2	0.4794		0.0016		0.3737	

Standard errors in parentheses

***$p < 0.01$, **$p < 0.05$, *$p < 0.1$.

Note: Model coefficients are referred to the reference group constituted by those voting for other parties than those analyzed.

In this sense, it seems that the religious vote stands not for a protest vote nor for a pious vote in that religiosity does not have a meaningful impact in determining the vote choice or in distinguishing Islamic parties' voters from all the others.

From the analysis of the organizational level (see the third column in Table 3.3), both trade union membership and mosque attendance behave as expected. The first is positively correlated with the secular vote but negatively associated with the vote for Islamist parties. The second, by contrast, is positively related with the religious vote and has a negative relationship with the secular one. Yet, no one of the coefficients associated with these variables is significant in discriminating these choices from the base outcome, nor are they statistically different across the two groups.

When considering all the aforementioned variables (and therefore the three dimensions) into a single model, the normative level emerges over the other dimensions previously analysed. As shown in Table 3.4, while some variables account for the vote choice of Islamist parties or Right/secular against the reference category, such as schooling years, house income, popular will, trade union membership, and Islamic law, only the latter is also statistically significant in distinguishing religious against secular voters. Indeed, only in this case the coefficient associated with the vote choice for an Islamist party rather those in the reference category is different from that distinguishing the vote choice for Right/secular parties from the base outcome.

Taken together, these findings suggest that the divide between Islamists and seculars that emerged in the occasion of the 2011–2 elections is not a genuine cleavage. First, the three dimensions do not overlap. Second, the empirical referent is totally missing in that there is no socio-economic differentiation between the two groups of voters and there is not a veritable differentiation in the organizational intermediaries. What seems to emerge in Egypt is not even an identity divide as suggested elsewhere (Pellicer and Wegner 2014, 2015; Wegner and Cavatorta 2016), in that personal issues related to identity and to the definition of society (exemplified by the variables on gender religiosity and cultural conservativism) are not relevant in discriminating the voters of the two factions opposing each other during the transition. Rather, there appears to be a divide on the 'rules of the game' opposing those who want more room for religion as a basis for legislation against those opting for secular law-making.

Tunisia

In the case of Tunisia, the analysis will also proceed stepwise. First, each component of cleavage politics is separately considered, then the focus shifts to the fully specified model. As far as the empirical level is concerned, socio-economic differences emerge in both countries. While age, gender, and regional marginalization do not have an impact on the vote choice for one faction or the other, house income and education significantly impact on the final decision at the ballot box. As Table 3.5 shows, the years of school variable positively impacts on the vote choice for left/secular parties with respect to the reference category. In particular,

Table 3.4 Vote determinants in Egypt

	Islamists	Right/Secular
Age	0.00702	0.00588
	(0.0217)	(0.0215)
Female	−0.276	−1.028
	(0.795)	(0.784)
Deprived	−0.345	0.137
	(0.629)	(0.571)
School years	0.0287	0.0857*
	(0.0507)	(0.0521)
House income	0.708**	0.120
	(0.356)	(0.310)
Religiosity	0.0266	0.0131
	(0.561)	(0.495)
Traditional index	1.009	0.295
	(0.665)	(0.535)
Islamic law	0.933**	−0.249
	(0.450)	(0.326)
Popular will	−0.609**	−0.230
	(0.306)	(0.289)
Suitability of democracy	0.119	0.249**
	(0.124)	(0.125)
Religious State	0.945	−0.314
	(0.786)	(0.887)
Trust in institutions	0.631	−0.176
	(0.470)	(0.331)
Mosque attendance	0.104	−0.395
	(0.329)	(0.302)
Trade unions membership	−1.839*	−1.092
	(0.956)	(0.810)
Constant	−9.004***	0.0169
	(3.452)	(2.855)
Observations	116	116
Pseudo R^2 0.1845		
Prob > Chi^2 0.0146		

Standard errors in parentheses

***$p < 0.01$, **$p < 0.05$, *$p < 0.1$.

Note: Model coefficients are referred to the reference group constituted by those voting for other parties than those analyzed.

the effect of one additional year of education is associated with a 0.104 increase in the relative log odds, meaning that for each additional year of school the probability to vote for left/secular parties instead of one in the reference category increases by 52%. At the same time, this variable seems to not have any statistically significant impact on the vote choice for Ennahda with respect to the reference category, even though a negative impact is suggested (a decrease of 49% for each additional year of school). The different effect education has on the categories

68 Analyzing the demand of representation

Table 3.5 Cleavage-dimensions-related multinomial models for vote choice in Tunisia

	Socio/economic level		Normative level		Organizational level	
	Nahdha	Left/Secular	Nahdha	Left/Secular	Nahdha	Left/Secular
Age	0.00785	0.0107				
	(0.00807)	(0.0114)				
Female	0.0976	0.436				
	(0.214)	(0.295)				
Deprived areas	0.0543	0.0364				
	(0.299)	(0.461)				
School years	−0.0153	0.104***				
	(0.0217)	(0.0325)				
House income	−0.0468	0.255				
	(0.116)	(0.159)				
Religiosity			0.441**	−0.311		
			(0.210)	(0.284)		
Cultural conservatism			−0.0367	−1.249***		
			(0.278)	(0.386)		
Shari'a			0.519***	−0.417*		
			(0.186)	(0.227)		
Popular will			0.0667	0.259		
			(0.179)	(0.225)		
Suitability of democracy			0.0601	−0.0597		
			(0.0542)	(0.0714)		
Religious state			0.860***	−0.375		
			(0.314)	(0.524)		
Trust in institutions			−0.229	0.00238		
			(0.145)	(0.194)		
Trade union membership					1.123	2.254***
					(0.800)	(0.856)
Mosque attendance					0.152**	−0.196**
					(0.0656)	(0.0951)
Constant	0.685**	−2.592***	−2.103*	2.890**	0.0329	−0.289
	(0.310)	(0.510)	(1.095)	(1.384)	(0.216)	(0.271)
Observations	464	464	355	355	457	457
Pseudo R^2	0.0376		0.1233		0.0279	
Prob > Chi^2	0.0001		0.0000		0.0000	

Standard errors in parentheses.

***$p < 0.01$, **$p < 0.05$, *$p < 0.1$.

Note: Model coefficients are referred to the reference group constituted by those voting for other parties than those analyzed.

of interest, Ennahda and left/secular voters, is also statistically significant for we can reject the null hypothesis that the coefficients associated with education are equal for the two categories vis-à-vis the one of reference with a confidence of 99%. The same trend appears to be followed also by the variable house income. An increase in perceived wealth increases by 29% the probability of voting for a left/secular party and decreases by 5% for Ennahda. Even though this effect is not statistically significant in discriminating from the base outcome 'vote for others', it is significantly different when comparing the effect house income has in determining a left/secular vote vs. the base outcome with the one it played in determining a vote for Ennahda vs. the base outcome. However, this does not imply that more educated and wealthier people have a greater probability of voting for a left/secular party instead of Ennahda. As a matter of fact, those with the highest self-reported income have a probability as high as 41% of being Ennahda voters and 28% of being left/secular voters. By the same token, those who possess a master's degree or more have 37% and 33% probability of voting for Ennahda or left/secular respectively.

Coming to the normative level, religiosity, cultural conservativism, support for Islamic law, and preference for a religious state appear to discriminate the vote choice among the different groups of voters. Unsurprisingly, an increase in the self-definition of religiosity is correlated with an increase of 60% in the probability of voting for Ennahda and a decrease of 27% in the probability of voting for Left/secular parties. Yet, even when people define themselves as 'not religious', there is a statistical significance in voting for one faction (39% probability of voting for Ennahda) or the other (23% probability of voting for left/secular) vis-à-vis the reference group. The finding that people defining themselves as not religious are still more likely to vote for a religious party than are for a left/secular one means that religiosity impacts on the magnitude but not on the fact that Ennahda is the most voted party among Tunisians, regardless their self-reported religiosity. In the same vein, a unit increment in the agreement that laws should be enacted in accordance with the Islamic law increases by 62% the probability of voting choice for Ennahda while significantly decreases of 39% those for left/secular factions with respect to the reference category. Paralleling this figure, the probability of voting for Ennahda is as high as 70% among those preferring a religious state instead of a civic state. Finally, and quite surprisingly, support for gender equality while statistically increasing (of 78% for unit) the probability of voting for a left/secular party, has no relevance on the propensity to vote for Ennahda vis-à-vis the reference category. Contrary to the expectations of finding a positive correlation between cultural conservativism (measured trough attitudes toward gender equality) and voting for Ennahda, it emerges that a unitary increase on this index is associated with a statistically insignificant decrease in the vote choice for Ennahda. The remaining variables, trust toward 'deep state institutions and suitability of democracy do not have any statistically relevant effect in discriminating the vote choice for Ennahda or left/secular parties with respect to the reference category and even if they have different effects on the different categories of the dependent variable,

70 Analyzing the demand of representation

such differences are not statistically significant, thus suggesting they are not helpful to discriminate the final vote choice.

At the organizational level, the two selected variables – mosque attendance and trade union membership – seem to both have a role in determining the vote choice. Mosque attendance is significantly correlated with voting for Ennahda and left/secular parties and, as expected, the direction of this correlation is positive in the first case and negative in the second one. Trade union membership increases by 90% the vote choice for left/secular parties with respect to the reference category. Interestingly, even if not meaningful, this variable is positively associated also with the vote choice for Ennahda, partially confirming Waltz (1986) and Wickham's (2004) findings that Islamists are particularly successful in penetrating trade unions and professional syndicates – despite the statistically difference between the effect trade union membership has in discriminating the two categories of interest (Ennahda and left/secular voter) against the base outcome.

When considering the full model integrating all three dimensions, much of what previously found within the different levels alone considered still applies. As shown in Table 3.6, education, house income, willingness to have Shari'a among the sources of law and preference for a religious state appear statistically significant in discriminating the vote choice in the direction seen above, even with a slightly different magnitude. Preference for Islamic Law ceases to be significantly correlated with a drop in the probability of voting for secular parties, but remains highly significant in determining a rise (64% for each unit increase) in the probability of opting for Ennahda. Similarly, other things being equal, the relative probability of voting for Ennahda rather than for parties in the reference category is more than double for those preferring to live in a religious state. Even if those variables are statistically significant only when contrasting one of the categories of interest of the dependent variable with the base outcome (education and house income are statistically significant only for left/secular outcomes while preferred source of law and preference for a religious state are significant only when considering Ennahda voters), the trends displayed are significantly different across left/secular and Ennahda voters. Nonetheless, the full model provides also for dissimilarities with the models examined earlier. First, cultural conservativism ceases to be significant for the left/secular outcome and its coefficients associated with left/secular and Ennahda voters are not statistically different. Second, the effects of the organizational predictors disappear. While the coefficients of mosque attendance still differ across Ennahda and left/Secular voters, this variable is no longer significant in discriminating Ennahda voters from the base outcome. Moreover, trade union membership loses statistical significance in discriminating the base category from the others considered and ceases to differ across Ennahda and left/secular voters. Compared to the case of Egypt, at first glance the Tunisian public is more deeply divided in that the division around the role Shari'a should have within the new regime is accompanied by a divide in the socio-economic conditions due to the statistical difference of the coefficient related to education and house income. The next section will provide a series of robustness checks to attest the reliability of such findings.

Table 3.6 Vote determinants in Tunisia

	Nahhda	Left/Secular
Age	−0.00998	0.00976
	(0.0107)	(0.0146)
Female	0.203	0.378
	(0.326)	(0.416)
Deprived	0.518	−0.0589
	(0.420)	(0.627)
School years	−0.0158	0.0722*
	(0.0291)	(0.0429)
House income	−0.0305	0.435**
	(0.148)	(0.205)
Religiosity	0.346	−0.415
	(0.225)	(0.310)
Traditional index	−0.132	−0.580
	(0.319)	(0.479)
Islamic law	0.582***	−0.315
	(0.193)	(0.240)
Popular will	0.0795	0.396
	(0.187)	(0.244)
Suitability of democracy	0.0493	−0.0306
	(0.0561)	(0.0776)
Religious state	0.795**	−0.177
	(0.325)	(0.551)
Trust in institutions	−0.224	−0.0250
	(0.152)	(0.208)
Mosque attendance	1.354	1.569
	(0.850)	(0.991)
Trade unions membership	0.162	−0.221
	(0.0990)	(0.141)
Constant	−2.335*	−0.547
	(1.344)	(1.851)
Observations	349	349
Pseudo R^2 0.1663		
Prob > Chi^2 0.0000		

Standard errors in parentheses.

***$p <0.01$, **$p < 0.05$, *$p < 0.1$.

Note: Model coefficients are referred to the reference group constituted by those voting for other parties than those analyzed.

The importance of organizational intermediaries

To assess the degree of reliability of the present findings, tests of robustness and representativeness are conducted here. The first kind of tests serves the purpose to ascertain whether the models used were suited to account for the vote choice in Tunisia and Egypt. The second ones are needed to assess whether the findings emerged from our analyses account for the entire population by controlling for possible selection bias due to the small size of the samples.

72 Analyzing the demand of representation

Above all, we might want to know the overall meaningfulness of the predictors included in the models by looking at their variance across the different categories of the dependent variable. This can be done using a Wald test for independent variables, which verifies whether all the coefficients associated with the independent variables are statistically different from zero, the null hypothesis. The results of this test, reported in Table 3.7, show that for most of the independent variables included in our models, this null hypothesis cannot be rejected – meaning that, from a formal point of view, those variables can be removed from the model for they add nothing to its fit. In Tunisia only religiosity, preference for Shari'a and an Islamic state, and mosque attendance have non-trivial effects on the dependent variable. In Egypt, the same can be said only for the Islamic law variable.

A similar test is also conducted on the dependent variables. In this case we want to know whether, in light of the predictors included in the model, different categories of the dependent variable can be combined. Indeed, if, as shown in Table 3.7, only few variables affect the odds of the different outcomes of the dependent variable, it might be the case that the different categories of the dependent variable are indistinguishable with respect to the variable in the model. To ascertain whether this is the case, another Wald test has been conducted to test the null hypothesis that all coefficients except the intercepts associated with a given pair of alternatives are equal to 0. In Tunisia, no one of the categories identified might be collapsed, as Table 3.8 shows. In Egypt, by contrast, all pairs of alternatives can be collapsed into one (see Table 3.9), meaning that there are no meaningful distinctions across the different groups of voters on the basis of the independent variables identified.

It then emerges that the fully specified model works quite well for Tunisia, but not for Egypt. What about the step-wise modeling then? The same figure emerges also

Table 3.7 Wald test for independent variables

	Tunisia			Egypt		
Vote choice	Chi²	df	P > Chi²	Chi²	df	P > Chi²
Age	2.031	2	0.362	0.569	2	0.752
Female	0.917	2	0.632	2.335	2	0.311
Deprived	1.861	2	0.394	0.495	2	0.781
School years	4.244	2	0.120	3.397	2	0.183
House income	5.662	2	0.059	5.160	2	0.076
Religiosity	6.354	2	0.042	0.109	2	0.947
Traditional index	1.467	2	20.480	2.237	2	20.327
Islamic law	15.313	2	0.000	6.954	2	0.031
Popular will	2.653	2	0.265	3.546	2	0.170
Suitability of democracy	1.352	2	0.509	4.614	2	0.100
State preference	7.792	2	0.020	2.491	2	0.288
Trust in institutions	2.374	2	0.305	2.522	2	0.283
Trade union membership	3.033	2	0.219	5.581	2	0.061
Mosque attendance	7.966	2	0.019	1.989	2	0.370
Constant	3.115	2	0.211	7.043	2	0.030

Note: The H_0 hypothesis tested is that all coefficients associated with given variables are 0.

Table 3.8 Wald test for combining outcome categories, Tunisia

	Chi²	df	P > Chi²
Others vs. Ennahda	39.575	14	0.000
Others vs. Left/Secular	30.200	14	0.007
Ennahda vs. Left/Secular	60.025	14	0.000

Table 3.9 Wald test for combining outcome categories, Egypt

	Chi²	df	P > Chi²
Others vs. Islamists	23.104	14	0.059
Others vs. Right/Secular	11.363	14	0.657
Islamists vs. Right/Secular	17.668	14	0.222

in this case, with the exception that, as expected, the normative model in the Egyptian case shows a significant distinction between Islamist voters and those opting for a party included in the reference category. Nonetheless, by making a comparison of the goodness of fit between the model with only the socio-economic determinants and the model with only the organizational factors, it emerges that the variables related to individuals' associational life better account for the vote choice than the socio-economic ones. This is what emerges by looking at two particular measures of goodness of fit, namely the AIC (Akaike information criterion) and BIC (Bayesian information criterion). Both measures provide information about the fit of the estimated model with the observed data by weighing model's likelihood functions for its parameters (and in the case of BIC, also the sample size is taken into account). The recourse to these measures is particularly suited to compare competing theories expressed by different models, and the one with lower scores on both AIC and BIC is to be preferred (Burnham and Anderson 2004). As Table 3.10 shows, in both Tunisia and Egypt, the organizational model outperforms the socio/economic one in both measures, thus corroborating network theories for vote choice.

Negative differences between the organizational and the socio/economic model in both AIC and BIC suggest that the first of the two models is to be preferred for it better fits the observed data, controlling for the number of the parameters included. Nonetheless, the difference of −14.725 observed in the BIC values for Tunisia suggests that the organizational model is far better than the other one in accounting for vote choice. The same goes for Egypt, even though none of the two models is reliable, for we cannot reject the null hypothesis that there is no effect of the independent variables, taken together, on the dependent variable (Prob > LR is greater than 0.05). Yet, the organizational model seems to perform better than the other ones.

As far as the representativeness of these findings is concerned, a test has been conducted by comparing the means of the independent variables between the sample constituted by those voting for a political party and all other respondents. By looking at the results in Tables 3.11 and 3.12, it emerges that while the variables accounting for individual beliefs and political preferences do not vary across the two

Table 3.10 Measures of fit for multivariate models

	Tunisia			Egypt		
	Organizational model	Socio/ economic model	Difference	Organizational model	Socio/ economic model	Difference
N:	457	464	−7	127	126	1
LR:	25.331(4)	38.487(12)	−13.156 (−8)	4.247(4)	9.566(10)	−5.319 (−6)
Prob>LR:	0.000	0.000	−0.000	0.374	0.479	−0.106
McFaden's Adj R^2:	0.008	−0.004	0.012	−0.050	−0.096	0.046
AIC:	1.972	2.006	−0.034	2.287	2.391	−0.104
BIC:	−1860.673	−1831.179	−14.725	−299.166	−257.066	−42.100

Table 3.11 T-test results on two independent samples, Egypt

Variable	Party voters	Others	$Pr(|T| > |t|)$
Age (mean)	37.42636	39.75413	0.0735
Female (mean)	.3100775	.5183486	0.0000
Deprived (mean)	.4418605	.5798165	0.0028
Schooling years (mean)	10.33333	8.623853	0.0037
House income (mean)	2.206349	1.836111	0.0000
Self-reported religiosity (mean)	2.338583	2.363383	0.6106
Traditional index (mean)	2.54080	2.608265	0.2254
Mosque attendance (mean)	3.425197	3.127679	0.0101
Trade union member (mean)	.1472868	.093578	0.0538
Preference for Shari'a (mean)	3.232558	3.232537	0.9998
Suitability democracy (mean)	6.897638	6.819139	0.7146

Table 3.12 T-test results on two independent samples, Tunisia

Variable	Party voters	Others	$Pr(|T| > |t|)$
Age (mean)	37.42918	41.81096	0.0000
Female (mean)	0.4270386	0.5410959	0.0001
Deprived (mean)	0.1523605	0.2589041	0.0000
Schooling years (mean)	9.381974	7.224658	0.0000
House income (mean)	2.172414	1.859944	0.0000
Self-reported religiosity (mean)	1.995633	1.956764	0.3108
Mosque attendance (mean)	2.886214	2.443515	0.0000
Trade union member (mean)	0.0429185	0.0219178	0.0382
Preference for Shari'a (mean)	2.770642	2.717822	0.2627
Suitability democracy (mean)	5.926606	6.043831	0.4415

groups, much of variation is at stake as far as the socio/economic and organizational variables are concerned. It is so because the probability that the means of those variable differ across the two groups is higher than 95%. In particular, in both countries, respondents declaring to vote for a political party tend to be younger, male and well positioned within the social and economic tissues. In particular, they are more affluent than the rest of the sample, more educated, do not reside in deprived areas and are more likely than others to be trade union members or mosque attendants.

This picture shows that individuals' reaction to elections, e.g., deciding whether to participate or not, voting for an independent candidate or a party, or remaining undecided, relies on their socio/economic background and their organizational networks. In light of this, while political preferences regarding the role of religion in politics – i.e., Shair'a as source of law and preference for a religious state – are the primary drivers accounting for the electoral preference between Islamist and their secular counterparts, socio/economic and organizational variables are relevant in accounting for how this preference is expressed and the degree of political awareness underneath.

Coming back to how the *SD* parameter of our model, that is the presence and the depth of social divisions, can be held accountable for the diverging patterns of transitions from authoritarianism in Tunisia and Egypt, the findings reveal that indeed no remarkable differences emerge in the two national patterns of vote choice. In both cases, the divide appears to be confined to the role of religion in politics as the result of individuals' proximity to particular networks. Yet, while these findings are sufficient to dismiss the hypothesis that deep and stratified social divisions have played a role in the two processes of transition, it is not sufficient to dismiss the hypothesis that the religious divide alone can be perceived as a threat to the achievement of any kind of agreement on the future of the *constituendum* political regime and its nation. In both cases, preferences for more religion in politics predict the vote for religious parties while its rejection is positively correlated with the electoral preference for their competitors. But was Islam the real and major concern? The next chapter will answer this question, thereby highlighting why Islamists dominated at the ballot box.

Notes

1 For a different conceptualization of cleavage, see: Bornschier (2009).
2 http://www.uis.unesco.org/Education/Documents/isced-2011-en.pdf.
3 Theoretically speaking the presence of the variable 'deprived areas' would require a multilevel multinomial model in that it is not an individual-level variable for it reports context-level information. However, being a dummy variable, it does not meet the formal criteria to proceed with multilevel modeling (Gelman 2005).
4 The coding procedure is reported in Table A.1 in the Annex.

References

Bâli, Aslı Ü., and Hanna Lerner. 2017. "Designing Constitutions in Religiously Divided Societies." In *Constitution Writing, Religion and Democracy*, edited by Aslı Ü. Bâli and Hanna Lerner, 373–96. Cambridge: Cambridge University Press.

Bartolini, Stefano, and Peter Mair. 1990. *Identity, Competition and Electoral Availability: The Stabilisation of European Electorates 1885-1985*. Cambridge: Cambridge University Press.

Başlevent, Cem, Hasan Kirmanoğlu, and Burhan Şenatalar. 2005. "Empirical Investigation of Party Preferences and Economic Voting in Turkey." *European Journal of Political Research* 44 (4): 547–62. https://doi.org/10.1111/j.1475-6765.2005.00238.x.

Berman, Chantal E, and Elizabeth R Nugent. 2015. "Regionalism in New Democracies: Sub-National Variation in Tunisia's 2014 Parliamentary Elections." Princeton University Working Paper.

Blaydes, L., and J. Lo. 2012. "One Man, One Vote, One Time? A Model of Democratization in the Middle East." *Journal of Theoretical Politics* 24 (1): 110–46. https://doi.org/10.1177/0951629811423121.

Blaydes, Lisa. 2010. *Elections and Distributive Politics in Mubarak's Egypt*. Cambridge: Cambridge University Press.

Boughzala, Mongi, and Mohamed Tli Hamdi. 2014. "Promoting inclusive growth in Arab countries: Rural and regional development and inequality in Tunisia." *Brookings Global Working Paper Series*.

Brown, Nathan J. 2017. "Islam and Constitutionalism in the Arab World." In *Constitution Writing, Religion and Democracy*, edited by Aslı Ü. Bâli and Hanna Lerner, 289–316. Cambridge: Cambridge University Press.

Burnham, Kenneth P., and David R. Anderson. 2004. "Multimodel Inference." *Sociological Methods & Research* 33 (2): 261–304. https://doi.org/10.1177/0049124104268644.

Chandra, Kanchan. 2005. "Ethnic Parties and Democratic Stability." *Perspectives on Politics* 3 (2): 235–52. https://doi.org/10.1080/01419870.1981.9993353.

Chandra, Kanchan, and Cilanne Boulet. 2003. "A Model of Change in an Ethnic Demography." *Unpublished paper, MIT*.

Choi, Jaehwa, Michelle Peters, and Ralph O. Mueller. 2010. "Correlational Analysis of Ordinal Data: From Pearson's r to Bayesian Polychoric Correlation." *Asia Pacific Education Review* 11 (4): 459–66. https://doi.org/10.1007/s12564-010-9096-y.

Clark, Janine. 2004a. *Islam, Charity, and Activism: Middle-Class Networks and Social Welfare in Egypt, Jordan, and Yemen*. Bloomington: Indiana University Press.

———. 2004b. "Social Movement Theory and Patron-Clientelism." *Comparative Political Studies* 37 (8): 941–68. https://doi.org/10.1177/0010414004267982.

Corstange, Daniel. 2018. "Kinship, Partisanship, and Patronage in Arab Elections." *Electoral Studies* 52 (April): 58–72. https://doi.org/10.1016/J.ELECTSTUD.2018.01.006.

Deegan-Krause, K. 2006. New Dimensions of Political Cleavage. *Oxford Handbook of Political Science*, eds. R. Dalton and H.-D. Klingemann. Oxford: Oxford University Press, 538–56

Driessen, Michael D. 2014. *Religion and Democratization: Framing Religious and Political Identities in Muslim and Catholic Societies*. New York: Oxford University Press.

Ellen Lust. 2009. "Competitive Clientelism in the Middle East." *Journal of Democracy* 20 (3): 122–35. https://doi.org/10.1353/jod.0.0099.

Elie Kedourie. 1994. *Democracy and the Arab Political Culture*. Geinsborough House: Frank Cass.

Elsayyad, May, and Shima'a Hanafy. 2014. "Voting Islamist or Voting Secular? An Empirical Analysis of Voting Outcomes in Egypt's 'Arab Spring.'" *Public Choice* 160 (1–2): 109–30. https://doi.org/10.1007/s11127-014-0173-3.

Elster, Jon. 1995. "Forces and Mechanisms in the Constitution-Making Process." *Duke Law Journal* 45 (2): 364–96.

Garcia-Rivero, C., and H. Kotze. 2007. "Electoral Support for Islamic Parties in the Middle East and North Africa." *Party Politics* 13 (5): 611–36. https://doi.org/10.1177/1354068807080088.

Gelman, Andrew. 2005. "Analysis of Variance: Why It Is More Important than Ever." *The Annals of Statistics* 33 (1): 1–53.

Gelvin, James L. 2004. *The Modern Middle East: A History*. New York: Oxford University Press.

Gunther, Richard, Paul A. Beck, Pedro Magalhães, and Alejandro Moreno. 2016. *Voting in Old and New Democracies*. Edited by Richard Gunther, Paul A. Beck, Pedro Magalhães, and Alejandro Moreno. New York: Routledge.

Gunther, Richard, and Anthony Mughan. 1993. "Political Institutions and Cleavage Management." In *Do Institutions Matter? Government Capabilities in the United States and Abroad*, 272–301. Edited by R. Kent Weaver and Bert A. Rockman Washington, DC: The Brookings Institutions.

Hashemi, Nader. 2009. *Islam, Secularism and Liberal Democracy*. New York: Oxford University Press.

Higley, John, and Michael G. Burton. 1989. "The Elite Variable in Democratic Transitions and Breakdowns." *American Sociological Review* 54 (1): 17–32. https://repositories.lib.utexas.edu/handle/2152/10296.

Horowitz, Donald L. 1993. "Democracy in Divided Societies." *Journal of Democracy* 4 (4): 18–38. https://doi.org/10.1353/jod.1993.0054.

Huntington, Samuel P. 1996. *The Clash of Civilizations and the Remaking of World Order*. New York: Simon and Schuster.

Jamal, Amaney A., and Mark A. Tessler. 2008. "Attitudes in the Arab World." *Journal of Democracy* 19 (1): 97–110. https://doi.org/10.1353/jod.2008.0004.

Kedourie, Elie. 1992. *Democracy and the Arab Political Culture*. Washington, DC: The Washington Institute for Near East Policy.

Kostenko, Veronica V., Pavel A. Kuzmuchev, and Eduard D. Ponarin. 2016. "Attitudes towards Gender Equality and Perception of Democracy in the Arab World." *Democratization* 23 (5): 862–91. https://doi.org/10.1080/13510347.2015.1039994.

Landau, David. 2012. "The Importance of Constitution-Making." *Denver University Law Review* 89 (2): 1–23.

Lerner, Hanna. 2011. *Making Constitutions in Deeply Divided Societies*. Cambridge: Cambridge University Press.

Lipset, Seymour Martin. 1959. "Some Social Requisites of Democracy: Economic Development and Political Legitimacy." *The American Political Science Review* 53 (1): 69–105.

Lipset, Seymour Martin, and Stein Rokkan. 1967. *Party Systems and Voter Alignments: Cross-National Perspectives*. New York: Free Press.

Masoud, Tarek. 2014. *Counting Islam: Religion, Class and Elections in Egypt*. New York: Cambridge University Press.

Merone, Fabio. 2015. "Enduring Class Struggle in Tunisia: The Fight for Identity beyond Political Islam." *British Journal of Middle Eastern Studies* 42 (1): 74–87.

Negretto, Gabriel L. 1999. "Constitution-Making and Institutional Design. The Transformation Presidentialism in Argentina." *European Journal of Sociology* 40 (2): 1–33. https://doi.org/10.1017/S0003975600007451.

Parolin, Gianluca Paolo. 2013. "(Re) Arrangement of State/Islam Relations in Egypt's Constitutional Transition." NYU School of Law, Public Law Research Paper No. 13–15.

Pellicer, Miquel, and Eva Wegner. 2014. "Socio-Economic Voter Profile and Motives for Islamist Support in Morocco." *Party Politics* 20 (1): 116–33. https://doi.org/10.1177/1354068811436043.

———. 2015. "Who Votes for Islamist Parties – and Why?" German Institute of Global Area Studies. 1:9.

Perkins, Kenneth J. 2004. *A History of Modern Tunisia.* Cambridge: Cambridge University Press.

Pierson, Paul. 2004. *Politics in Time: History, INstitutions and Social Analysis.* Princeton, NJ: Princeton University Press.

Randall, Vicky. 2001. "Party System and Voter Alignments in the New Democracies of the Third World." In *Party System and Voter Alignment Revisited,* edited by Lauri Karvonen and Stein Kuhnle, 238–60. London and New York: Routledge.

Rustow, Dankwart A. 1970. "Transition to Democracy: Toward a Dynamic Model." *Comparative Politics* 2 (3): 337–63.

Samuel P. Huntington. 1996. *The Clash of Civilizations and the Remaking of World Order.* New York: Simon and Schuster.

Stepan, Alfred C. 2000. "Religion, Democracy, and the 'Twin Tolerations.'" *Journal of Democracy* 11 (4): 37–57. https://doi.org/10.1353/jod.2000.0088.

Stepan, Alfred, and Juan J. Linz. 2013. "Democratization Theory and the 'Arab Spring.'" *Journal of Democracy* 24 (2): 15–30.

Stephen Whitefield. 2002. "Political Cleavage and Post-Communist Politics," *Annual Review of Political Science* 5(1): 181–200

Strauss, Roger. 1938. "The Relations of Religion to Democracy." *Public Opinion Quarterly* 2: 37–38.

Tessler, Mark A., and Eleanor Gao. 2005. "Gauging Arab Support for Democracy." *Journal of Democracy* 16 (3): 83–97.

Van Hamme, Gilles, Alia Gana, and Ben Rebbah Maher. 2014. "Social and Socio-Territorial Electoral Base of Political Parties in Post-Revolutionary Tunisia." *The Journal of North African Studies* 19 (5): 751–69.

Vermunt, Jeroen K., and Jay Magidson. 2005. "Factor Analysis With Categorical Indicators: A Comparison Between Traditional and Latent Class Approaches." In *New Developments in Categorical Data Analysis for the Social and Behavioral Sciences,* edited by L. Andries van der Ark, Marcel A. Croon, and Klaas Sijtsma, 41–62. Mahwah, New Jersey: Lawrence Erlbaum Associates.

Waltz, Susan. 1986. "Islamist Appeal in Tunisia." *Middle East Journal* 40 (4): 651–70. https://www.jstor.org/stable/4327425?seq=1#page_scan_tab_contents.

Wegner, Eva, and Francesco Cavatorta. 2018. "Revisiting the Islamist–Secular Divide: Parties and Voters in the Arab World." *International Political Science Review* 40 (5): 558–75. https://doi.org/10.1177/0192512118784225.

Weingast, Barry R. 1997. "The Political Foundations of Democracy and the Rule of Law." *The American Political Science Review* 91 (2): 245–63. https://doi.org/10.2307/2952354.

Whitefield, Stephen. 2002. "Political Cleavage and Post-Communist Politics." *Annual Review of Political Science* 5 (1): 181–200. https://doi.org/10.1146/annurev.polisci.5.112601.144242.

Wickham, Carrie Rosefsky. 2004. "The Path to Moderation : Strategy and Learning in the Formation of Egypt ' s Wasat Party." *Comparative Politics* 36 (2): 205–28.

Zeghal, Malika. 2013. "Competing Ways of Life: Islamism, Secularism, and Public Order in the Tunisian Transition." *Constellations* 20 (2): 254–74. https://doi.org/10.1111/cons.12038.

4 Unfair patterns of competition and transitional parties' power resources

Both the transitology literature and our reassessment presented in the model for parties' agency in transition processes conceive of actors' power positions as a variable to take into consideration for making the final outcome of such processes more intelligible. Other things being equal, an uneven distribution of power among the actors involved diminishes the prospects of a successful transition. From this perspective then, far from what we can say about social divisions – which turned out to not have had a role – it is out of question that the different power configuration of the political elite involved in the transition has played a role in the difference of outcomes observed in Tunisia and Egypt. In fact, the power of the Egyptian Islamist factions, which has no parallel in Tunisia, is regarded as one of the main reasons for the failed transition. Commanding the absolute majority of seats in the Parliament, the Egyptian Islamists had no incentive to include other political forces in decision-making for the simple reason that they had the numbers to pass their desired legislation. In contrast, the Tunisian transition is deemed to be inclusive and consensual because the main party, the Islamist Ennahda, did not control the absolute majority of seats and was therefore forced to come to terms with other political parties, as it eventually did when it coalesced with the leftist and secular CPR and Ettakatol.

As will be shown in the next chapter, this is only a partial reading since it does not consider the fact that successful installations have occurred even in situations of unequal distribution of power among the actors involved. It is also an erroneous reading in that it overlooks the fact that Islamists' absolute majority in Egypt was the result of a coalition between different Islamist parties. Nonetheless, when thinking in terms of Islamist/secular cleavage, this understanding contains self-evident elements of truth and has the merit of turning our attention to the reasons behind the overwhelming success of Islamist parties in the two countries and, possibly, to cross-country variations between Tunisia and Egypt. Such an inquiry will not only unveil possible joint causes of the different transitional outcomes observed but will also help us to understand the puzzling issue of how it was possible for Islamist parties to take control of processes of transitions that initially had seen them only playing a very marginal role. In fact, the mass protests were articulated through historically leftist claims, which were dominant in the 1970s. Leftist parties, though, performed incredibly poorly in subsequent decades and in the 2011–2

80 *Competition and transitional parties' power resources*

elections as well. After ascertaining that Arab societies were particularly receptive to Leftists' messages, this part is dedicated to the investigation of the institutional determinants behind the electoral gap between Islamists and secularists observed at the 2011 elections. The latter is indeed at the roots of different parties' power resources which in turn, accordingly to the model exposed in Chapter two, contribute to the formation of parties' strategy profiles within processes of democratic installation and might contribute to enlightening why transitions fail or succeed. In line with a regional trend, in both Tunisia and Egypt the cooptation, manipulation, and repression of oppositions during the previous authoritarian regimes contributed to the electoral successes of Islamist parties and determined the irrelevance of the leftist ones, thus undermining, albeit to a varying degree, the prospects for a democratic installation.

From leftist protests to Islamist dominance: explaining the gap of the founding elections

Intriguingly, the success of Islamist parties, even though with different degrees of magnitude in the two countries, came about shortly after the eruption of mass protests articulated around claims historically promoted by leftist parties. While it is not the objective of this chapter to investigate whether the Arab uprising was actually a revolution led by leftist-inspired forces against neo-capitalistic liberal regimes (Achcar 2013; Zemni, De Smet, and Bogaert 2013), it is nonetheless true that the uprisings across the region, and particularly in Tunisia and Egypt, "spoke" a leftist jargon which can be summarized in the revolutionary claims "change, freedom and social justice" and "bread, jobs and dignity." As per the data from the Arab Barometer, these claims were nothing but the tip of the iceberg. In fact, ABII data highlight not only that the religious cleavage that emerged from the elections does not reflect the perceived priorities of Tunisians and Egyptians, but also that left and secular values seemed well entrenched within the broader public, making the Islamist dominance of the 2011/2012 period quite puzzling, at least from the perspective of the demand of representation coming from those societies.

To begin with, ABII data show that when the previous regime was toppled and a new one was yet to be built, the citizens of Tunisia and Egypt were mostly concerned with the economic environment, and not with religious issues. Figure 4.1 illustrates these priorities. As it emerges, 69.34% and 82.79% of Tunisians and Egyptians respectively perceived unemployment and poverty as the major challenges their country faced despite the precarious institutional and political conditions. These findings are in line with the socio-economic reading of the 2010/2011 uprisings and, at least retrospectively, renders the subsequent turmoil in the region more intelligible. In contrast, concerns over regime stability and internal security were regarded as the major challenge only by 7.36% of Tunisians and 6.97% of Egyptians, coming after the desire to fight administrative and financial corruption.

Finally, and from a broader perspective, in the immediate aftermath of the dictators' downfall and right before the call for the first free and fair elections, the majority believed that a parliamentary system, wherein all parties can compete,

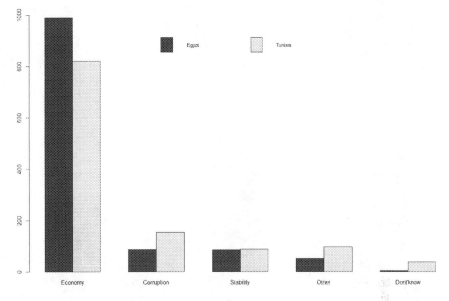

Figure 4.1 Perceived priorities in Tunisia and Egypt, 2011.
Source: Arab Barometer, Wave II.

would be appropriate for their country (see Figure 4.2). Even though this is not a uniquely leftist claim, leftist parties across the North African region have nonetheless championed the introduction of a genuine parliamentary system and political pluralism since the earlier days of national independence in the mid-50s. At the same time, the majority of respondents believed that religion should be disentangled from social and political life (see Figure 4.3), and that women should have the same opportunities and rights as men (see Figure 4.4). The variables used to understand personal attitudes toward these issues are all ordinal categorical variables ranging from 1 (total detachment) to 4 (complete attachment). The fact that in all cases the means of such variables are beyond the two score threshold speaks to the fact that the progressive values measured through these variables are well entrenched in both the Tunisian and the Egyptian societies. Moreover, these figures are in line with a regional trend whereby Arab publics' social and political attitudes are gradually shifting toward more pluralist and secular stances (Resta 2018).

Yet, these findings appear like a paradox in that the rise (or the discovery) of a society supportive of redistributive measures and progressive values corresponds to the resurgence of Islamist parties both in terms of mass support and parliamentary representation within transitional regimes. According to Hinnebusch (1981), the causes of the emergence of some parties and the rollback of others are to be attributed either to the social environment or to the structures of the state, or a combination of both. Since the social environment would have predicted a massive Left vote in both Tunisia and Egypt instead of an "Islamist dominance," the remaining

82   Competition and transitional parties' power resources

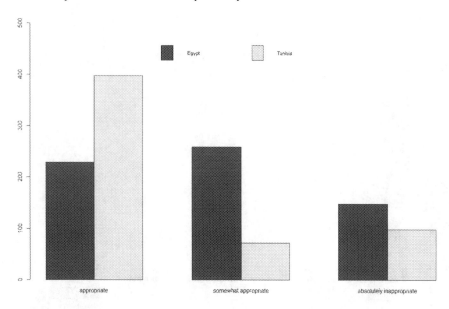

Figure 4.2 Suitability of a Parliamentary system wherein all parties can contest elections, 2011.
Source: Arab Barometer, Wave II.

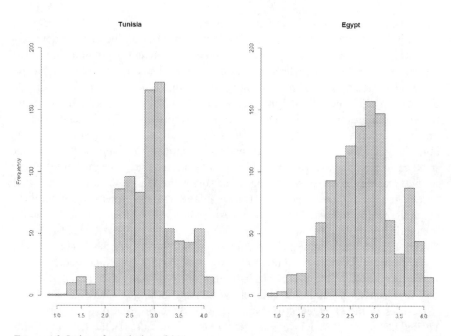

Figure 4.3 Index of secularism, 2011.
Source: Arab Barometer, Wave II.

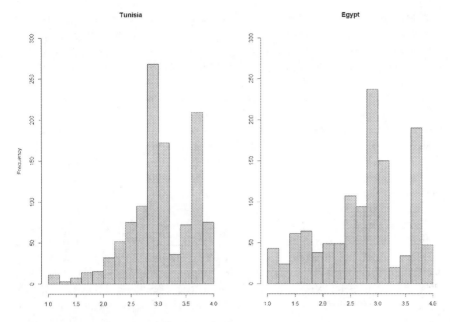

Figure 4.4 Support for gender equality, 2011 index.
Source: Arab Barometer, Wave II.

part of the chapter will discuss the structural causes of this "electoral paradox" (Resta 2018). This gap is of foremost importance not only because it has played a crucial role in the outcome of the transition in the two countries, but also because, from a broader perspective, it is responsible for the lack of political representation of this new Arab public (Achcar 2013).

Blame the founding electoral systems?

The electoral systems used for the founding elections are naturally the prime suspects for the gap observed between people's attitudes and the elections' results. The impact of the electoral systems on the political life of a given country is a hotly debated theme in political science and their effects are all the more salient when founding elections are at stake. This is even more so if the transition from authoritarian rule is rapid and dramatic because, first and foremost, they determine the composition of the elected parliaments entrusted with constitution-making prerogatives and the kind of relationship between MPs and voters. Variations in these two dimensions have profoundly different implications for the constitution-making processes (Carey 2014). On the basis of the decisions around the three constitutive elements of an electoral system – the electoral formula, the structure of the vote, and the dimension of electoral districts – it is possible to arrive at different kinds of electoral systems depending on their simplicity, their effects on inclusiveness, distortion, incentives in building coalitions, and individual accountability (Carey and Reynolds 2011). In this perspective, any given electoral systems can favor (or not) a democratic transition by creating (or not) excessive disproportions of power positioning among competing parties, by encouraging (or not) party–voters relations based on clientelism, kinship, and patronage, and by conceding room (or not) to manipulations and frauds.

The proportional closed-list electoral system associated with Hare's quota formula with highest remainders (HQLR) chosen in Tunisia strongly contributed to the installation of democracy, acting on two levels. First, the closed-list electoral system encouraged parties' discipline and organization in filing candidates in all the 33 Tunisian districts (Carey 2013). Second, inside the elected parliament the HQLR electoral formula encouraged the search for compromise and collaboration inasmuch as it drained seats bonuses from Ennahda, who managed to capture 'only' 41% of seats (Carey 2014). By simulating seats' allocations from the vote Tunisian voters cast at the 2011 elections under different electoral formulas, Carey notices that the one chosen by the Higher Commission proved to be more suitable for the founding elections because it magnified political pluralism while denying the largest party the absolute majority in the parliament, that other proportional formulas (such as the D'Hont) would have otherwise provided (Carey 2014).

In Egypt, in contrast, the fuzziness surrounding the design of the transitional roadmap was reflected in a jumbled voting procedure. The military opted for a mixed electoral system: two-thirds of each house were to be elected by closed-party lists, while the remaining third through individual candidacies. Districts differed from one system to the other and the elections were conducted in six rounds. As far as the strategic effects of this electoral system are concerned, the combination of two symmetrical systems for the election of the same body

> pulled [parties] in two different directions. On the one hand, individual districts incentivized parties to pool resources, negotiate certain districts, and come together on the basis of ideological affinity. On the other hand, the high magnitude of the districts in list districts encouraged party proliferation and provided disincentives to coordination.
>
> (Tavana 2011, 563–64)

Hence, the Egyptian electoral system triggered the emergence of three distinct ideological groups (the religious, the right/liberal, and the leftist camps) with poor party discipline. Yet, inter-parties migration in the aftermath of the founding elections is a phenomenon that also occurred in the Tunisian ANC. More likely is that individual districts penalized partisan mechanisms, such as ideological and issue affinity, at the expense of mechanisms typical of Mubarak's liberalized autocracy, namely networks of kinship, clientelism, and so on (Albrecht 2010; Masoud 2014). This perverted the very nature of representation for the founding elections charged with electing the body that, directly or indirectly, had to write the new constitution. Further, coming to the analysis of the mechanic effects, the Egyptian electoral formula benefited major parties at the expense of the smaller ones, thus magnifying the unbalance of power between the Islamists and their opponents (Carey 2014).

From this, it followed that the Tunisian electoral system has been often presented as the poster case for its positive impact on the Constituent Assembly, while the Egyptian one has been repeatedly pointed to as one of the principal causes of the failed transition. Yet, as the remaining part of this section will show, while the electoral systems can account for relative differences in parties' representation, displaying more or less distortive effects, they fall short in accounting for the regional (beyond Tunisia and Egypt) success of Islamist formations and the concomitant failure of leftist parties which, from the above survey data, seemed to be the natural vehicle for the realization of people's political ambitions.

The Tunisian electoral system

The choice of the electoral system made by Ben Achour's commission has been deemed to be particularly inspired by many observers (Carey 2013; Carey and Reynolds 2011; Stepan and Linz 2013). It is so because the provisions around its constitutive element assured "high scores on almost all key markers" (Carey and Reynolds 2011, 40) mentioned above. As far as the structure of the vote is concerned, the closed-list vote providing for the gender quota has had good effects on inclusiveness but noxious effects on individual accountability. On the one hand, the provision of lists with alternated representation of men and women had the effect of including in the circuit of passive electorate women who otherwise would have been possibly left at the margins. On the other hand, this deprived citizens of the possibility to choose their own candidates – whereas party did – thus reducing MPs' accountability vis-à-vis their electorates. This effect appears clearly by looking at the parties' outflows inside the ANC in the months following the elections. Coming further to the most substantive features, the recourse to the HQLR, which is the most proportional electoral system among those available, was enhanced by the district magnitude. Indeed, at the time of elections, the 33 electoral districts were to elect the members of the constituent assembly (for a total of 217) in proportion to their population. Districts' magnitude thus ranged from 1 to 10, but often districts were entrusted with the election of five or seven MPs. In the absence of a legal threshold, such a magnitude allowed the representation of small parties also. It is so because under the HQLR formula, the electoral quota, that is the number of votes needed to obtain a seat, is calculated by dividing the number of votes casted in each district by the numbers of seats assigned in the district itself. The more the seats up for grabs in a given constituency the lesser the number of votes needed to gain a seat. Moreover, the remaining seats are assigned according to the largest remainders. The combined effect of the HQLR with the size of the district allowed even smaller parties to compete for votes with the concrete hope of entering parliament (Duverger 1954). In this way, as Carey notes,

> the HQLR method awarded Ennahdha 41% of the seats in the Assembly, or 4% above its vote share. It is noteworthy that, despite dominating the field of parties, Ennahdha's seat bonus was not the largest. The bonuses of much smaller alliances were as large – and in one case, even larger – than Ennahdha's in

absolute terms, and many times larger in relative terms. Together, these seat bonuses for small alliances determined that Ennahdha fell well short of a majority of the seats in the Constituent Assembly and, consequently, had to negotiate with other alliances in the process of drafting a constitution. By contrast, had Tunisia chosen differently – for example, had it chosen the other most common PR formula for converting votes to seats, the d'Hondt Divisor (DHD) method – Ennahdha would have won 69% of the Assembly seats and been in a position to impose a new constitution unilaterally.

(Carey 2014, 10)

The Egyptian electoral system

The Egyptian transitional roadmap to oversee the passage from SCAF's control to civilian rule has been seen as an example of how not to conduct a transition (Awad 2013). Similarly, the electoral system adopted for the founding elections has been described as "headed for failure" (Carey and Reynolds 2011, 39) for the purpose of a democratic transition. The SCAF envisaged a complex electoral system for the founding elections whereby one third of the Parliament would have been elected trough individual candidacies, while the remaining two-third according to a closed-list system. As far as the elections of individuals was concerned, the law provided for 83 and 30 two-member districts for the People Assembly and the Shura Council respectively. Coming to the closed-list part, 46 districts were to elect 332 members of the People Assembly, while 30 districts were designed to assign a total of 120 seats in the Shura Council. The electoral formula to convert votes in seats for closed-list districts was, as in Tunisia, the HQLR, but with the provision of a legal threshold as low as 0.5% of the nationwide vote. To make things more complex, each branch of parliament was elected in six separate rounds across three distinct regions for a total of 12 election days.

Coming to the effects of this electoral system, the structure of vote providing for individual candidacies was similar to the electoral system adopted in the same Egypt before 1984 and 1990, which had "increased the importance of money in elections" (Carey and Shugart 1995; Masoud 2014, 68) and paved the way for the reassertion of patronage practices, networks of kinship, and vote-buying over policy programs while weakening all but the biggest political parties. As for the electoral formula, it is indeed quite difficult to assess the overall impact of such a complex system, wherein two symmetrically different kinds of vote (majoritarian and proportional) coexist. On the one hand, Masoud (2014) welcomed this system because, in his opinion, the combined effect of large district size for the majoritarian vote and the PR part would have brought politics back in allowing even smaller parties to compete on the base of their political platforms. On the other hand, other scholars emphasize the distortive effects of the majoritarian vote and call into question the district magnitude, pointing to the fact that several proportional districts were "too small to offer voice to fledging parties outside the dominant players" (Carey and Reynolds 2011, 38). Tavana (2011), for his part, notes that as a result of the two opposite pushes triggered by the electoral system "parties will coalesce into three distinct ideological groups, they will be both weak and loosely organized" (Tavana 2011, 564).

A final controversial point has to do with the fact that the electoral days were spaced out. Even though the rationale behind this decision was that of overcoming the lack of personnel to supervise the conduct of elections, this opened the room to excessive distortions, frauds, manipulation of the electoral results, and strategic vote following the announcement of previous results. The Egyptian electoral system – as expected – is certainly responsible for the creation of unbalanced power distribution, allowing Egyptian Islamists to rule alone and thus nullifying the incentives to bargain and compromise, as the Tunisian Ennahda had to do. But the electoral system cannot account on its own for Egyptian Islamists gaining such a large percentage of the vote. Why did they perform so well both under the proportional rule, which emphasizes "politics" and programs, and under the majority one, which rewards the importance of candidates' popularity? And why is this phenomenon observable, even if on a smaller case, also in Tunisia?

The double standard: patterns of competition between leftists and Islamists before the Arab Spring

As already mentioned, the power advantage of Islamists parties, underpinned by electoral results, appears like a paradox (Cavatorta and Storm 2018; Resta 2018). Dominant opposition forces in the 1970s, leftist parties have consistently lost appeal across the Arab world while political Islam has imposed itself as a major political force. Despite all this, the Arab uprisings seemed to unveil the existence of a rather progressive society in line with the values and policies of the Left. Yet, in post-uprising democratic elections in Tunisia and Egypt, leftist parties have been largely marginalized by the success of their competitors: the Islamist parties. Drawing from Hinnebusch, political parties in the Middle East, as their counterparts in western consolidated democracies, can be considered as barometers of "the nature and the development of politics in the region" (Hinnebusch 2005, 335). In particular, parties are deemed to: (i) reflect the inherited societal tradition, and with it the power of sub-national and trans-national identities; (ii) reflect social change, in terms of *composition, ideologies, and organizational capacit*[ies]; and (iii) reflect and affect the process of *state formation* (ibid., italics in original). Following on from this theoretical framework, the very reasons for the decline of leftist parties and the concomitant resurgence of the Islamists are to be found within the society, intended as its inner characteristics and its perception of political changes, and within the national polities. It might then be the case that either leftist politics no longer chimed with mass aspirations, while Islamism did, or that the evolution of the two regimes under consideration has been detrimental to leftist parties, but not to Islamists.

Indeed, each of the explanations attributed to the decline of leftist parties falls within one between the social and the institutional environments. As for the former, some have argued that the importance of trans-national identities the Left embodied, namely Communism, Socialism, and Nasserism, lost their attractiveness because of the failure of the URSS and of the Nasserist socio-economic and political experiments (Graham 2004; Hilal 2014; Ehteshami and Murphy 1996). Others see in the organizational rigidity of leftist parties a problematic Soviet importation that undermined the capacity of the Arab Left to accommodate social dynamism (Yacoub 2014). In contrast, others point to the reliance of leftist parties on the charisma of their leaders, thus reflecting the regional praxis of the personalization of politics (Shteiwi 2014). Along similar lines, the decline of Leftist parties has been attributed to their poor institutionalization (Hilal 2014; Storm 2014). This goes hand-in-hand with the claim that leftist parties were too elitist and too concerned with intellectual work to develop any meaningful link with their societies (Gessoumi 2014). Although all these accounts enhance our comprehension of the phenomenon under investigation, a reappraisal is needed.

On the one hand, arguing that leftist politics has lost appeal because of its past failures is misleading. Firstly, as Masoud puts brilliantly, "such arguments assume that the Egyptian peasant or the Yemeni tribesman (or the American political science professor) decide whom to vote for by weighting the historical records of alternative worldviews" (2014, 57). Indeed, the experience of several Latin American countries after 1991 proves that leftist politics has not been buried under the ruins of the URSS. Secondly, history-based readings completely disregard the fact that many people in the Arab World self-place on the left side of the political spectrum (Masoud 2014; Tessler 2011) and that their personal attitudes support leftist agenda, as our data confirm. On the other hand, conceiving the decline of leftist parties as a result of their organizational deficiencies that translate into their detachment from the public might be shortsighted. Considering the mobilization capacities these parties enjoyed up to the late 1970s, such accounts confound the causes with the effects of other intervening variables. And this leads to the introduction of institutional explanations.

Tunisia and Egypt gained their independence from foreign domination through revolutions inspired by a leftist ideology imbued with nationalism, but whose fight against the oppression of capital was translated into a fight against the oppression of colonization. Since the 1960s, people and political elites gathered around the leaders – soon turned into the head of states – of those revolution, still galvanized by the cause of independence and the challenges ahead for nation- and state-building. Yet, signals of uneasiness with power concentration and economic policies began to surface soon after independence, finding political expression in left parties. Confronted with internal sustained political dissent and international pressures, Tunisia and Egypt's authoritarian regimes were then obliged to put in place other devices than a single party rule in order to survive. This brought to the process of "authoritarian upgrading" (Heydemann 2007), which consisted in a semblance of political liberalization entailing a mix of controlled political competition and repression that has, more or less intentionally, advantaged Islamist parties, thus partially explaining their overwhelming electoral victories in 2011 and 2012.

Leftist and Islamist oppositions in authoritarian Egypt

In the aftermath of the Free Officers' revolution in 1952, Nasser put in place a considerable effort in creating a consensual environment suitable for the one-person rule. The period going from 1952 to mid-1960s witnessed the creation of a single party-system, the Liberation Rally (LR), later named Arab Socialist Union (ASU) in 1962, which merged with state institutions (Brownlee 2007). This took place through control, co-optation, and repression of opposition movements and the depoliticization of the polity. As Lust-Okar notes,

> a new constitution, put to a referendum in 1956, created a presidency with vast powers. The 1956 "Law on the Exercise of Political Rights" established state control over all forms of political participation; the 1958 Law no. 162 confirmed the president's right to declare and terminate states of emergency; the 1960 Law no. 156 nationalized the media, effectively eliminating freedom of the press; a 1963 law stipulated that union leaders must be members of the ASU; and the 1964 law no. 32 allowed the government to prohibit organizations that threatened 'morality' and the 'interest of the republic'.
> (Lust-Okar 2005, 61)

With the exception of the ruling party, all pre-existent political parties, including the Communist party, were abolished while other forms of associationism, first and foremost, the Muslim Brotherhood (MB), met harsh repression. Further, in 1961, pre-existent trade unions (already under state control) were merged into the Egyptian Trade Union Federation (ETUF), falling under the direct control of the government (Posusney 1997). Finally, the 1967 state of emergency, issued with the objective of coping with the Arab–Israeli war, was protracted with only small interruptions until the Arab uprisings, allowing incumbent dictators to have a free hand.

Sadat's accession to power following Nasser's death in 1970 witnessed major changes inasmuch as he presented himself as the man for a new – and more open – political era. He adjusted Egypt's international position by joining the Western sphere of influence and in so doing he also opened the door to cosmetic political liberalization. Major adjustments occurred both within the centers of power and in the polity, moving Egypt away from the institutional setup inherited from Nasser. First, to pursue his ambitious agenda, he reorganized the cabinet; appointed key governors; purged both the National Assembly and the security forces; reformed the ASU's structure and established a committee to write a new constitution. Second, he relaxed the grip of the regime on the organization and participation of opposition movements with special consideration for the Muslim Brotherhood. In his mind, the MB was a potentially important ally to "counterweigh the combined opposition to his regime mounted by Nasserite and leftist elements" (Ibrahim 1982, 76), as they were opposed to his neoliberal economic policies. At this moment, Islamists leaders "reemerged from prisons" (Brown 2012, 87) or returned from abroad to revive their organization benefiting from Sadat's tolerance, "if not outright blessing" (Ibrahim 1982, 76).

By 1976, times appeared then suited to calm internal and international demands of democratization with the rise of (limited) pluralism and multipartyism. In that year, the National Progressive Union Party (NPUP), also known as Tagammu, and the Liberal Socialist Union saw the light as ASU's splinters under the impulse of Sadat to introduce a semblance of political liberalization (Hinnebusch 1981) and the first multiparty elections were held. As expected, the ASU gained the overwhelming majority of seats, while its competitors achieved only modest results (15 and 3 seats for the Liberal Socialist Union and Tagammu respectively) and independents, mostly MB's candidates, earned 47 seats. This kind of results – i.e., the large victory of the ruling party accompanied by the small parliamentary representation of tolerated opposition parties – characterized Sadat's presidency until his death. This came with significant efforts to contain the left, represented by the NPUP, through repression and through encouraging the expansion of the MB to counterbalance leftist movements within the broader opposition champ.

Because of the circumstance surrounding its creation, the NPUP – up to now the oldest (and at times the most vibrant) leftist opposition – was initially regarded with ambiguity. Soon after though, the party's involvement in 1977 bread riots signed a clear rupture with the regime and its position as opposition party was reinforced. Its following went far beyond an already politicized constituency and the party obtained the support of the wider working class, the middle class, progressive intellectuals and professionals. In particular, the NPUP had strongholds among the working class in the major districts of Cairo and Alexandria. As Hendriks reports,

> Of approximately one hundred eighty registered party members in one Cairo qism (district), thirty-one percent were workers, forty-one percent were muwazzafin [clerks, rev], and the remaining twenty-eight percent were students. The official figures underestimate actual workers' support. In this district, one worker, who was a member of the local leadership group (lejnat el qism), collected membership fees from thirty-one colleagues, many of whom did not want to register officially. Given the risk of being known as a Tajammu'awi for people who feel more vulnerable vis-a-vis the authorities than do educated muwazzaf, it is probable that this underenumeration occurs elsewhere as well.
>
> (1983, 267)

In a relatively short period of time, the party had succeeded in developing a complex organizational structure and in penetrating trade unions, the professional association of journalists, the bar and it also made inroads into the countryside despite government interferences (Hendriks 1983). This made the NPUP "(with the possible exception of the Ikhwan) [...] the only political force in Egypt which possesse[d] cadres and basic units on a serious scale" (Hinnebusch 1981, 338). However, the party's increasing appeal drew Sadat's attention. Both in terms of proposed political agenda and of support, in his mind the party had simply gone beyond the threshold of the political pluralism his regime could tolerate. In September 1978, a wave of repression began against NPUP members and the party was banned.[1] At the same time, a tame leftist alternative to the NPUP, the Socialist Labor Party (SLP), was created. Finally, in 1980, the "law of Shame" stated that anyone trying to corrupt the youth by denying religious values or criticize state policy could be punished in the Court of Values. This law targeted Nasserist elements, even inside the ruling party, and the NPUP for their secular ideology, portrayed as a "denial of divine laws," and for its oppositional stance, depicted as "disloyalty to the nation."[2]

At the same time, legitimized by regime's ideological revision along more pious stances, the Islamist organizational machine continued to grow despite, or thanks to, the fact that it was still a movement lacking legal recognition. University activism shifted from leftist venues to Islamist ones without triggering the regime's reaction. Islamists were also highly successful in penetrating civil society organizations, through "religious coloration" (Brown 2012, 88; Masoud 2014), establishing new ones, and entering into professional associations (Wickham 2002). In line with their mobilization strategies, characterized by incredible flexibility and opportunism, MB members also ran the elections by filing independent candidates in the ranks of other lists, such as that of the Socialist Labor Party in 1979.

The advent of Mubarak to power in 1981 after Sadat's assassination at the hands of an extremist Islamic group, seemed at first to rebalance the organizational opportunities among opposing factions. Initially, the new president eased the pressure on the NPUP but, probably because of the fear of following the fate his predecessor, did not intervene in the Islamist champ. As Albrecht and Wegner (2006) note, Mubarak adopted toward it a double standard. On the one hand, it used heavy-handed pressure toward the more radical and violent groups such as Islamic Jihad and *Jama'a Islamiyya*. On the other hand, he left Islamist moderates alone, allowing them to be a player in formal political institutions and to participate in parliamentary and professional associations' elections as independent candidates. Following Sadat's politics, the relations between Mubarak and the Brotherhood during the 1980 have been described as a "political honeymoon." This environment had the effect of boosting MB's political ambitions and led to the presentation of the Islamic Alliance list at the 1987 elections. Formed by the MB (still not a legal party), the Liberal Socialist Party and the Socialist Labor party, the Islamic Alliance won 60 seats.

On the other side of the opposition front, the Left, represented by the sole NPUP, continued to decline irredeemably due the significant obstacles placed in its path concerning both the channels of mobilization available to it and access to parliament. On the one hand, despite the alternation of different electoral systems, electoral dynamics during Mubarak's rule were particularly detrimental to the NPUP. From 1984 to 1987, Egypt used a proportional system with a closed list. Even though priority was given to parties, the NPUP was badly defeated, gaining no seats in both elections due to its inability to compete with the ruling party in terms of both political and economic resources. The situation worsened for the NPUP when, from 1990, Egypt returned to a majoritarian system that for opposition parties was "something close to a death knell" (Masoud 2014, 68). It is so because the winner-take-all system, wherein all qualified persons could be candidates without constraints – first and foremost a party affiliation – inflated the influx of local notables and businessmen, who had more economic resources to meet the demands of voters, and pushed opposition parties at the margins of the electoral competition. In addition, as in the past, there was a resurgence of networks of patronage and kinship – networks that were also detrimental to the NPUP's hope of expanding beyond its cradle-districts (Masoud 2014). On the other hand, the Left's natural channels of mobilization, such as trade unions, professional syndicates, and networks within deprived areas were controlled by Islamists and the regime. The latter, in particular, managed to secure the allegiance of the poor people through vote-buying and patronage practices and completely colonized the trade unions (Posusney 1997). Serving as channel of mobilization under Nasser, these became, under Sadat and Mubarak, channels of demobilization to control the working class. This strategy of demobilization reached its apex in 1995 with the trade union law, which prevented workers employed on temporary contracts to vote in union elections, thereby easing the re-election of incumbent union leaders loyal to the regime (Kienle 2000; Posusney 1997; Shehata 2010).

Meanwhile, since the early 1990s, the regime became increasingly opposed to the MB. The escalation of violence in the first years of the 1990s at the hands of armed radical Islamist groups generated mistrust toward the MB, accused of being the "front organization for armed Islamist groups" (Kienle 1998, 229). With the pretext of fighting violence, but with the deliberate purpose of silencing the mass protests following the economic crisis of the mid-80s and the failure of market-oriented reforms, Mubarak put in place a series of measures conducive to a "net loss of positive and negative liberties" (Kienle 2000). In 2005, however, things appeared to change again, and elections occurred under "an unprecedented international spotlight" (Brown 2012, 92) as external pressure for moving toward genuine liberalization and to end the persecution of political opponents increased. On that occasion, the left, represented by the NPUP, gained only two seats signaling its impossibility of reaching the masses. In contrast, the MB, which fielded independent candidates, gained 88 seats. As had happened in 1989 Tunisia, the MB's strength alarmed the regime, which responded with violence and forced the group to operate underground until the 2011 uprisings. Yet, the Brotherhood managed to develop at the margins of state control, while during the same years, leftist parties further demobilized. This opened the space for the creation of acephalous issue-based movements that while promoting leftist claims and fighting leftist battles always rejected any explicit political affiliation to formal organizations. In light of the debacle of parties belonging to the Egyptian Left, these new forms of activated citizenship simply regarded such forms of participation as counterproductive.

Leftist and Islamist oppositions in authoritarian Tunisia

The problem of oppositions' management arose in all its salience in Bourguiba's Tunisia in the late 1960s. From 1956 – the year of independence – to that moment, "politics was dominated by the Neo-Destour's evolution from a mass-based nationalist movement into an authoritarian ruling party" (Alexander 2016, 34). Not that in this period political opposition was absent, but was rather confined within the ruling party and silenced through the personalization of politics. As observed, "part of Bourguiba's genius laid in his ability to play competing factions and personalities off against one another and to use promotions to pull people under his thumb" (ibid. 38). When this did not work, individual expulsions (as happened to Ben Youssef and Ben Salah) or physical elimination (as was eventually Ben Youssef's fate) of opponents followed (Vandewalle 1980). The only opposition party present and active at that time was the Tunisian Communist Party (PCT). Established the 1920s, it was outlawed in 1963. In order to occupy also the far-left political space that was left after PCT's ban and to host leftist dissident voices, the Neo-Destour underwent a socialist turn that was sanctioned in 1964 at the Bizerte Congress. On that occasion not only the party was renamed, becoming the Socialist Destourian Party (PSD, out of it French acronym), but it coalesced with the Tunisian General Labor Union (UGTT) and, sure of having defused any potential resistance, blended with the state.

However, this did not suffice to placate the mounting discontent both outside and inside the PSD due to desperate economic conditions and unattained promises of democratic openings. In line with the global trend, mass protests erupted in 1968. In that same year, Ahmed Mestiri, a minister of state and a leading figure within the party, began to denounce the failure of Bourguiba's economic policies and the lack of democracy within the PSD and in the country and eventually left the PSD to create the Movement of Socialist Democrats (MDS) in 1978. Moreover, as the "paradox of performance" (Huntington 1991) mandates, Bourguiba's reform of education produced an "unprecedented numbers of a young people [who] received secondary and university educations at home or in Europe" (Alexander 2016, 43). This generation was more politicized and inclined to protest, particularly as the distribution of wealth became uneven and as Bourguiba's grip on the country grew tighter, culminating in the 1974 Congress of Monastir which designated him President for life. In 1978, mass protests spread again around the country with unparalleled participation and violence. These events pushed even the Islamists, which up to that moment were only concerned with intellectual debates and preaching, to undertake political activity (Tamimi 2001).

With several political movements beyond the PSD popping up, and in need of restoring his ascendancy, Bourguiba accepted the popular demand for more democracy by calling the first contested elections in 1981. However, this did not mean that political parties other than PSD became legal. Indeed, this would have followed only if they had obtained at least 5% of nationwide votes (Alexander 2016). Encouraged by this opening, the Islamists, initially perceived by the government as a potential ally for their non-involvement in the 1978 protests and therefore not yet repressed, decided to go public by setting up in that same year the Islamic Tendency Movement (MTI) to participate in the political life of the country. Frightened by the great following the Movement was displaying, the government organized mass arrests against its members and the MTI was banned. In contrast, MDS, MUP, and the PCT ran for elections hoping this would be conducive to legal recognition. However, Bourguiba intervened by "manipulate[ing] the voter rolls, intimidate[ing] oppositions observers at polling places and falsify[ing] the vote count" (Alexander 2016, 45). In the end, a plebiscitary victory was constructed for the PSD while the others didn't manage to reach the 5% of national vote necessary for legal recognition. In this way, Bourguiba ended the pluralistic experiment and returned to a single-party autocracy where all the oppositions were systematically and equally repressed.

Ben Ali's "medical coup," deposing Bourguiba in 1987, seemed to inaugurate a new beginning characterized by democratic openings both in terms of political competition and expansion of political and civil rights. This was at least what resulted from the 1987 Declaration and, more importantly, from the National Pact of the following year. While the Declaration, pronounced on the day of Ben Ali's takeover, meant to signal a clear rupture with the hegemonic and paternalistic management of power,[3] the National Pact was presented as a programmatic document establishing the new government's direction in the fields of national identity, political regime, economic development, and foreign policy agreed upon also by the oppositions. The project provided for both the accommodation of Islam in society and the creation of a democratic political system. Sixteen among opposition parties and civil society organizations signed the 1988 Pact, including the Islamists, with the hope this would lead to a relaxation of relations with the regime and to a pluralistic society. As a matter of fact, beyond the pact there were good reasons to believe in this new beginning (Angrist 1999). In the days following Ben Ali's accession to power, men closed to Bourguiba were removed from key power positions and the PSD became the National Constitutional Rally (RCD) to mark the distance with the single-party regime. More than 5,000 political prisoners – including the leaders of opposition parties – were released and political exiles were invited to come back to the country. Further, the UN Convention against Torture was ratified to prevent the reiteration of common practices under Bourguiba. When it came to institutional reforms, on December 15, 1987, a Constitutional Council was created – albeit with a merely consultative role – and life presidency came to an end.[4] As for political liberties, political parties were allowed to form and operate enjoying new freedoms of expression and association.[5] The MTI, for instance, established a student union, the General Union of Tunisian Students (UGET), and was allowed to publish its own newspaper (Allani 2009).

In such a context, the 1989 elections were infused with great expectations (Anderson 1991). However, the majoritarian electoral system "worked a tremendous hardship on small, new parties that did not have national organizations" (Alexander 2016, 53). Ben Ali proposed to the parties signing the National Pact that they would run jointly with the RCD and eventually accede to the following spoils system. Even though this offer was a clear departure from the spirit of democratic elections, some parties took it into serious consideration as it possibly constituted the only way for them to enter representative institutions. Yet, Mestiri's decision to run alone induced all other opposition parties to realize that their credibility would have been really undermined if they had run with the RCD. Although they followed Mestiri's line, all leftist parties were upset by his initiative and ran each under separate lists. Such fragmentation paved the way for a total disaster in that no party managed to surpass the 5% threshold thus missing the opportunity to obtain legal recognition. As for the Islamist camp, the MTI, now named Ennahda, obtained the permission to field its candidates as independents and obtained impressive results winning 14% of nationwide votes, reaching a peak of 30% in some urban areas (Alexander 2016). That was simply too much for the pluralism Ben Ali had in mind. A new wave of harsh repression hit again the Islamists. The 1989 elections thus proved that Ben Ali's regime was no more inclined than the previous one in allowing pluralism, genuine political liberalization, and that, more importantly, the hegemony of the opposition front had shifted from the left to Islamist camp (Hibou 2011; Khiari and Lamloum 1999; Sadiki 2002).

From this moment on, the Islamists continued to operate underground until the 2011 revolution. The regime alternated periods of tolerance with periods of persecution (as happened after the adoption of laws against terrorism following September 11, 2001), but they have been always prevented from contesting elections, even as independents. In contrast, from 1994, several leftist parties – the MDS, Ettajdid, Unionist Democratic Union, and the Party of People Unity –, have been allowed to participate in the political and institutional life of the country, but always within the boundaries established by the regime. By so doing, these parties moderated their oppositional stances but at the cost of their electoral support, thus augmenting their dependency on the regime's benevolence for their survival. This journey to irrelevance is also the result of the regime's success in closing off the Left from its natural channels of mass mobilization and electoral support. While trade unions were coopted or annihilated and professional associations easily infiltrated, the poor areas of the country, which would have supported the Left's redistributive policy programs, relied on practices of vote-buying and electoral patronage to obtain a minimum of services and attention, as the success of the RCD in those areas prove. As consequence, from the 2000s onwards the Tunisian Left found expression in a series of urban civil society's initiatives which nonetheless rejected any kind of partisan and ideological affiliation. Instances of this trend are the Palestinian Youth Association for Leadership and Rights Activation and the Tunisian League for Human Rights (LTDH), already active since 1977 but which gained new momentum in those years.

Islamists' supremacy after the Arab Spring: organizational advantages and reputation

The political developments of Tunisia and Egypt from independence to the 2011 uprisings follows a similar dynamic that is crucial for understanding parties' power resources at the time of the founding elections, which – as emerged from the above investigation of people's beliefs and political convictions – is in no way reflective of Tunisians and Egyptians' policy preferences and political aspirations. In both countries, the growth of the political attractiveness of Islamism parallels the rollback of leftist parties, which in the 1960s and 1970s were really strong both in terms of mass support and ideological appeal and thus constituted the major opposition force. By the beginning of the new millennium, in both countries the left displayed all the symptoms. Tarrow (1998) attributes to decline of collective action, namely withdrawal, fractionalization, and institutionalization. In contrast, the Islamist camp was sound and well.

Looking at the evolution of the political systems in both countries, and in line with other contributions (Heydemann 2007; Lust-Okar 2005; Masoud 2014), it is here argued that such disparity is to be attributed to the way dictators structured political competition and this is also at the heart of the electoral results observed at the 2011/2012 founding elections. First, the previous authoritarian structures of political competition rewarded previous illegal opposition forces, i.e. the Islamists, with 'power reputation'. In fact, while the division of the opposition between legalized and banned had the goal of preventing the unification of oppositions, in the aftermath of the 2010 uprisings it had the consequence of depicting previously legalized parties – like leftist ones – as part of the previous regime and of infusing the perception that previously banned parties – i.e. the Islamists – were really independent and a genuine alternative to the previous regime even though in some cases they had a stake in the institutional, social, and economic life of the authoritarian regime. Second, regime repression impacted differently the oppositions' mobilization capacities. This was due not only to the fact that it was conducted with a different resolve depending on the target, but also, and more importantly, because its efficiency depended on the organizational structures the oppositions relied on. These dynamics are in turn responsible for (i) the inconsistency of the electoral offer and (ii) individuals' misperception of the electoral offer leading to the representativeness gap during the 2011 founding elections.

Authoritarian repression and transitional parties' organizational advantages

In Tunisia and Egypt, one of the first measures in the construction of the single-party regime, lasting until the 1970s, was the repression of the left opposition, which had partaken in the struggle of national independence. This was the fate of Communist parties, which had been present since the 1920s, and of other leftist factions, critical of how incumbents ruled, within the ruling parties. In addition to this, both Nasser and Bourguiba secured their grip on sectors of society by blending their party with established trade unions. This development is actually in line with the regional trend, which pushed scholars to speak of these regimes as authoritarian populist (and later post-populist) corporatisms (Ayubi 1995; Hinnebusch 2005, 2010). Trade unions were subordinated to the state which sought to include the different social forces within one organization in order to make class conflict irrelevant in favor of state-building and regime stability (Ehteshami and Murphy 1996; Hinnebusch 2010; Murphy 1999). In this regard, the ruling party functioned as the intermediary between the state and corporate groups by co-opting all other intermediary associations (Murphy 1999). Further, following the introduction of measures of economic liberalization, trade unions, and all other intermediate associations served the purpose of accommodating growing demands of representation, thus functioning as means of demobilization and social control (Heydemann 2007; Hinnebusch 2010; Posusney 1997). This was for instance the case of the creation of leftist parties like the NPUP in Egypt or MDS's participation at the 1981 elections in Tunisia and the reorganization of state labor-relations in both countries. As mentioned earlier, from the 1980s onward, the formalistic interpenetration of state, party and union was in varying degrees substituted with less visible means of co-optation through legal restrictions on the civils and political liberties, clientelistic relations and, in ultimate instance, repression.

From national independence to the Arab uprisings then, the potential constituencies of leftist parties were simply closed off to them. Sectors of the workforce and the poorer strata of the society were virtually insulated from leftist politics. The former were under the direct control of the ruling elite since trade unions leaders were selected by top cadres of the state apparatus and ordinary militants were aware of important restrictions on its freedom of self-organization and demonstration (Hinnebusch 2005), even though in some cases some of them found a way to denounce this system, as the 2008 Gafsa protests in Tunisia prove (Allal 2009). The latter, who would favor leftist claims for redistribution and social justice, was controlled by the ruling party through patronage and clientelistic practices (Schedler 2002, 2006). In this respect, the left could not compete with the economic resources available to regimes and necessary to secure the support of this constituency (Hinnebusch 1981; Masoud 2014). Given this setup, leftist parties, once legalized, faced insurmountable obstacles to penetrate this key constituency like the NPUP had succeeded in doing in the late 1970s before being harshly repressed.

A totally different picture is the one regarding the mobilization opportunities for Islamist formations. From being communities of proselytism and theological debates, these groups grew by entering pre-constituted associational networks, such as charitable associations and youth organizations revolving around the mosques. At first, as many authors note, such expansion was even encouraged by Sadat and Ben Ali to counterbalance the power of leftist opposition at a time of radical changes in the national political economy from state planning toward the free market. Yet, when the expansion of the "parallel Islamic sector" (Wickham 2002) stepped over the boundaries of regimes' toleration, it had become just too complex and too heterogeneous to be effectively dismantled. In Egypt it entailed "private mosques; Islamic voluntary associations, including welfare societies, cultural organization, health clinics; and Islamic-profit commercial and business enterprises, such as Islamic banks, investment companies, manufacturing firms, and publishing houses" (ibid., 97). The reasons for this spread are due to both the will of the incumbent rulers and to intrinsic features of the Islamist camp. On the one hand, Ben Ali, Sadat and Mubarak, who first saw in the Islamists an ally in the containment of the Left, when confronted with the problem of containing the Islamists themselves opted for a policy of selective accommodation (Bianchi 1989). Thus, they repressed more radical Islamist groups and closed an eye on the moderate ones, with the latter effectively benefiting from the political liberalization inaugurated in the 1970s (Wickham 2002). This kind of policy was more evident in Mubarak's Egypt than in Tunisia where Ben Ali intermittently targeted moderates as well. On the other hand, since late 1980s, Islamists' policy programs offered some vague form of democracy grounded on religion as guarantor of national moral integrity, but with no clear plan on economic issues (Pahwa 2013). Contrary to leftist parties, whose political and economic program is naturally oriented toward just some segments of society (the same constituency the state wanted under its control), Islamists were more naturally inclined to reach different segments of society through different means, ranging from those taking advantage of the services provided by charitable associations to those benefiting from profit-oriented commercial enterprises.

For Masoud (2014) and Cammet and Luong (2014), this organizational advantage is at the heart of Islamist strength and the concomitant weakness of the Left, ultimately sanctioned at the ballot boxes during the post-revolutionary founding elections. This reading is also in line with the findings presented in Chapter 3 where the explanatory power of the organizational models outweighs that of the socio-economic ones in both countries. In this regard, if the argument about the irrelevance of political parties within transitions (Collombier 2013; Eyadat 2015) is to be dismissed, it is nonetheless true that some of the tenets grounding this position, like for instance the claim that political parties were not allowed to genuinely proliferate, explain why this organizational advantage has been crucial in 2011–2 Tunisia and Egypt. In fact, at the time of founding elections following decades of authoritarianism or semi-authoritarianism, voters are required to choose across a multitude of parties, many which are new or distant from voters due to the strict conditions under the previous regime. In such cases, it is too naive to believe that voters will cast their preference by picking the party which best suits their policy preferences, for they simply lack the time to develop the required knowledge of the entire spectrum constituting the electoral offer (Dalton and Weldon 2007). Instead, voters' choice will be influenced by agents of political intermediation (Dalton and Klingemann 2007).

This recent field of studies holds that the "varying channels and processes through which voters receive information about partisan politics" influence voting behavior itself (Gunther et al. 2016, 3). For the founding elections in Tunisia and Egypt, this claim is further confirmed by the fact that voters were not able to properly locate parties on a policy space (Masoud 2014) and that, therefore, there was no correlation between parties'–voters' convergence on salient issues and the final vote choice (Çarkoğlu, Krouwel, and Yıldırım 2013). Unable to appraise correctly different political alternatives, voters simply choose the only party they probably really had been "in touch with." This implies that after the ousting of the Left from its natural channels of mobilization in parallel with the accommodation of Islamist associations pursued in both Tunisia and Egypt, Tunisian and Egyptian voters had simply more opportunities to come across an Islamist organization rather than a leftist one. Because of this, they were more likely to vote for an Islamist party. In Masoud's words,

> though the majority of poor Egyptian voters prefer significant redistribution and a large welfare state, they are unable to connect these preferences with parties that most espouse them [i.e. the Left parties], voting instead for Islamist politicians who, by virtue of their embeddedness in dense

networks of religious organization, are able to speak to voters in way that leftists are not.

(Masoud 2014, 181)

In this regard, Islamists' advantage was more significant in Egypt than in Tunisia because the "assets" Ennahda controlled were in no way comparable to those of the Muslim Brotherhood and, to a lesser extent, of the Salafist Nour party. In fact, while, as we have seen, for the 2011 elections Ennahda, which was systematically repressed prior to that moment, relied only on the activation of its underground cells, the FJP could count on a broader and much more varied network that was allowed to prosper under Sadat and Mubarak.

Divided structures of competition and transitional parties' reputation

Beyond the arbitrary recourse to repression, another important tool underpinning the survival of authoritarian rulers was the arbitrary division of the opposition between legal and illegal parties. This altered parties' reputational resources, and hence electoral support, with tangible consequences for the 2011 elections (Cammett and Luong 2014). As mentioned earlier, under electoral authoritarianism, the competition was structured to prevent the creation of a united opposition front by drawing arbitrary lines between those allowed to compete in the elections and those who were banned. The result of this structuring was that that the political parties that were legalized under the previous regime suffered a reputational crisis once authoritarianism collapsed and that, in contrast, those who were previously outlawed could present themselves as a truly new alternative to the previous regime.

Drawing from Dahl (1971), Lust-Okar (2005) notes that the entrance into formal political competition, for very different reasons (Cavatorta 2007) in context of mixed political systems (wherein some groups are included but not others), is subordinated to the acceptance of limits on political participation and competition. Even though this might not be explicit, it is always the product of playing by the established rules of the game. Opposition parties admitted into the political space of electoral authoritarianism and its governing institutions gave up on their claims for radical change and on their ambition of provoking an alternation of government altogether. This pushed legalized parties into a vicious circle. By moderating their stances, they started losing their political relevance in terms of programmatic platform, and as consequence, in terms of electoral support, making their survival more dependent on regimes' benevolence, which in turn led them to further align with the regime and lose further voters. At the same time, banned parties increased their popularity by criticizing the immobility of the political system and the connivance of legal opposition parties. Hence, once electoral authoritarianism collapsed, the different opposition forces not only enjoyed varying levels of support, but could also present to voters different reputational standings.

In authoritarian Tunisia and Egypt, legal opposition parties were mainly leftist: MDS and lately the Ettajdid (the once PCOT) in Tunisia, and the NPUP in Egypt, just to name the ones that in the past had been able to mobilize mass protests. Since they had been included into the political competition, they began losing their popularity because, in order to enter the legal political space and its governing institutions, they no longer represented a clear alternative to the regime. After about three decades of electoral authoritarianism, the effects of such mechanisms were all the more evident at the beginning of the 2000s. The disaffection toward legal political parties was such that the new millennium brought with it the creation of a myriad of new parties, in large part of the Left, and, more importantly, a shift of balance between political parties and civic associations in favor of the latter as far as genuine opposition to the regime was concerned. In light of the inefficacy of partisan engagement, the new generation of leftist activists chose the path of engagement in civil society (Abdalla 2015; Albrecht 2010; Langohr 2004).

Islamists, in contrast, were never legalized even though they were allowed to develop organizational networks and, at times, to field candidates as independent. This distinction created great unbalances in political parties' reputation, rewarding Islamists and disadvantaging the Left. While the latter was perceived as part of the system, the former's alleged distance from the authoritarian machine allowed them to present themselves as the true alternative to the previous regime and with the ability to grant citizens a new beginning once it collapsed. This trend can be seen in the emergence of movements such as the "*Kifaya*" or the Palestinian Youth Association for Leadership and Rights Activation in Egypt. Despite their leftist leanings, these new activists did not describe themselves as leftist, finding it useless to have partisan or ideological affiliations (Cavatorta 2012; Langohr 2004). However, new leftist parties also arose. They barely represented the working classes – thus acknowledging the rupture with their natural constituencies that had occurred during the 1980s and 1990s – and focused instead on the wider themes of democratization, social justice, and human rights. The creation of the *Congrès pour la République* (CPR) in Tunisia, and the emergence of the *Al Karama* in Egypt are instances of this development.

Before 2011, the camp of illegal opposition forces was monopolized by Islamists in both Tunisia and Egypt. Even though they were allowed to contest elections at times, their status of banned opposition paradoxically allowed them to openly criticize the status quo and this strengthened their legitimacy in the eyes of public opinion, gaining increasing following. Hence, from this perspective, they could offer potential voters during the founding elections their reputational capital accumulated in the preceding years. Since their 'brand' was never linked to the regime, they represented the only 'new' alternative to the previous political system. In this regard, in the aftermath of the Arab uprisings, Tunisian and Egyptian Islamists enjoyed a double advantage with respect to their counterpart, and in particular leftist parties. Not only they could count on a wide organizational network, they also could count on a positive reputation because their status of illegality had allowed them to maintain a certain autonomy from the regime.

Shape and reasons of the 2011 electoral gap awarding Islamist parties

True enough, during the 2010 uprisings and in the following months, the Tunisian and Egyptian publics appeared open to, if not cherishing, the installation of a civic state able to deal with uneven economic development and unequal wealth redistribution. Even though many observers expected Islamists to have a role in the transition process, few forecast their eventual electoral dominance. After surveying citizens' political attitudes and beliefs, this account confirms the presence of a gap of representativeness in that what people appeared to want was far from what they voted for. This discrepancy is at the heart of stunning disparities in parties' power, which concur to the formation of their strategy profile at the time of installation. Indeed, the more the seats controlled inside the decision-making body, the lesser the payoff for compromising with the other political forces. And this is a piece of the puzzle accounting for the different transition's outcome in Tunisia and Egypt. In the first case, Islamists had the relative majority of seats but needed the cooperation of other parties to pass any kind of legislation and approve a new constitutional text. In Egypt, Islamists controlled the absolute majority of seats and did not need to negotiate with others.

There are two reasons for the electoral gap leading to the uneven distribution of power among the decision-making actors. The contingent one has to do with the different degree of distortion produced by the electoral systems adopted in Tunisia and Egypt can account for cross-countries' differences in the distribution of power among the political parties involved in the 'constitutive phase'. In this respect, the electoral systems are the immediate cause for Egyptian failure and Tunisian success. Yet, this explanation falls short in fully accounting for the dominant role of Islamists across the region and for the different strength they had across the two countries. Structural explanations show how authoritarian regimes favored the proliferation of Islamists at the expense of the Left, thus contributing to the electoral gap at the time of the 2011 founding elections.

First, the cooptation of leftist parties through their legalization, combined with their eradication from leftist mobilization channels, undermined their effectiveness. In the end, leftist parties were reduced to empty shells and leftist political opposition fragmented in a myriad of small organizations. The leftist electoral offer in 2011 was then absolutely inconsistent, for it was dispersed across several new parties with little following or support in society. This effect was remarkable in Tunisia where the sum of the broad left vote amounted to around 50%, but the most popular leftist party only obtained 8% of the vote. In contrast, the Islamists' illegal status allowed them to maintain autonomy from the regime and avoid (or contain) splintering, especially within the boundaries of the moderate camp. In this way, Islamists' ability and resources to be a true alternative were never questioned and their 'brand' never knew reputational crises. Second, regimes' repression undermined the Left severely, but it passively allowed the growth of an Islamist sector. Such disparity is at the roots of the misperception of the political offer, which is the second component of the aforementioned electoral gap. Indeed, people with the political attitudes outlined earlier 'voted for jobs, not Islam' (Robbins and Tessler 2011). The very fact that voters identified Islamist parties as more redistributive than leftist ones (Çarkoğlu, Krouwel, and Yıldırım 2013; Masoud 2014) is due to the fact that the former had more channels to get to voters than the latter. This effect was particularly pronounced in Egypt, where Islamist structures and networks had come to constitute a wide 'parallel sector'.

The unbalanced distribution of power among the different transitional parties as a product of the previous authoritarian structures of competition might alone be deemed sufficient to explain why Tunisians were able to give themselves a democratic constitution while in Egypt Islamist parties, with their total control of parliament, were tempted to impose their own agenda, thus triggering the strong reaction of the left and secular opposition. The latter gave up on attempting a dialogue with the Islamists and consistently resorted to mass demonstrations in the major cities of the country and to judicial adjudication. It was precisely this exclusionary and non-consensual transition that paved the way to the 2013 military coup. Yet, the mere counting of the seats transitional political parties controlled cannot account alone for the success of the Tunisian transition and the failure of the Egyptian one, since this reading presents a number of flaws. First, to conceive the parliamentary power of Egyptian Islamists as monolithic is incorrect inasmuch as what we refer to as the "Islamist dominance" is the result of the sum of the parliamentary seats controlled by different parties, notably the FJP and al-Nour, which ran the elections from within different coalitions and whose alliance proved fragile. Second, even if we accept the idea of an internally coherent Islamist camp, looking at parties' power relations alone might be misleading since in Eastern Europe, for instance, transitions from authoritarian rule ended with the installation of democracy even with one party dominating over the others, as the case of Czech Republic, where, after the founding elections, the Civic Forum controlled 104 alone out of the 200 parliamentary seats, shows. Finally, accounts relying exclusively on actors' power positions disregard the role of actors' ideological orientation and policy preferences, which is indeed the driving (and guiding) force of political action. True enough, actors' power configuration was more encouraging to the search of a dialogue in the Tunisian case than in the Egyptian one. Yet, what about the role of ideas? Following from this question, the next chapter investigates whether the two different transitional outcomes can be also in part attributed to the varying degree of political polarization across the two countries or to the presence of "committed democrats" (McFaul 2002) in Tunisia and their absence in Egypt.

Notes

1 In 1979, the Parliament was dissolved because of "irresponsible oppositions."
2 See Law 95/1980.
3 The most salient passage reads "Our people has reached a degree of responsibility and maturity where every individual and group is in a position to constructively contribute to the running of its affairs, in conformity with the republican idea which gives institutions their full scope and guarantees the conditions for a responsible democracy, fully respecting the sovereignty of the people as written into the Constitution. This Constitution needs urgent revision. The times in which we live can no longer admit of life presidency or automatic succession, from which the people is excluded. Our people deserves an advanced and institutionalized political life, truly based on the plurality of parties and mass organizations."
4 See Constitutional Law n. 88–88, 25th July 1988.
5 See Organic Law 89–90, 2nd August 1988 which modifies and completed law n. 59–154 of November 7, 1959.

References

Abdalla, Nadine. 2015. "Youth Movements in the Egyptian Transformation: Strategies and Repertoires of Political Participation." *Mediterranean Politics* 9395 (February): 1–20. https://doi.org/10.1080/13629395.2015.1081445.
Achcar, Gilbert. 2013. *The People Want: A Radical Exploration of the Arab Uprising*. Oakland, CA: University of California Press.
Albrecht, Holger. 2010. *Contentious Politics in the Middle East : Political Opposition under Authoritarianism*. University Press of Florida. https://upf.com/book.asp?id=9780813034744.
Albrecht, Holger, and Eva Wegner. 2006. "Autocrats and Islamists: Contenders and Containment in Egypt and Morocco." *The Journal of North African Studies* 11 (2): 123–41. https://doi.org/10.1080/13629380600704688.
Alexander, Christopher. 2016. *Tunisia: From Stability to Revolution in the Maghreb*. New York: Routledge.
Allal, Amin. 2009. "Les Mobilisations Protestataires Dans La Région Minière de Gafsa En 2008." In *L'état Face Aux Débordements Du Social Au Maghreb: Formation, Travail et Protection Sociale*, edited by Miriam Catusse, Blandine Destremau, and Éric Verdier, 173–86. Paris: Editions Karthala.
Allani, Alaya. 2009. "The Islamists in Tunisia between Confrontation and Participation: 1980–2001." *The Journal of North African Studies* 14 (2): 257–72. https://doi.org/10.1080/13629380902727510.
Anderson, Lisa. 1991. "Political Pacts, Liberalism, and Democracy: The Tunisian National Pact of 1988." *Government and Opposition* 26 (2): 244–60. https://doi.org/10.1111/j.1477-7053.1991.tb01136.x.
Angrist, Michele Penner. 1999. "Parties, Parliament and Political Dissent in Tunisia." *The Journal of North African Studies* 4 (4): 89–104. https://doi.org/10.1080/13629389908718381.
Awad, Ibrahim. 2013. "Breaking out of Authoritarianism: 18 Months of Political Transition in Egypt." *Constellations* 20 (2): 275–92.
Ayubi, Nazih. 1995. *Overstating the Arab State: Politics and Society in the Middle East*. New York: St Martin Press.
Bianchi, Robert. 1989. *Unruly Corporativism: Associational Life in Twentieth-Century Egypt*. New York: Oxford University Press.
Brown, Nathan J. 2012. *When Victory Is Not an Option: Islamist Movements in Arab Politics*. Ithaca, New York: Cornell University Press.
Brownlee, Jason. 2007. *Authoritarianism in an Age of Democratization*. Cambridge: Cambridge University Press.
Cammett, Melani, and Pauline Jones Luong. 2014. "Is There an Islamist Political Advantage?" *Annual Review of Political Science* 17 (1): 187–206. https://doi.org/10.1146/annurev-polisci-071112-221207.
Carey, John M. 2013. "Tunisia Electoral Formula." Tunisia Electoral Formula – Carey – May 2013. bpb-us-e1.wpmucdn.com
Carey, John M., and Andrew Reynolds. 2011. "The Impact of Election Systems." *Journal of Democracy* 22 (4): 36–47. https://doi.org/10.1353/jod.2011.0072.
Carey, John M., and Matthew Soberg Shugart. 1995. "Incentives to Cultivate a Personal Vote: A Rank Ordering of Electoral Formulas." *Electoral Studies* 14 (4): 417–39.
———. 2014. "Party Systems and the Choice Sets Voters Confront in Transitions to Democracy." In *Workshop on Democracy and Regime Change*, 1–31. Istanbul: Sabanci University.

Çarkoğlu, Ali, André P.M. Krouwel, and Kerem Yıldırım. 2013. "Post-Arab Spring Elections: A Comparison of Voting Advice Application Results." In *ECPR General Conference*, Boredaux, 1–35.
Cavatorta, Francesco. 2007. "'More than Repression: The Significance of Divide et Impera in the Middle East and North Africa –The Case of Morocco.'" *Journal of Contemporary African Studies* 25 (2): 187–203. https://doi.org/10.1080/02589000701396223.
———. 2012. "Arab Spring: The Awakening of Civil Society. A General Overview"." *European Institute for the Mediterranean (IEMed)*, 75–85.
Cavatorta, Francesco, and Lise Storm. 2018. *Political Parties in the Arabic World: Continuity and Change*. Edited by Francesco Cavatorta and Lise Storm. Edinburgh: Edinburgh University Press.
Collombier, Virginie. 2013. "Politics without Parties. Political Change and Democracy Building in Egypt Before and After the Revolution." 35. Max Weber Programme for Doctoral Studies (MWP). Firenze. eui.eu.
Dahl, Robert A. 1971. *Polyarchy: Participation and Opposition*. New Haven and London: Yale University Press.
Dalton, R. J., and S. Weldon. 2007. "Partisanship and Party System Institutionalization." *Party Politics* 13 (2): 179–96. https://doi.org/10.1177/1354068807073856.
Dalton, Russell J., and Hans-Dieter Klingemann. 2007. "Citizens and Political Behavior." In *The Oxford Handbook of Political Behavior*, edited by Russell J. Dalton and Hans-Dieter Klingemann, 3–27. New York: Oxford University Press.
Duverger, Maurice. 1954. *Political Parties*. London: Methuen.
Ehteshami, Anoushiravan, and Emma C. Murphy. 1996. "Transformation of the Corporatist State in the Middle East." *Third World Quarterly* 17 (4): 753–72. https://doi.org/10.1080/01436599615362.
Eyadat, Zaid. 2015. "A Transition without Players: The Role of Political Parties in the Arab Revolutions." *Democracy and Security* 11 (2): 160–75.
Graham, Fuller. 2004. *The Future of Political Islam*. London: Palgrave.
Guessoumi, Mouldi, and Mouldi Gessoumi. 2014. "The Map of the Tunisian Left." In *Mapping of the Arab Left*, edited by Khalil Kalfat, 16–43. Rosa Luxemburg Stiftung North African Office.
Gunther, Richard, Paul A. Beck, Pedro Magalhães, and Alejandro Moreno. 2016. *Voting in Old and New Democracies*. Edited by Richard Gunther, Paul A. Beck, Pedro Magalhães, and Alejandro Moreno. New York: Routledge.
Hendriks, Bertus. 1983. "The Legal Left in Egypt." *Arab Studies Quarterly* 5 (3): 260–75.
Heydemann, Steven. 2007. "Upgrading Authoritarianism in the Arab World." *The Saban Center for Middle East Policy at the Brooking Institution*. Vol. 13. Washington, D. C.
Hibou, Béatrice. 2011. *The Force of Obedience: The Political Economy of Repression in Tunisia*. Cambridge: Polity Press.
Hilal, Jamil. 2014. "Introduction: On the Self-Definition of the Left in the Arab State." In *Mapping of the Arab Left: Conteemporary Leftist Politics in the Arab East*, edited by Jamil Hilal and Katja Herman, 8–34. Rosa Luxemburg Stiftung Regional Office Palestine Ramallah.
Hinnebusch, Raymond. 1981. "The National Progressive Unionist Party : The Nationalist-Left Opposition in Post-Populist Egypt." *Arab Law Quarterly* 3 (4): 325–51.
———. 2005. "Political Parties and Trade Unions." In *A Companion to the History of the Middle East*, 334–54. Malden, Oxford and Carlton: Blackwell Publishing Ltd.
———. 2010. "Toward a Historical Sociology of State Formation in the Middle East." *Middle East Critique* 19 (3): 201–16. https://doi.org/10.1080/19436149.2010.514470.

Ibrahim, Saad Eddin. 1982. "An Islamic Alternative in Egypt : The Muslim Brotherhood and Sadat." *Arab Studies Quarterly* 4 (1/2): 75–93.
Khiari, Sadri, and Olfa Lamloum. 1999. "Tunsie: Des Élections En Trompe-l'œil." *Politique Africaine* 76 (4): 106–15.
Kienle, Eberhard. 1998. "More than a Response to Islamism: The Political Deliberalization of Egypt in the 1990s." *Middle East Journal* 52 (2): 219–35. https://doi.org/papers2://publication/uuid/4280E0FE-C3B5-4D08-AFAE-6F12FCCB2BF8.
———. 2000. *A Grand Delusion: Democracy and Economic Reform in Egypt*. London: IB Tauris.
Langohr, Vickie. 2004. "Too Much Civil Society, Too Little Politics: Egypt and Liberalizing Arab Regimes." *Comparative Politics* 36 (2): 181. https://doi.org/10.2307/4150142.
Lust-Okar, Ellen. 2005. *Structuring Conflict in the Arab World: Incumbents, Opponents, and Institutions*. Cambridge: Cambridge University Press.
Masoud, Tarek. 2014. *Counting Islam: Religion, Class and Elections in Egypt*. New York: Cambridge University Press.
McFaul, Michael. 2002. "The Fourth Wave of Democracy and Dictatorship: Noncooperative Transitions in ThePostcommunist World." *World Politics* 54 (2): 212–44.
Murphy, Emma C. 1999. *Economic and Political Change in Tunisia: From Bourguiba to Ben Ali*. London: Palgrave Macmillan UK.
Pahwa, Sumita. 2013. "Secularizing Islamism and Islamizing Democracy: The Political and Ideational Evolution of the Egyptian Muslim Brothers 1984–2012." *Mediterranean Politics* 18 (2): 189–206. https://doi.org/10.1080/13629395.2013.799324.
Posusney, Marsha Pripstein. 1997. *Labor and the State in Egypt: Workers, Unions and Economic Restructuring*. New York: Columbia University Press.
Resta, Valeria. 2018. "Leftist Parties in the Arab Region before and after the Arab Uprisings: Unrequited Love?" In *Political Parties in the Arab World: Continuity and Change*, edited by Francesco Cavatorta and Lise Storm, 23–48. Edinburgh: Edinburgh University Press.
Robbins, Michael, and Mark Tessler. 2011. "Tunisians Voted for Jobs, Not Islam." *Foreign Policy*, 2011.
Sadiki, Larbi. 2002. "Bin Ali's Tunisia: Democracy by Non-Democratic Means." *British Journal of Middle Eastern Studies* 50 (3): 497–513. https://doi.org/10.1111/1467-9248.00381.
Schedler, Andreas. 2002. "The Menu of Manipulation." *Journal of Democracy* 13 (2): 36–50. https://doi.org/10.1353/jod.2002.0031.
———. 2006. *Electoral Authoritarianism: The Dynamics of Unfree Competition*. Edited by Andreas Schedler. Boulder, CA and London: Lynne Rienner Publishers.
Shehata, Dina. 2010. *Islamist and Secularists in Egypt: Opposition, Conflict and Cooperation*. New York: Routledge.
Shteiwi, Musa M. 2014. "The Jordanian Left: Today's Realities and Future Prospects." In *Mapping of the Arab Left: Conteemporary Leftist Politics in the Arab East*, edited by Jamil Hilal and Katja Herman, 58–83. Rosa Luxemburg Stiftung Regional Office Palestine Ramallah.
Stepan, Alfred, and Juan J. Linz. 2013. "Democratization Theory and the 'Arab Spring.'" *Journal of Democracy* 24 (2): 15–30.
Storm, Lise. 2014. *Party Politics and the Prospects for Democracy in North Africa*. Boulde, CO: Lynne Rienner.
Tamimi, Azzam S. 2001. *Rachid Gannouchi: A Democrat within Islamism*. New York: Oxford University Press.
Tarrow, Sidney. 1998. *Power in Movement: Social Movements, Collective Action and Contentious Politics*. 2nd ed. Cambridge: Cambridge University Press.

Tavana, D. 2011. "Party Proliferation and Electoral Transition in Post-Mubarak Egypt." *The Journal of North African Studies* 16 (4): 555–71. https://doi.org/10.1080/13629387.2011.639142.

Tessler, Mark. 2011. *Public Opinion in the Middle East: Survey Research and the Political Orientations of Ordinary Citizens*. Bloomington: Indiana University Press.

Vandewalle, Dirk. 1980. "Bourguiba, Charismatic Leadership and the Tunisian One Party System." *Middle East Journal* 34 (2): 149–59.

Wickham, Carrie Rosefsky. 2002. *Mobilizing Islam : Religion, Activism, and Political Change in Egypt*. Columbia University Press.

Yacoub, Hussein. 2014. "The Lebanese Left: The Possibility of the Impossible." In *Mapping of the Arab Left: Conteemporary Leftist Politics in the Arab East*, edited by Jamil Hilal and Katja Herman, 82–101. Rosa Luxemburg Stiftung Regional Office Palestine Ramallah.

Zemni, Sami, Brecht De Smet, and Koenraad Bogaert. 2013. "Luxemburg on Tahrir Square: Reading the Arab Revolutions with Rosa Luxemburg's The Mass Strike." *Antipode* 45 (4): 888–907.

5 Authoritarian learning and transitional party systems' politicking

The religious divide and polarization parties work out

The pernicious effects of polarization within installations

Thus far, it has emerged that the different distributions of power within the Egyptian and Tunisian party systems, forged by the structures of the previous authoritarianisms, had a role in explaining the different paths undertaken during the transition processes. While in Tunisia Ennahda won the relative majority of seats, in Egypt the Islamist parties, notably the FJP and Nour, controlled the absolute majority of seats. The Egyptian failure in engineering a self-enforcing democracy is therefore in line with Przeworski's claim that in cases of known and uneven power distribution, the 'constitutive phase' will only be aimed at consolidating winners' power advantage and not a self-enforcing democracy (1991). However, previous records of transitions from authoritarian rule show that enduring democracy can also be a possible outcome in such situations, and several explanations have been put forth. Some scholars look at the ideological orientation of the winning coalition looking for 'committed democrats' (McFaul 2002; Ozzano 2013). Others point to the ideological distance between the actors involved in the installation phase (Lesch 2014). Even though these two readings rest on very different assumptions – the first one builds on the idea that democracy can be one faction's unilateral imposition while the second conceives it as a win-win solution for all the parties involved – when it comes to appraising the processes of transition in the MENA region after the Arab uprisings, they overlap bringing back, albeit in a different manner, a sort of "myth of moderation." In fact, by merging the main tenets of the inclusion-moderation hypothesis, according to which Islamist parties tend to moderate their stances when allowed to participate in elections, with transitology's lesson that the absence of polarization fosters a compromise among the actors involved in the installation, it is widely believed that the prospects for democracy in transitions from authoritarian rule led by Islamist parties depend on the political moderation attained during the transition itself (Schwedler 2013). In this perspective, the absence of political polarization is regarded as an indicator of Islamists' moderation and, at the same time, as a good sign for the success of the transitional bargaining. In fact, in principle, the concept of polarization, here understood as the ideological distance among

DOI: 10.4324/9781003269717-6

the political parties in a party system, is perfectly apt at predicting whether or not the actors involved in the transition will agree on a set of norms to which everybody accept to be bounded by inasmuch as actors' positioning on the political space draws the boundaries of what aspects an actor is ready to negotiate with others. The greater the distance among actors' political preferences, the smaller the possibility for any sort of pact to see the light.

From this, the hypothesis that can be deduced is that party system polarization has had a role as well in explaining the different transitional outcomes in Tunisia and Egypt. More precisely, as per the model presented in Chapter 2, it might be the case that in Egypt the uneven resources between the Islamists and secular parties have not been counterbalanced by parties' ideological proximity, or that, even worse, there was a very significant distance between them, as some authors have argued (Cross and Sorens 2016; Lesch 2014). At the same time, the expectation about the Tunisian case is that the dialogue among the parties involved, which needed to coalesce since none of them had the absolute majority, was eased by the absence of significant party-system polarization. Were this hypothesis be corroborated by the empirics, as per the new 'myth of moderation', it would, in turn, also convey information about Islamist parties' moderation in both countries. More specifically, the presence of polarization in Egypt would indicate the presence of extremist and still-anti-system Islamist parties and the lack of polarization in Tunisia would suggest the fact that Ennahda managed to turn into a moderate Islamist party (or a party inspired by Islamism, as their members repeatedly said).

Due to the crucial role polarization has within transition processes and because the information it conveys about party systems, parties' spatial distribution informs a rich literature in most parts of the world, but it is totally missing in the MENA region, whose comprehension of a wide array of party-politics related issues is still beyond the reach of the extant discipline. The next pages will contribute to filling this knowledge gap. Yet, before jumping to the measurement of political polarization in Tunisia and Egypt, a reappraisal of the sources of polarization is needed to grasp its causes.

Parties as countervailing mechanisms to polarization?

Whatever the content of the divide, conventional wisdom understands party systems' polarization as the result of mass attitudes channeled into the political system through the institutional context, first and foremost the electoral system. This latter, in particular, has catalyzed researchers' attention for its role in fostering party system polarization at two different, but entangled, levels. First, electoral systems influence the degree of polarization by acting on parties' strategic incentives. In this sense, electoral rules in a more proportional voting system (by providing, for instance, for large size districts without an electoral threshold) are deemed to disincentivize parties' strategic positioning toward the center of the political space, which is the terrain of contention of majoritarian systems because that is where the median voter is expected to be. Second, electoral systems are deemed to foster polarization because of the mechanic effects they exert on the size of the party system itself. The more the parties in a given party system, the greater the polarization because, in such circumstance, political parties will have an incentive in moving away from centrist positions and seek viable niches available elsewhere to maximize their vote. The opposite applies in party systems with a limited number of parties, as these will move toward the center to maximize their votes therefore decreasing the chances of polarization developing.

Recent contributions have more or less explicitly emphasized the active role political parties play in determining the degree of polarization in democratization processes. In this sense, what is salient is not the political demand for representation as shaped by the inner attributes of society, nor the strategic and mechanic effects produced by the institutional context. Rather, attention falls on parties' creative role when it comes to peoples' organization of interests by means of their representative agency (Enyedi 2005; Kitschelt et al. 1999; Mair 2002). In Enyedi's words:

> In their attempt to mold the political landscape, parties face institutional and social constraints and adjust their appeal accordingly, but they also invent, facilitate and destroy political identities, underplay social divisions and shift group boundaries. The clusters of pre-political life-experiences and dispositions present both opportunities and constraints for politicians. They can mobilize these structural and attitudinal differences, but they can also identify symbols that unite various groups by tapping what is common in them. The potential room for maneuver is considerable since individual interests and values can be combined with other values/interests in a large number of ways.
>
> (Enyedi 2005, 700)

Such a reading adds new light on the role of political parties within transitions because their saliency within such processes is not only the result of the decisions they take in their governmental capacities during the installation phase (Katz 2014; Mair 2002), but also of their hitherto organization of the interplay between pre-existent social and political divisions and political institutions (Kitschelt et al. 1999). It follows that political parties not only play an active role in determining which cleavages will be politically represented within the party system by brokering among disperse allegiances, values, and interests (Deegan-Krause and Enyedi 2010; Enyedi 2005, 2008; Evans and De Graaf 2013; Raymond 2014), but in so doing they also have an active and decisive role in fostering party systems' polarization (Bermeo 1990; Kitschelt et al. 1999; Tepe 2013). Political entrepreneurs' decisions about the salience attributable to certain issues (offered by national critical junctures or simple political developments) and the position to take about them determine the nature of party alignments and the programmatic competition at the base of different kinds of representation. In this latter regard, parties may decide to reduce the political distance or to increase it, thus affecting considerably, in a way or another, the prospects for a democratic agreement to come about.

Earlier account of transitologists have pointed to the active role of political parties in mitigating the political polarization arising from the public, thereby smoothening the processes of transition and, ultimately, making democratization viable. Examples of such kind are Italy, Portugal, and Spain. In such cases the pact-making process was conducted despite sustained pressure from below in terms of extremism and ideological polarization. Nonetheless, the political parties involved in the transition successfully managed to converge on a set of basic norms, but were also crucial, in the medium run, in moderating the masses by integrating them in the new political regime.

However, the opposite can also occur and they can also act as agents of polarization, as the recent developments in consolidated democracies show (Carothers and O'Donohue 2019; McCoy and Somer 2021). In the absence of a clear ideological cleavage in both societies, as the data show, the reading stressing the active role of political parties in fostering political polarization will therefore be employed in explaining the differences in the level of polarization across Tunisia and Egypt.

Party systems polarization in 2011 Tunisia and Egypt

Locating parties on a political space

Questions about the structure and the polarization of party systems in many parts of the world are addressed through a variety of methods, like expert surveys, the Comparative Manifesto Project (CMP), or computer assisted techniques. The common trait behind these research efforts is the attempt to locate parties on a Euclidean space in order to physically appreciate the distance that separates them along with the dimension(s) where such political competition occurs. In this respect, a significant difference emerges when it comes to the determination of what informs the political space between supervised and unsupervised approaches (Benoit and Däubler 2014). The former, which informs the majority of studies on party systems across the word, starts from a pre-defined definition of the substantive content informing the political space. The political space is then conceived along a right–left continuum (RILE), wherein parties are located according to their distance from what is deemed to be left or right. The CMP, for instance, moving from pre-defined categories of left and right that are provided to coders, assigns parties a score that locate them on a left–right continuum according to the ratio of right vs. left quasi-sentences contained in their party manifestos. In a slightly different manner, but relying nonetheless on left/right categories, country experts, through expert surveys, assign parties a score on the left–right continuum out of their knowledge of the party system in question.

The methods based on an ex-ante definition of left/right categories have immensely advanced our knowledge on parties and party systems in large parts of the world and still contribute to the literature in important ways. Yet, in recent years, they have faced mounting criticisms. To begin with, the validity of CMP' reference categories has been questioned for their anchoring in outdated patterns of political divisions, which are deemed to miss the emergence of new lines of contention and, with it, the genuine nature of the current political contention (Mölder 2016).

In addition, such categories are deemed to be unsuitable when applied to countries outside the Western political tradition (Kraetzschmar and Zollner 2020). Because of these shortcomings, and thanks to the development of computer-assisted machine learning techniques, a new approach, known as 'unsupervised', is becoming more common when analyzing parties' positions. With the unsupervised approach, the content of the political space is one of the results of the empirical investigation as well. In fact, when adopting this approach the parties' positioning on a political space is derived by "scaling observable party behavior" (ibid. 5) and the substantive layer(s) informing the political space are treated as a latent variable. An example of a successful tool adopting an unsupervised approach is the Wordfish algorithm, which locates political parties on a political unidimensional space according to their relative use of words with respect to that made by other parties (Slapin and Proksch 2008). In this case then, the political space will move along a left/right continuum, but these two categories are defined as such only for their spatial connotation and no longer have an ideological one. In this respect it is not that information about the drivers of political contention are not given; they are inferred from the word distribution across parties on the left and on the right of the spatial continuum. Of course, even this approach is not immune from shortcomings. For instance, its results are entirely driven by the features of a given party system at a given time, it does not allow for cross-country comparisons and it leaves to the single researcher the determination of the nature of political contention.

Nonethless, the unsupervised appraoch appears to be suitable for the study of the party ststems in 2011/2012 Tunisia and Egypt. It so not only because CMP left/right categories are not applicable to these cases, but also because of the absence of reference categories valid for enhancing our comprehension of party systems across the MENA region. The literature in fact is still divided in the determination of the political cleavages driving political competition in the MENA region, and of course this indecision characterizes the study of the transitional party systems in Tunisia and Egypt. For some, the left/right political cleavage in Tunisia and Egpyt (as elsewhere in the MENA) is supplanted by a religious/secular one (Aydogan 2020; Çarkoğlu, Krouwel, and Yıldırım 2018). For others, the religious/secular divide conceals a divide between opponents (the Islamists) and supporters of the authoritarian status quo (the secularists) (Lust 2011), a centre-periphery rift (Van Hamme, Gana, and Maher 2014; Gana and Maher 2014), or a class divide (Elsayyad and Hanafy 2014; Merone 2015). As the impossibility of solving this puzzle is due in large part to the lack of data providing for knowledge accumulation and systematization, the use of the Wordfish algorithm on the electoral programs presented by political parties in Tunisia and Egypt at founding elections will hopefully start to fill this gap, while advancing our understanding of the transtion processes in the two countries. In this latter regard, Wordfish perfectly suits the agency-based approach here adopted to understand polarization, in that it assumes that party manifestos embody overall party ideology resulting from the bargain and the strategic choices of political parties' elites (Proksch and Slapin 2014; Slapin and Proksch 2008).

Measuring polarization in 2011/2012 Tunisia and Egypt

Wordfish is a scaling method for estimating parties' positions on a political space that relies on a "bag of words approach" according to which documents are treated as input and broken into words, which constitute the real data grounding text analysis, regardless of their order or context. From this, Wordfish assumes that the use of some words but not others in party manifestos contributes to discover parties' positioning on a political space without defining it *a priori*. Instead, this might be inferred at a later stage by looking at the estimated words' parameter. This characteristic makes Wordfish particularly appealing for having an idea of the political space in Tunisia and Egypt because, as saw earlier, we are left indeed with little authoritative guidance in assessing what political competition is really about. To define the political space and locate political parties in it, Wordfish relies on a scaling model whereby words distribution is assumed to follow a Poisson naïve Bayes distribution, formally put as:

$$y_{ijt} \sim Poisson(\lambda_{ijt})$$

$$\lambda_{ijt} = exp(\alpha_{it} + \psi_j + \beta_j * \omega_{it})$$

where y_{ijt} is the count of word j in a party i's manifesto at a time t. From this model, the placement of a political party within a political space at a specific time is a function of party elections' fixed effect (α_{it}), word's fixed effects, (ψ_j) and the specific weight β_j that a word has in discriminating between party i's manifesto positions at a time t (ω_{it}).

In estimating the model (for more details see Slapin and Proksch 2008), Wordfish then returns two sets of results. The first is is about the estimates of political parties' positioning on the latent dimension. The second consists in the parameters accounting for the role each word has in determining parties' placement within the political space. On the one hand, words' fixed effects are deemed to "capture the fact that some words are used much more often than other words by all parties" (ibid. 709). On the other hand, words' weights highlight which words were crucial in discriminating parties' positioning. While Wordfish proves really useful in placing political parties on a political space over time, in our case only one electoral race is considered, so party-election fixed effects and party position across time will be constant. Henceforth, the function to be here estimated becomes:

$$\lambda_{ij} = exp(\psi_j + \beta_j * \omega_i)$$

Party manifestos as data

The data are of course constituted by the party manifestos in Arabic collected during field research or through political parties' official websites. Because in both countries several political parties did not publish an electoral manifesto, the criterion followed has been that of using only those of parties that gained at least ten seats in parliament. By so doing, this allows to cover 50% and 80% of parliamentary seats in Tunisia and Egypt respectively, while also surveying more parties than are effective parliamentary ones (4,6 in Tunisia and 1,9 in Egypt).[1] In Tunisia the surveyed parties are Ennahda, the Congress for Republic (CPR), the Progressive Democratic Party (PDP), Ettakatol, and Aridha Chaabia, while for Egypt the selected manifestos are those of the Freedom and Justice Party (FJP), Nour, the Building and Development Party (BD), the Socialist Democratic Party (SPD), the Free Egyptians, and of the New Wafd party. Not only are there parties that gained more seats and are therefore representative of parliaments' political composition, but these are also the most important parties as far as the contemporary political history of Tunisia and Egypt is concerned.

Ennahda is the main Islamist party in Tunisia. In its earlier incarnation as the Movement of the Islamist Tendency (MTI, from its French acronym), it was invited to partake in the 1989 elections in the wake of Ben Ali's attempt at giving the Tunisian regime a more democratic appeal through the reconciliation with opposition parties after a period of repression and political ban. Yet, the party was immediately outlawed after its impressive results at the polls and its members were forced to operate underground or go into exile. After the fall of the regime, the party was legalized in March 2011 and at the founding elections of the same year it became the leading party gaining 34.81% of the vote. The CPR arose from civil society associationism inasmuch as it was founded in 2001 by Moncef Marzouki, the leader of the Tunisian League for Human Rights (LTDH) and future interim president of Tunisia during the transition (2011–4). Outlawed the following year, the CPR remained active from abroad and was legalized again in 2011. It received the 8.19% of votes in the October elections. For its attention to human rights, gender equality and the provision of constitutional guarantees along with a focus on social equality and reconciliation of the different souls of *Tunisianité* (Marzouki 2009), the party is considered as occupying the center-left of the political space. Ettakatol (also known as the Forum Démocratique pour le Travail et les Libertés, FDTL) is a social democratic party founded in 1994 but officially recognized only in 2004. Having failed to win any seats under Ben Ali, the party won 6.63% of votes at the 2011 elections, in third place. It subsequently entered in coalition with Ennahda and the CPR, forming what is known as the Troika government, which drove the Tunisian transition until 2013. The PDP, founded (with the name of Progressive Socialist Rally) in 1983 but legally recognized only in 1988 (and renamed as Progressive Democratic Party in 2001), was one of the few legalized opposition parties under Ben Ali and, at that time, was considered the major left-secular political force. At the 2011 elections the PDP gained a meagre 3.73% that pushed it to launch a new political initiative to counterbalance the power of the Troika parties. This resulted in the creation of the centrist and liberal Republican Party. The other party included in the analysis is Aridha Chaabia (also known as Popular Petition or al-Aridha), which was formed after the fall of Ben Ali's regime under the impulse of Mohamed Hechimi Hamdi, a media tycoon. Thanks to its populist program, which envisaged, among others, the provision of material goods to those in need, and to the fact that Hamdi was a native of Sidi Bouzid, the poor internal governorate where the revolt first erupted, Aridha Chaabia scored a surprising 6.63% at the 2011 elections, thus becoming the fourth largest party of Tunisia. Yet, shortly after, the parliamentary and electoral strength of party began to fade and in 2013 Aridha Chaabia became the current of Love, but the change did not stop its declining trend and the party is now at the margins of the political scene.

As for the Egyptian political scene, the Freedom and Justice Party (FJP) was the major Islamist party. Formally constituted in 2011 after the fall of Mubarak, the FJP is the political arm of the Muslim Brotherhood (MB), which has been a potent political force since the 1970s. Even if it never established an independent political party, the MB had controlled independent candidates, sometimes from within the ranks of other parties, since the late 1970s. At the founding elections the FJP, which led the Democratic Alliance electoral list, gained 36.6% of the vote becoming the leading Egyptian party and securing 213 seats out of 508 at the lower house. The Nour party is the largest Egyptian Salafi party and in 2011 it headed the Islamic Alliance electoral list, which included several parties adhering to Salafism. To the surprise of many, Nour secured 27.8% of votes and was the second most voted party, controlling 108 parliamentary seats at the lower chamber. The Building and Development party, which also ran with the Islamic Alliance, traces its origin in the militant organization of the Islamic Group, embodying a more radical (and Jihadist) view of Salafism. The BD managed to win 13 parliamentary seats. On the other side of the political spectrum, the Socialist Democratic Party (SPD) is a secular and leftist formation. Formally founded in 2011, the SPD includes several groups sharing a liberal and social democratic outlook. These groups had been politically active in the years preceding the revolution and came from different experiences ranging from formal politics (like for instance the Social Democratic Party) to civil society associations (like ElBaradei's National Association for Change), to new forms of activated citizenship (like the Revolution's Youth Coalition). The party headed the Egyptian Bloc electoral coalition which had the objective of counterbalancing the strength of political Islam, but it gained only 16 seats. Also running with the secular Egyptian Bloc was the Free Egyptians party which obtained 15 seats. Finally, there is the New Wafd Party, which was established in 1973 with the aim of reviving the old Wafd Party, banned after the 1952 revolution. The New Wafd claims to be a nationalist and liberal party located at center of the political space and advocates the separation between religion and state. In the post-Mubarak elections, the New Wafd emerged as the third most voted political party and gained 38 parliamentary seats.

Each document of party manifesto produced by these parties has followed a pre-processing that consisted in cleaning the text from useless elements. This procedure is very common in text analysis (Krippendorff 2013) and is aimed at retaining only what is strictly necessary by getting rid of numbers, punctuation, and so on. For the same reason, words are usually processed so as to reduce them to their roots through the stemming process. For some languages, such as English, German, Italian, these procedures are very accurate. However, the stemming for the Arabic language is 'not a solved problem' (Nielsen 2013, 111) yet because it is a highly inflected language with a high rate of infixing. Contrary to most common languages, the same roots may then have very different meanings not only depending on the prefix or suffix, but also on a single letter within the word itself (which is for instance the case for plurals or active forms). Following a rather conservative approach, the stemming package used here is the 'arabicStemR' recently developed for R users by Richard Nielsen. Given below is an example of how it works (Table 5.1).

Results

After having preprocessed the relevant texts, the Wordfish model algorithm is applied in the two countries separately. As reported in Figure 5.1, in both countries, Islamist parties, namely Nour, Wasat, Building and Development party, FJP in Egypt, and Ennahda in Tunisia, fall on the left side of the political spectrum, while more secular parties occupy the other extreme of the political spectrum. In Egypt, the right side of the political space is occupied by the Social Democratic Party and right/secular parties occupy the center. In Tunisia, Ennahda is isolated on the left side of the spectrum, while the PDP is located in the center and on the other extreme there are Ettakatol, CPR, and Aridha Chaabia.

Parties' distribution along the political space seems to suggest that the left–right political space is the product of the religious-secular cleavage. In order give

Table 5.1 Stemming process with arabicStemR

Original text	الثورة باسم الديمقراطية
	The revolution in name of democracy
Stemmed text	ثور ديمقراط
	Revolution democracy

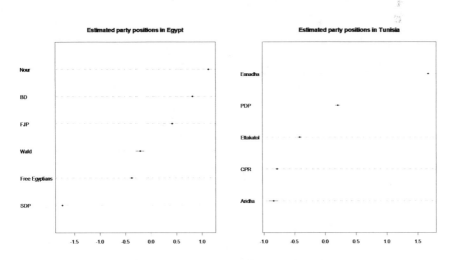

Figure 5.1 Estimated party positions in 2011 Egypt and Tunisia[2].

a substantive content to this political continuum and to assess what determines what is "left" and what is "right," it is then necessary to look at the estimated word parameters shown in the word plot (Figures 5.2 and 5.3). Here the words contained in the corpus made up of all the party manifestos follow an "Eiffel Tower" distribution. Words on the top-center of the plot are those with higher fixed effects but low betas because they are indifferently used from all the parties and therefore constitute the content of the center of the political space. By contrast, the words with greater weights, considered in absolute values, are those that discriminate greatly the placement of a given party in the political space (and therefore have low fixed effects). In our case, words with negative betas determine party positioning on the

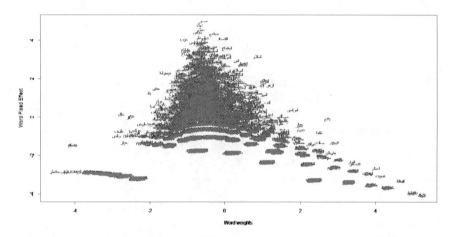

Figure 5.2 Word weights vs. word fixed effects on the Islamist/secular divide in Egypt[3].

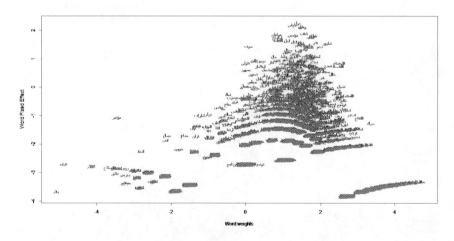

Figure 5.3 Word weights vs. word fixed effects on the Islamist/secular divide in Tunisia[4].

Left in Figure 5.1 while words with positive betas are those affecting the positioning of parties on the right side.

By looking at the word plot in Egypt – Figure 5.2 – there is a difference in the topics addressed in party manifestos and, therefore, of language. Among the words with lower betas having a role in determining parties' positioning on the Left, are "economy," "election," "activism," and "citizenship." By contrast, among the words with highest betas, that therefore are responsible for the placement of a party on the right of the political space, we find "homeland," "Hamas," and "Israel." Words with highest fixed effects, on the top-center of the word plot, and that therefore are widely used by all the Egyptian parties are, from the highest PSI's scores "Egypt," "state," "job," and "politics." Furthermore, on the center of the plot, "stability" and "change" emerge indiscriminately as major concerns of all parties along with the reference to "our identity" (yes, the stemming package sometimes fails), meaning that for Egyptian political entrepreneurs, identity politics goes hand in hand with transitional politics.

In the case of Tunisia (Figure 5.3), the words having the highest fixed effects which therefore appear more frequently with the same emphasis on all the parties' manifestos are (in order of psi values): "state," "politics" (indeed the root of the word politics), and "nation." Other words of common use (in the center) are "challenge" and "elections," which denote the awareness of the historical moment and the priorities flowing from it. Differences though emerge in the attention devoted by parties to certain issues. By looking to the beta coefficients, it emerges that parties on the left side of the spectrum devote more attention to the themes of employment and independence (from the French economy and from free market policies, but also from the political paradigms of western countries) as denoted by words "jobs" and "independence." On the other hand, among the top 50 words with positive betas there are "occupations," "exclusion," and "marginalization" denoting Ennahda's attention to the issues of social justice probably due to its entrenchment across Tunisia and especially in the poorer areas. Yet, a strong reference to the religious tradition embodied by the words "Islam," "haji," and "our identity" also emerges. Nonetheless, there has been an attempt at speaking the revolutionary jargon and reassuring the public about the party's moderation on gender issues, as is evident by the frequent use of the words "dignity" and "women" (sic for the stem).

A matter of polarization?

These analyses confirm that political competition in Tunisia and Egypt mainly appears to revolve around the religious continuum inasmuch as Islamist parties occupy one portion of the political space while the secular parties stand in the other one. Yet, an interesting finding emerges about party system polarization in the two countries that contradicts the mainstream understanding according to which the Egyptian transition failed because of the polarization of its party system while the Tunisian one succeeded because of its absence. Indeed, quite the contrary emerges from this analysis. In Tunisia, there was significant polarization insofar as Ennahda is located at one extreme of the political spectrum far away from the other parties.

In contrast, Egyptian political parties appear more homogenously distributed across the political spectrum, with only SPD distancing itself from other parties. More interestingly, the FJP is as distant from the other secular parties, namely the Wafd party and the Free Egyptians, as it is from the other Islamist parties ascribing to salafism, namely al-Nour and the Building and Development party. From this perspective then, the eventual coalition between FJP and Nour cannot be understood in pure ideological terms, as previously held, but calls into question other factors that go beyond the pure political positioning.

At the same time, these findings lead to question the main tenets (and implications) of the inclusion-moderation hypothesis inasmuch as this hypothesis (for some already a theory – for an overview see (Tepe 2019) links the moderating effects of inclusion on parties' platforms with a democratic-prone environment. In fact, the expected effects of inclusion are evident in Egypt but not in Tunisia in terms of harmonization of parties' political positioning, but they are evident in Tunisia but not in Egypt in terms of overall democratizing impact. It is so because in Tunisia, where the ideological distance among the key parties appears greater, the transition was characterized by inclusion and consensus. In Egypt, in contrast, where the ideological distance among parties is not that wide, the transition was characterized by exclusion and inability to hold dialogue. Given these findings, the remaining part of the book will be devoted to looking for alternative explanations as why FJP rejected the opportunity of becoming the pivot to the transition both in political and electoral terms and, with it, to explain why Egyptian parties' political moderation did not lead to a different direction in the process of transition.

Parties' structuring politics: the importance of the past

Formal structures, political learning, and polarization

Since parties' behavior, especially in Egypt, cannot be understood by looking only at their ideological positioning, the factors influencing their strategic choices during the transition must be found elsewhere. In constituting themselves as 'combiners' of the interplay between society and institution, thus determining both the nature and the depth, i.e. polarization, of political divisions, transitional parties play a 'signaling game' bounded by social political attitudes and previous political legacy. While some authors downplay parties' ability in mastering individual interests and values – because the conditions characterizing previous semi-authoritarianism prevented the organization of political parties by imposing on them severe limits on their activities or outlawing them (Albrecht 2010) and pushed individuals to dissimulate their preferences (Kuran 1991) – it might be interesting to look at the determining role of previous political learning in accounting for large part of parties' choices when molding the political landscape (Bermeo 1990).

Because the role of religion in politics and society has emerged during the transitions here considered as a divisive issue catalyzing the political debate, the scholarly tradition on the authoritarian resilience and the inclusion-moderation hypothesis point to both the structures and the dynamics shaping the political learning of the political parties involved in the critical phase of installation. These studies hold that the polarization of the religious divide depends on the previous relationships between religion and the state and between the state and its oppositions. For Lust (2011), whether or not undemocratic regimes of the MENA region base their legitimacy on Islam determines the secularists' perceived threat of political Islam and, therefore, the mistrust toward them eventually leading them to distance themselves from these groups. This hypothesis applies to the Muslim-majority countries, in that the inception of the 'liberalization' phase coincided with the Iranian revolution and witnessed later the civil war in Algeria. In this regard, the incentives for secularists to push in the direction of democratic reform varied, depending on whether the regime already based its legitimacy on Islam or not. In the former case, there was little fear of more room afforded to the Islamist opposition because, as far as the relations between religion and state are concerned, this was not perceived as a major change with the status quo. In contrast, when authoritarianism hinges on secular legitimation, secularists will be far more hesitant in banding together with the Islamist oppositions to advance their stances for more political openings. In this case, if these political overtures actually occur and Islamists become the major winner, the risk is that of moving away from a secular structuring of the relationship between the religion and state, thus putting the very survival of secularists in jeopardy.

Yet, religious polarization can also derive from how the regime shapes its relation with its oppositions. As seen in the previous chapter, Arab autocracies usually rely on divided structures of competition with the aim of increasing the costs of cooperation between the varying opposition groups. The mechanisms triggered by such divisions are conducive to mutual distrust, and hence, polarization around the topics through which the regime justifies the division between legal and illegal groups. In Tunisia and Egypt, up to the 1970s, the division was between parties considered 'too leftist' and acquiescent ones, but from that moment on the lines of inclusion and exclusion relied on the division between Islamists and secularist, thus polarizing the religious divide. When conflict is structured in such a manner within regimes relying on a secularly legitimated system, the effects on the polarization of the religious divide are simply magnified. As Lust (2005) notes, Islamists' illegal oppositions will try to exploit mass demonstrations organized by the legal ones so as to avoid the ax of repression. However, precisely because they were excluded from formal contestation, secular legalized opposition will be unsure about Islamists' strength and true intentions and therefore will opt to avoid any form of mass demonstration in order not to run the risk of losing their acquired privileges as a consequence of either regime repression or Islamists' takeover. At the same time, their exclusion from the formal sphere will push Islamists to radicalize their political programs and their means of contestation, thus further precluding any form of dialogue, or collaboration with other oppositions and/or dividing both fronts on the issue of whether to join forces against the regime or not (Lust 2011; Lust-Okar 2005). This reading is completely complementary to that provided by the inclusion-moderation hypothesis according to which Islamist formations will moderate their agenda, thus reducing the polarization of the overall party system, inasmuch as they are allowed to contest elections following their inclusion into the formal political sphere (Kurzman and Naqvi 2010; Schwedler 2011, 2013).

Before the transition, Tunisia and Egypt had similar formal structures of contestation. In both countries access to formal politics was granted to a limited number of secular parties, while Islamists were formally excluded. Despite the ban, in both countries Islamist parties had the chance to operate underground (as was the case of Tunisia) and even expand (as was the case of Egypt). In this latter case, Islamists had also the opportunity of contesting elections as independents and/or within larger electoral blocs. Hence, following this line of reasoning, it would be expected that during the transition the Egyptian party system is less polarized than the Tunisian one given Egyptian Islamists' longstanding participation in the electoral arena and, as such, more prone to achieve a successful democratic transition. Yet, the experiences of Egypt and Tunisia contradict the main implication of the inclusion-moderation hypothesis. In fact, the more moderate configuration of the Egyptian party system led to a military coup, while the more polarized Tunisian party system constituted the cradle of democratic installation. Such findings speak to the need of reappraising the inclusion-moderation hypothesis by going beyond the mere facts of format and mechanics of party systems and by considering also the very content upon which they build. To account for both cases where inclusion in the political sphere is not conducive to moderation and cases in which Islamists undergo an ideological revision of their stances regarding pluralism and democracy in the absence of any involvement in the formal political sphere, less configurational and more contextual explanations have been proposed by either revisiting the inclusion-moderation hypothesis or radically departing from it.

Beyond mere configurational explanations: political center and polarization

From within the inclusion-moderation paradigm, a revision has occurred around the definition of moderation. As per its most widespread formulation, moderation has been understood as "movement from a relatively closed and rigid worldview to one more open and tolerant of alternative perspectives" (Schwedler 2006, 3). From this, the very term 'moderation' has been then simply used as a substitute for 'more democratic' (Ly Netterstrøm 2015) and conceived as ancillary to that of democratization (Bermeo 1990, 1997), suffering from the normative and tautological biases often attributed to the entire stream of democratization studies (Anderson 2006; Clark 2006; Schwedler 2007; Wegner and Pellicer 2009). In fact, among the critiques moved to the inclusion-moderation hypothesis the most important has to do with the fact that it disregards the context wherein inclusion occurs. Indeed, this hypothesis has been formulated to describe and explain the behavior of communist parties in Europe after the WWII. In those cases, the inclusion of previously anti-system parties took place in consolidated democracies or ongoing consolidation following re-democratization and the norms political parties participating in political life had to come to terms with and eventually internalize were democratic ones. The longer anti-system parties were allowed to play a role in the political arena, the more they ended up accepting the rules of the game they were playing. This dynamic was deemed to have enhanced the process of democratization, or the quality of democracy, of the political systems in two respects. First, parties that initially considered (liberal) democracy as illegitimate ended up in recognizing it as 'the only game in town'. Second, the involvement in democratic systems of previously anti-system parties had the effect of integrating into such systems also the supporters of those parties, thus enhancing the consolidation of civic culture and civic societies (Merkel 1998). This is in no way the case of political systems across the Middle East and North Africa where the inclusion-moderation hypothesis has been used to explain Islamists' behavior. While it is true that allowing them to be part of the political arena has led to the abandonment of their more radical stances, it is equally true that such a shift was not always (rarely indeed) conducive to the enhancement of the democratic credentials of the political systems in which they operate.

Acknowledging the relational nature of the concept of moderation and clearly spelling out the conditions under which it can be equated with democratization can help to understand why the mainstream formulation of the inclusion-moderation falls short in accounting for the case studies at hand and, possibly, to reappraise it. For Somer, then, moderation is "an adjustment to at least some attributes of the centrein a particular country at a certain time" (2014, 246) where the center is the overall political outlook of a given country in a given time. In his words:

> I maintain that the concept of centre has three components. The political-institutional component refers to the characteristics, values and interests of the dominant state institutions and agents, and of the dominant actors in "political society", such as the main political parties. The social component involves the characteristics, values and interests of the median voters and of the dominant actors in civil society, including the main economic power holders and the intelligentsia. The international component captures the external context of moderation, and denotes the main international alliances and position of the country in global politics and economy.
>
> (2014, 248)

As the case of Turkey shows, the inclusion of Islamist movements into a given formal political sphere is not automatically conducive to their acceptance of democratic norms and values, nor it is conducive to democratization. What really matters are the effects exerted on parties' political adaptation and political learning by this complex center. As a consequence, the real gateway to democratization is not the inclusion of anti-system parties into the political competition, but rather the construction of a democratic center. This can happen through hegemony or cooperation of opposition forces. Even though this reading calls back the problem of the feasibility of cooperation highlighted by Lust and other hard-core structuralists, it nonetheless has the merit of broadening the scope of the analysis beyond the simple inclusion into electoral competition while radically narrowing the extent to which moderation is conducive to democratization by contextualizing it.

In line with the notion of 'center' but totally departing from the inclusion-moderation approach, Cavatorta and Merone (2013) argue instead that the moderating path of the Tunisian Ennahda is not to be attributed to its institutional inclusion, which never occurred, but rather to the characteristics of the Tunisian society and its political tradition. Tunisians, the authors claim, were inherently hostile to both assertive political Islam and to radicalization, their social and political culture rooted instead on the peaceful co-existence of different and varied identities under the notion of 'Tunisianité'. Therefore, they were ill-disposed toward Ennahda in the 1970s and 1980s. Confronted with its initial exclusion from both the institutional arena and broader society, the authors contend that the journey toward moderation was due to the necessity of escaping alienation and irrelevance both in society and the political arena. Contrary to the mainstream inclusion-moderation hypothesis, the push factor to moderation was not inclusion but rather exclusion. Nonetheless, according to Tepe's version of the inclusion-moderation hypothesis, Ennahda's moderation took the form of an adjustment to some attributes of the Tunisian society.

While the reference to the nature of Tunisian society in constituting the democratic center might appear only partial (or too culturalist) to confidently equate moderation with democratization, and underplay the capacity of political parties to act as countervailing mechanisms to centrifugal pushes within society (Bermeo 1990; Tepe 2013), this contribution has the merit of shifting the focus from the formal structures of competition to the informal factors triggering nonetheless moderation above and beyond them. In so doing, the authors locate the conditions making Islamists' moderation conducive to the mutual recognition and acceptance with secularist forces in "the common destiny of repression" (Cavatorta and Merone 2013, 870), which could be a fruitful point of departure to grasp cross-country differences in the degree of polarization across Tunisia and Egypt.

Divided they stood, divided they failed

If the structuring of politics is a signaling game wherein past political experiences serve as focal points, then it might be useful to look at the relationships between Islamists and secularists under the authoritarian rule. This topic is not new indeed. Attempts at coalition-building between the different oppositions have constituted the focus of several studies under the assumption that their unity would have undermined the survival of the incumbent dictators (Abdelrahman 2009; Haugbølle and Cavatorta 2011). As the following review will show, while in Tunisia attempts at coalition-building under Ben Ali were quite successful, in Mubarak's Egypt they were not. Even though this commonality speaks to the fact that dictators fall even in the absence of unified opposition front (thus suggesting that this is not a necessary condition), past records of attempts at coalition-building undertaken by different opposition groups can account for understanding the different outcomes of the transition across Tunisia and Egypt. In particular, past track records of attempts at coalition-building have repercussions on the installation phase in two respects. First, as predicted by Somer (2014), a fruitful dialogue among different political forces might enable the construction of a 'democratic center' – and such a construction might be accompanied by the fact that the parties included in the coalition- building process tend to moderate thus reducing transitional party systems' polarization. Second, and more importantly, different patterns of coalition-building are at the base of the resolution (or not) of commitment problems among the parties involved.

The different experiences across Tunisia and Egypt confirm that what indeed mattered for the success of such attempts was not only the formal division of oppositions between legal and illegal groups, but also the informal manipulation of the oppositions by the dictator. The case of Egypt exemplifies this point. On the one hand, the regime successfully co-opted legal oppositions each and every time these engaged in coalition-building with other (legal and illegal) opposition groups. On the other hand, the FJP, which enjoyed a twofold power advantage for its informal inclusion into the polity and its control of the largest part of the mobilized public, had little incentives to engage in any kind cooperation with others. First, it did not need any change in the status quo to be admitted into the political competition. Second, it regarded with increasing mistrust successful opposition movements, such as Kefaya, for they were likely to deprive its monopoly over opposition voices – and therefore it tried to undermine them. In Tunisia, by contrast, the regime rarely undermined attempts at coalition-building by inducing specific groups to break rank. Rather, it recurred to indiscriminate violence toward the entire coalition. Further, Ennahda, which was the strongest opposition group in terms of mass support, in light of its total exclusion from formal politics, needed to change the status quo if it wanted to institutionalize such power.

Coalition-building in Tunisia

Relations between Islamists and their secular counterparts have never been as hostile as some describe them (Marzouki 2009; Tamimi 2001). Indeed, Islamists' engagement in politics was partly triggered by labor protests and coincided with the birth of the Movement of Socialist Democrats (MSD) that since the beginning constituted itself as an interlocutor thus influencing the same political agenda of Islamists (Salem 2020). As mentioned already, the Islamists' awareness of social problems, and therefore the need to go beyond preaching and theological debates to make a difference for believers' lives, arose in the mid-1970s along with the labor protests of those years, which encountered Islamists' sympathy. As Ghannouchi (Ennahda's leader) said:

> The workers' revolt […] had awaken us to the importance, and to the social and economic ramifications, of the problems the workers had been complaining of. Prior to that moment, we had only been preoccupied with the issues of *da'wah* [preaching] and *tabligh* [sacred message] and with pure intellectual debate.
>
> (Tamimi 2001, 50)

Since that moment, Islamists realized that Tunisians' problems were more related to the failure of Bourguiba's economic policies and its ruling style than to a lack of piety. Ghannouchi and its clique soon felt the need to intervene in politics by proposing policy alternatives. In so doing, the impact of the Left played a role of paramount importance. Jama'a al-Islamiya, at that time the Islamists' political platform, welcomed Mestiri's initiative to found a new party and a dialogue between these two factions began. This had the effect of introducing to Islamists themes alien to them up to that moment such as political liberalism, redistribution, human rights, and democracy. The realization that the lack of democracy was the ultimate cause of Tunisia's hard times created a meeting point with some opposition movements, the ones that never proactively sided with regime's anti-Islamist campaigns. Some of these movements even manifested solidarity with the Islamists when violent waves of repression hit them. On the one hand, departing from government's rhetoric, the MSD never regarded the Islamists as threat and refused to ally with the RCD in order to form a common front against Ennahda at the 1989 general elections, the only election Ghannouchi's party was allowed to contest. On the other hand, between 1989 and 1992, during the regime's harsh repression of the Islamist movement, the Tunisian League for Human Rights, led at that time by Moncef Marzouki, the future interim president of Tunisia (2011–4) appointed by the Tunisian Constituent Assembly, defended Ennahda and firmly denounced the violations of human right perpetrated on party's members and sympathizers by the regime.

These early instances of a mutual recognition eventually led some opposition parties to genuine cooperation, if not to an alliance, as was the 2003 "Call from Tunis." On this occasion, for the very first time, Islamists and secularists signed a common document to "rally the Tunisian citizens around the democratic alternative, to which they all aspire."[5] After expressing deep concern for the current political situation, all the subscribers to this document committed to adopt a new constitution, thus establishing a political regime whose legitimation would be exclusively rotted in popular sovereignty; to guarantee freedom of belief, and to fight against the perverse effects of both globalization and subjugation of the country's economy. One year later, Ennahda, the PDP and CPR joined forces to boycott the elections and encouraged by this successful experience created, in 2005, the 18 October Coalition. This had the aim to "lay the foundations for a democratic transition and [...] build a strong civil society that is capable of withstanding and throwing back all attempts at undermining the foundations of the democratic system."[6] Worried by the escalation of repression, carried out through the 10 December 2003 Anti-Terror Law, directed against personal freedoms and freedoms of association and expression, the Tunisian Communist Labour Party, Islamists – i.e., Ennahda – and liberal parties, such as the MDS, PDP, and the CPR, joined again their forces against the authoritarian regime. At first, it was just a hunger strike for freedom of information and expression, the release of political prisoners and, the adoption of a law on a general amnesty, but later it became a permanent platform for discussion. Compared with the 2003 "Call for Tunis," the new coalition presented very few substantial differences. Most importantly, it inaugurated a new style of cooperation, based on a steady confrontation between the different factions of the coalition, under the assumption that a unifying spirit, along with the right to disagree, would better enable them face the regime. The political parties and movements participating in this coalition decided to guide their efforts in the establishment of clear political principles and political proposals, which would allow them to steer a potential transition from the incumbent authoritarian regime. The Coalition was able to survive, despite regime repression, up to the uprising, periodically gathering the different political parties, which over time discovered in each other a partner in the fight for democracy. Part of their efforts resulted in the publication of a volume from the sibylline title *Our way to democracy*, in 2010.

Coalition-building in Egypt

Relationships between Islamists and secularists in Egypt, in contrast, were not as good, nor meaningful as those of their Tunisian counterparts. Contrary to the case of Tunisia, the politicization of the Muslim Brotherhood occurred fully in 1952, when it played an active role from the ranks of the Free Officers. Probably because the quietist strategy initially adopted by the Brotherhood, in the first years of the new republic it never engaged into open criticism with it, but it nonetheless pursued political activities in competition with the Left for the support of some segments of masses, notably students and professionals. For this reason, up to the 1990s, the relationships between Islamists and secularists, in particular leftists, were quite antagonistic and two episodes are worth remembering. First, during the 1977 the labor strike, the Brotherhood sided with the regime, which ultimately repressed the protesters while blaming on leftist parties behind it. Second, the Left welcomed the initiative of the regime to intervene in trade unions' elections, with the 1993 Unified Law for unions, with the aim of containing the Islamist presence in them (Abdelrahman 2009).

Attempts at alliance-building between all the Egyptians opposition forces can be subdivided into two periods. From early 1980s to late 1990s attempts at joining forces against the regime were led by political parties pursuing grand reforms, but proved largely unfruitful. Later, from the 2000s, opposition cooperation took the form of spontaneous issued-based movements guided by the principles of consensus and independence (Abdelrahman 2009).

The first series of ventures of alliance -building were characterized by the centralism of political parties which nonetheless had to come to terms with an environment largely hostile to the organization and the proliferation of grassroots political initiatives that made them largely vulnerable to regime's mercy in order to survive. In 1983, promises of undertaking the road to pluralism and multipartyism were in fact balanced by several restrictions contained in the electoral law which nullified the introduction of a closed-list proportional system. The law in question stipulated indeed an 8% legal threshold, prevented electoral alliances between opposition parties and excluded independents from the electoral race. As we saw in the previous chapter, such provisions hampered the capacity for oppositions to gain electoral seats, either because if legalized they had few chances to go beyond the electoral threshold alone or, if illegal, they could not field independent candidates (Blaydes 2011; Masoud 2014; Posusney 2002). In light of these limitations, all opposition groups – legalized or not – joined forces to form the National Committee for the

Defense of Democracy (NCDD) with the aim of pushing the regime to return to the previous system or at least adopting an "unconditional open list proportional representation system" (Shehata 2010, 93). However, this initiative had the unintended consequence of forcing the regime's hand. Parliament was dissolved and early elections were called. In response, the members of the NCDD announced their intention to boycott elections. However, the Wafd party broke ranks and decided to participate, thus provoking the dissolution of the NCDD. The same dynamics applied both in 1986 and 1988. In both cases, the NCDD revived its activities following the constitutional court's pronouncements about the unconstitutionality of the electoral law (that regulating the 1983 elections in the first case and that regulating the 1986 elections in the second one). In both cases, parties within the NCDD saw in SCC's rulings the opportunity to make their voice heard and to finally take part in the electoral race. However, in both cases coordination failed. In the first case, Wafd disowned the pact according to which opposition leaders would have run elections under its list. In the second case, another party, namely the NPUP, decided to contravene NCDD's decision to boycott elections, this time burying the NCDD for good. Interestingly, the repetition of the same dynamics pushes Shehata (2010) to wonder with Shukr whether it was a coincidence that in each instance a party broke ranks, that same party gained a large number of seats in the upcoming elections. Another attempt for opposition parties to form a common front against the regime came under the impulse of the Committee for Coordination of Professional Syndicates in 1989. Concerned by the loss of liberty in several areas, the Committee succeeded in inviting the major political opposition forces, along with other civil society associations and NGOs, to draft shared principles and goals that would have coordinated their political conduct. In its scope and *modus operandi*, this attempt was the one which most resembles the Tunisian 18 October Coalition. After one year of discussions, this so-called National Consensus Project came up with a document very similar to the Tunisian *Our way of democracy*, asserting that pluralism, civic and political freedoms, limited government, popular legitimation, and secularism were the fundamental and guiding tenets. Agreed by the majority of participants, the draft document left Nasserists and Islamists unhappy. The first denounced the absence of specific provisions making the state responsible for national development. The second refused the principle of secularism and pushed for the insertion of a specific clause making Shari'a the principal source of legislation. None of these requests was satisfied. The two groups defected and the project of adoption of a national consensus charter collapsed. The Committee for Coordination among Political Parties and Forces (CCPPF), established in 1995, constitutes a further attempt to have Egyptian political parties partaking in shared initiatives. This drew much from both the NCDD and from the National Consensus Project. Very much like the former, it tried to coordinate parties' behavior at elections. As the latter, it had also the ambition of working out an "agreed program for political and constitutional reform" (Shehata 2010, 97). While all parties agreed to such political program, even if largely paralleling that of the national consensus project – nor shari'a neither state interventionism were mentioned – electoral coordination failed, again, both in 1997 and in 2000 ending also the experience of the CCPPF.

The new millennium saw the inception of a new phase of opposition coordination characterized by the absence of political parties, which had proved really bad at making a common front (Abdelrahman 2009; Kraetzschmar 2011). Membership within these forms of civic activism was open to individuals but not to political parties, whose members could nonetheless participate. Since these environments of activated citizenship spoke a leftist jargon and adhered to democratic, socialist and liberal principles, they were largely populated by activists coming from leftist parties. However, even the moderate Islamists parties, remarkably the FJP and Wasat, partook such initiatives through the activism of their members. By contrast, no radical religious group were involved.

Two remarkable examples of attempts at joining forces from within the civil society were the Egyptian Popular Committee for the Support of the Palestinian Intifada (EPCSPI) and the more popular Kifaya. The first, created in the aftermath of the Palestinian Intifada and still dominated by political parties, even though not officially, avoided pursuing grand political reforms and inaugurated a new form of issue-based political activism, which in this case was the affirmation of Egypt's distancing itself from Israel. Despite MB members' uneasiness in finding itself in a coalition dominated by the Left, this formula allowed the EPCSPI to survive for almost five years, up to its confluence into Kifaya. The latter directed activists' attention on internal policy issues, pushing toward greater pluralism, freedom, and democracy, but it insisted on the principles of individual membership and deliberative consensus. In light of this and of its success in gathering mass support and bringing popular activism to the masses, the major opposition parties conceived it as a competitor and were always ambivalent toward it (Shehata 2010). Yet, this hostility did not prevent Kifaya from surviving despite major internal disagreements upon its position vis à vis political Islam, which occasionally resurge.

Common destiny of repression, incentives for joining forces, and the resolution of the commitment problem

In Tunisia, opposition parties ventured into coalition-building only a few times, but they proved all, even though at varying degree, successful and instructive. After the 2011 elections, the importance of finding a "common ground" led to several debates in and out of state institutions and was also one of the grand themes of an international conference organized by Center for Study of Islam and Democracy in March 2013. In all these occasions, the spirit of the 18 October Coalition was, and still is, evoked with the hope this can be infused also into other political forces that were absent at that time, like Nidaa (CSID 2016). Even though some consider it as a political work of 'outdated history' (ibid.), and others do not see it as particularly remarkable in its political achievements (Haugbølle and Cavatorta 2011), the 18 October Coalition is nonetheless rightly considered crucial for Tunisia's democratization processes because it served as a forum for discussions, which helped secularists and Islamists to overcome their mutual mistrust. The very fact that both factions engaged on a five-years political debate whereby they agreed on a common political program largely helped them to resolve their commitment problems thus moderating the salience of religion in the aftermath of the uprisings – or at least to contain it in the framework of a political conflict inside within a democratic institutional context. In Egypt, in contrast, the many attempts at coalition-building among all opposition parties proved largely unsuccessful. The NCDD and the CCPFF failed because of parties' expectations of immediate gains, while the National Consensus project was aborted due to the lack of agreement between Islamists and seculars upon the role of religion in politics.

In looking at the two countries' party systems, the polarization in Egypt is due to the presence of more radical Islamist parties (Nour and BD) than the mainstream ones (FJP and Wasat), which never had the opportunity to moderate for they were never included in electoral competitions, nor in broader political debates, nor were they ever engaged in the several attempts at coalition-building. For some, this might be considered a sufficient to explain why the Egyptian transition aborted (Cross and Sorens 2016). However, the presence of extremist parties, yet not anti-system (Cavatorta and Resta 2020) alone cannot sufficiently account for the lack of a coalition of national unity for leading the transition, as the one formed in Tunisia by Ennahda, CPR, and Ettakatol. Indeed, as Figure 5.1 showed, the FJP, which alone controlled around 40%, was equally distant from both other Islamist parties as it was from the secular ones. Thus, ideological proximity would have allowed two kinds of coalitions. Why did the FJP then not opt for a government of national unity that would have facilitated the installation process? The answer has to do with both external opportunities and past records of confrontation with other oppositions. The availability of other strong parties belonging to the same political family made FJP's choice to coalesce with them all the more natural, even though Nour would subsequently back the military coup. Further, the FJP, contrary to Ennahda, despite its moderation, did not manage to solve its commitment problems with secular oppositions. The many attempts at coalescing have always been sabotaged by either the regime, which succeeded in coopting minor parties by promising them more seats, or by the FJP itself. Indeed, it saw in such initiatives a potential enlargement of its competitors' following risking to dip into the basin of voters it managed to secure precisely because of regime's benevolence, as the previous chapter showed. Confronted with this, not only the seculars never arrived at having a clear idea of FJP's true intentions, but the FJP itself could not credibly trust the secular oppositions in light of their past propensity to withdraw from coordination initiatives. In this regard, FJP's experience proves that moderation is not conducive to democratization unless commitment problems are solved. However, this does not only apply to religious parties, as emphasized by Kalyvas (2000) and the major part of inclusion-moderation theorists, but all parties involved in a given political system.

The fact that Tunisians succeeded where Egyptians failed does not mean that the former were simply better at compromising than the latter. Regime's strategies are crucial in this case too. While in Tunisia the regime responded with indiscriminate repression to coalition-building, in Egypt the regime remained faithful to the *divide-et-impera* strategy, or what Brumberg (2013) referred to as the regional variant of the protection-racket policy, that is the reliance of the regime on its ability to manipulate identity conflicts by playing one group against the others and to subsequently providing its protection as a guarantee for their survival. Having been socialized and politicized within such environment, Egyptian political parties replicated this behavior also during the transition, alternatively referring to the judiciary – as the secular left did – or to the military -as every party, FJP included, did during the different stages of the transition. This ultimately culminated with the call for a military coup from the vast majority of the political parties against the Muslim Brothers, which was not perceived by its opponents, as it was, just a political adversary but rather as a menace to their existence precisely because this is the way Egyptian political parties were used (and induced) to think about each other's.

Notes

1 The number of relevant parties is calculated as follow: $N = \dfrac{1}{\sum_{i=1}^{n} p_i^2}$ where p represents the proportion of seats gained by each party (Laakso and Taagepera 1979).
2 Appeared in Valeria Resta (2022) "The 'myth of moderation' following the Arab Uprisings: polarization in Tunisia and Egypt's founding elections" *British Journal of Middle Eastern Studies*. DOI: 10.1080/13530194.2021.2023353.
3 Ibid.
4 Ibid.
5 Extract from the French version of the issues Declaration. See: "Déclaration de Tunis." 17 Juin 2003, Aix-en-Provence.
6 See: "Founding Charter of the 18 October coalition."

References

Abdelrahman, Maha. 2009. "'With the Islamists?—Sometimes. With the State?—Never!' Cooperation between the Left and Islamists in Egypt." *British Journal of Middle Eastern Studies* 36 (1): 37–54. https://doi.org/10.1080/13530190902749556.
Albrecht, Holger. 2010. *Contentious Politics in the Middle East: Political Opposition under Authoritarianism*. Gainesville: University of Florida Press.
Anderson, Lisa. 2006. "Searching Where the Light Shines: Studying Democratization in the Middle East." *Annual Review of Political Science* 91 (1): 189–214.
Aydogan, Abdullah. 2020. "Party Systems and Ideological Cleavages in the Middle East and North Africa." *Party Politics*, no. November 2018: 1–13. https://doi.org/10.1177/1354068819894299.
Benoit, Kenneth, and Thomas Däubler. 2014. "Putting Text in Context : How to Estimate Better Left-Right Positions by Scaling Party Manifesto Data Using Item Response." *"Mapping Policy Preferences from Texts" Conference, May 15–16, 2014, Berlin*.
Bermeo, Nancy. 1990. "Rethinking Regime Change." *Comparative Politics* 22 (3): 359–77.
———. 1997. "Myths of Moderation: Confrontation and Conflict during Democratic Transitions." *Comparative Politics* 29 (3): 305–22.
Blaydes, Lisa. 2011. *Elections and Distributive Politics in Mubarak's Egypt*. New York: Cambridge University Press.
Brumberg, Daniel. 2013. "Transforming the Arab World's Protection-Racket Politics." *Journal of Democracy* 24 (3): 88–103. https://doi.org/10.1353/jod.2013.0042.

Çarkoğlu, Ali, André Krouwel, and Kerem Yıldırım. 2018. "Party Competition in the Middle East: Spatial Competition in the Post-Arab Spring Era." *Https://Doi.Org/10.1080/13530194.2018.142462*046(3):440–63.https://doi.org/10.1080/13530194.2018.1424620.

Carothers, Thomas, and Andrew O'Donohue. 2019. *Democracies Divided: The Global Challenge of Political Polarization* (pp. 1–14). Edited by Thomas Carothers and Andrew O'Donohue. Washington, DC: Brookings Institution Press.

Cavatorta, Francesco, and Fabio Merone. 2013. "Moderation through Exclusion? The Journey of the Tunisian Ennahda from Fundamentalist to Conservative Party." *Democratization* 20 (5): 857–75. https://doi.org/10.1080/13510347.2013.801255.

Cavatorta, Francesco, and Valeria Resta. 2020. "Beyond Quietism: Party Institutionalisation, Salafism, and the Economy." *Politics and Religion* 13 (4): 796–817. https://doi.org/10.1017/S1755048320000292.

Clark, Janine. 2006. "The Conditions of Islamist Moderation: Unpacking Cross-Ideological Cooperation in Jordan." *International Journal of Middle East Studies* 38 (1): 539–60. https://doi.org/10.1017/S0020743806412460.

Cross, Ester, and Jason Sorens. 2016. "Arab Spring Constitution-Making: Polarization, Exclusion, and Constraints." *Democratization* 23 (7): 1292–1312. https://doi.org/10.1080/13510347.2015.1107719.

CSID (Center for the Study of Islam and Democracy) 2016. "The Movement 18 October 2005 to 2016."

Deegan-Krause, Kevin, and Zsolt Enyedi. 2010. "Agency and the Structure of Party Competition: Alignment, Stability and the Role of Political Elites." *West European Politics* 33 (3): 686–710. https://doi.org/10.1080/01402381003654742.

Elsayyad, May, and Shima'a Hanafy. 2014. "Voting Islamist or Voting Secular? An Empirical Analysis of Voting Outcomes in Egypt's 'Arab Spring.'" *Public Choice* 160 (1–2): 109–30. https://doi.org/10.1007/s11127-014-0173-3.

Enyedi, Zsolt. 2005. "The Role of Agency in Cleavage Formation." *European Journal of Political Research* 44 (5): 697–720. https://doi.org/10.1111/j.1475-6765.2005.00244.x.

———. 2008. "The Social and Attitudinal Basis of Political Parties: Cleavage Politics Revisited." *European Review* 16 (03): 287–304. https://doi.org/10.1017/S1062798708000264.

Evans, Geoffrey, and Nan Dirk De Graaf. 2013. *Political Choice Matters: Explaining the Strength of Class and Religious Cleavages in Cross-National Perspective*. Oxford: Oxford University Press.

Haugbølle, Rikke Hostrup, and Francesco Cavatorta. 2011. "Will the Real Tunisian Opposition Please Stand Up? Opposition Coordination Failures under Authoritarian Constraints." *British Journal of Middle Eastern Studies* 38 (3): 323–41. https://doi.org/10.1080/13530194.2011.621696.

Kalyvas, Stathis N. 2000. "Commitment Problems in Emerging Democracies: The Case of Religious Parties." *Comparative Politics* 32 (4): 379–98. http://www.jstor.org/stable/422385.

Katz, Richard S. 2014. "No Man Can Serve Two Masters: Party Politicians, Party Members, Citizens and Principal-Agent Models of Democracy." *Party Politics* 20 (2): 183–93. https://doi.org/10.1177/1354068813519967.

Kitschelt, Herbert, Zdenka Mansfeldova, Radoslaw Markowski, and Gábor Tóka. 1999. *Post-Communist Party Systems: Competition, Representation and Inter-Party Cooperation*. New York: Cambridge University Press. http://www.amazon.com/dp/052165890X.

Kraetzschmar, Hendrik. 2011. "Mapping Opposition Cooperation in the Arab World: From Single-Issue Coalitions to Transnational Networks." *British Journal of Middle Eastern Studies* 38 (3): 287–302. https://doi.org/10.1080/13530194.2011.621687\r(null).

Kraetzschmar, Hendrik, and Barbara Zollner. 2020. "We Are All Wasatiyyun: The Shifting Sands of Center Positioning in Egypt's Early Post-Revolutionary Party Politics." *Middle East Critique* 29 (2): 139–58. https://doi.org/10.1080/19436149.2020.1732010.

Krippendorff, Klaus. 2013. *Content Analysis: An Introduction to Its Methodology*. Third. London: Sage Publications. http://www.sagepub.in/textbooks/Book234903.

Kuran, Timur. 1991. "Sparks and Prairie Fires : A Theory of Unanticipated Political Revolution." *Public Choice* 61 (1): 41–74.

Kurzman, Charles, and Ijlal Naqvi. 2010. "Do Muslim Vote Islamic?" *Journal of Democracy* 21 (2): 50–63.

Laakso, Markku, and Rein Taagepera. 1979. "'Effective' Number of Parties: A Measure with Application to West Europe." *Comparative Political Studies* 12 (1): 3–27.

Lesch, Ann M. 2014. "Troubled Political Transitions: Tunisia, Egypt and Libya." *Middle East Policy* 21 (1): 62–74.

Lust, Ellen. 2011. "Missing the Third Wave: Islam, Institutions, and Democracy in the Middle East." *Studies in Comparative International Development* 46 (2): 163–90. https://doi.org/10.1007/s12116-011-9086-z.

Lust-Okar, Ellen. 2005. *Structuring Conflict in the Arab World: Incumbents, Opponents, and Institutions*. Cambridge: Cambridge University Press.

Ly Netterstrøm, Kasper. 2015. "The IslamIsts' Compromise in Tunisia." *Journal of Democracy* 26 (4): 110–24. https://doi.org/10.1353/jod.2015.0055.

Mair, Peter. 2002. "Populist Democracy vs. Party Democracy." In *Democracies and the Populist Challenge*, edited by Yves Mény and Yves Suret, 81–98. Basingstoke UK: Palgrave.

Marzouki, Moncef. 2009. *Dictatuers En Soursis: Une Voie Démocratique Pour Le Monde Arabe*. Paris: Les Editions de l'Atelier.

Masoud, Tarek. 2014. *Counting Islam: Religion, Class and Elections in Egypt*. New York: Cambridge University Press.

McCoy, Jennifer, and Murat Somer. 2021. "Overcoming Polarization." *Journal of Democracy* 32 (1): 6–21.

McFaul, Michael. 2002. "The Fourth Wave of Democracy and Dictatorship: Noncooperative Transitions in ThePostcommunist World." *World Politics* 54 (2): 212–44.

Merkel, Wolfgang. 1998. "The Consolidation of Post Autocratic Democracies : A Multi Level Model." *Democratization* 3 (3): 37–41.

Merone, Fabio. 2015. "Enduring Class Struggle in Tunisia: The Fight for Identity beyond Political Islam." *British Journal of Middle Eastern Studies* 42 (1): 74–87.

Mölder, Martin. 2016. "The Validity of the RILE Left–Right Index as a Measure of Party Policy." *Party Politics* 22 (1): 37–48. https://doi.org/10.1177/1354068813509525.

Nielsen, Richard. 2013. *The Lonely Jihadist: Weak Networks and the Radicalization of Muslim Clerics*. Doctoral dissertation: University of Harvard.

Ozzano, Luca. 2013. "The Many Faces of the Political God: A Typology of Religiously Oriented Parties." *Democratization* 20 (5): 807–30. https://doi.org/10.1080/13510347.2013.801253.

Posusney, Marsha Pripstein. 2002. "Multi-Party Elections in the Arab World: Institutional Engineering and Oppositional Strategies." *Studies in Comparative International Development* 36 (4): 34–62.

Proksch, Sven-Oliver, and Jonathan B Slapin. 2014. "Ideological Clarity in Multiparty Competition : A New Measure and Test Using Election Manifestos." *British Journal of Political Science* 46 (3): 591–610. https://doi.org/10.1017/S0007123414000192.

Raymond, Christopher. 2014. "Party Agency and the Religious-Secular Cleavage in Post-Communist Countries: The Case of Romania." *Political Studies* 62 (2): 292–308. https://doi.org/10.1111/1467-9248.12061.

Salem, Maryam Ben. 2020. "'God Loves the Rich.' The Economic Policy of Ennahda: Liberalism in the Service of Social Solidarity." *Politics and Religion* 13 (4): 695–718. https://doi.org/10.1017/S1755048320000279.

Schwedler, Jillian. 2006. *Faith in Moderation: Islamist Parties in Jordan and Yemen*. New York: Cambridge University Press.

———. 2007. "Democratization, Inclusion and the Moderation of Islamist Parties." *Development* 50 (1): 56–61. https://doi.org/10.1057/palgrave.development.1100324.

———. 2011. "Can Islamists Become Moderates? Rethinking the Inclusion-Moderation Hypothesis." *World Politics* 63 (2): pp. 347–376.

———. 2013. "Islamists in Power? Inclusion, Moderation, and the Arab Uprisings." *Middle East Development Journal* 5 (1): 1350006-1-1350006–18. https://doi.org/10.1142/S1793812013500065.

Shehata, Dina. 2010. *Islamist and Secularists in Egypt: Opposition, Conflict and Cooperation*. New York: Routledge.

Slapin, Jonathan B, and Sven-Oliver Proksch. 2008. "A Scaling Model for Estimating Time-Series Positions from Texts." *American Journal of Political Science* 52 (3): 705–22. https://doi.org/10.1111/j.1540-5907.2008.00338.x.

Somer, Murat. 2014. "Moderation of Religious and Secular Politics, a Country's 'Centre' and Democratization." *Democratization* 21 (2): 244–67. https://doi.org/10.1080/13510347.2012.732069.

Tamimi, Azzam S. 2001. *Rachid Gannouchi: A Democrat within Islamism*. New York: Oxford University Press.

Tepe, Sultan. 2013. "The Perils of Polarization and Religious Parties: The Democratic Challenges of Political Fragmentation in Israel and Turkey." *Democratization* 20 (5): 831–56. https://doi.org/10.1080/13510347.2013.801254.

———. 2019. "The Inclusion-Moderation Thesis: An Overview." *Oxford Research Encyclopedia of Politics*, September. https://doi.org/10.1093/ACREFORE/9780190228637.013.788.

Van Hamme, Gilles, Alia Gana, and Ben Rebbah Maher. 2014. "Social and Socio-Territorial Electoral Base of Political Parties in Post-Revolutionary Tunisia." *The Journal of North African Studies* 19 (5): 751–69.

Wegner, Eva, and Miquel Pellicer. 2009. "Islamist Moderation without Democratization: The Coming of Age of the Moroccan Party of Justice and Development?" *Democratization* 16 (1): 157–75. https://doi.org/10.1080/13510340802575890.

Conclusions

The transition processes of Tunisia and Egypt offer a unique opportunity to contribute to the study of transitions from an authoritarian rule. On the one hand, the two cases are similar in many ways but differ in the outcome of the transition. In light of a most-similar research design, this circumstance is deemed to facilitate the search for the independent variable(s) that might explain the success of the Tunisian transition and the concomitant failure of the Egyptian one. On the other hand, and from a broader perspective, the two cases here analyzed contribute to the study of comparative politics, and in particular to the body of scholarship on democratization, with new empirics and analytical dimensions. First, they broaden the scope of existing democratization theories to the MENA region, which had not experienced sustained and widespread democratization processes before. Second, they instantiate cases of transitions from electoral authoritarianism, a type of regime never previously examined in democratization studies precisely because it is the first time that a process of transition replaces an electoral authoritarian regime. The work presented in this book is thus a way to enrich the body of scholarship on transitions from authoritarian rule while also shedding more light on the politics of the Arab MENA.

Since the first series of protests, the two countries followed more or less a similar path up to the moment when political parties took control of the transition. In Tunisia, albeit not without turmoil, they managed to agree on a set of procedural and substantive rules supporting the establishment of a new democratic regime. In Egypt, the conduct of political parties actually paved the way for the military coup that set the country back to authoritarian rule. Once elected, the parties sitting in the Egyptian Parliament and entrusted with the appointment of a Constitutional Commission were in profound disagreement on the rules guiding its composition. The Islamists (i.e. the Freedom and Justice party and Salafi parties) contended that it had to reflect the balance of power inside Parliament, while the secular front maintained it had to represent the different political sensibilities in the country. Unable to overcome this divergence through political means, the left-secular oppositions persistently resorted to judicial adjudication, which eventually led to the disbandment of the whole Parliament. In this way, the intra-parliamentary conflict among the different political forces shifted into an inter-institutional one with tremendously negative effects. To fill the legal void created by the decision of the

DOI: 10.4324/9781003269717-7

Supreme Constitutional Court, the Supreme Council of the Armed Forces assumed all legislative powers thus interfering with the development of the rule of law and, in particular, with the governing activity of elected president Mohammed Morsi. The latter soon found himself struggling against the SCAF for control of the transition, a battle he eventually lost when he was deposed through a military coup.

Parties' conduct is then at the roots of the different outcomes of the transition from authoritarian rule in Tunisia and Egypt and, for this reason, they constitute the unit of analysis of our research. To fully understand how parties could have impacted the two transition processes, a model for parties' agency in transitions from authoritarian rule has been employed. The extant models are used by transitologists to explain why and how a set of actors arrive, or not, at a compromise on the basic norms of the new political regime and conceive the aforementioned actors as having full freedom of action. From such a reading, the determinants behind the feasibility and the content of transitional pacts are actors' interests and power positions. This understanding emerged from earlier processes of transitions from authoritarianism wherein democracy was actually 'pacted' among a restricted set of nonpartisan actors between reformers and defenders of the authoritarian status quo. In the cases of Tunisia and Egypt, in contrast, the basic rules of the new democratic regime were formulated, directly as was the case for Tunisia or indirectly as happened in Egypt, by the political parties sitting inside parliaments elected through founding elections. Hence, transitologists' original conception of agency has been reappraised to better understand political parties' unique nature as intermediate and intermediary institutions. From this, the model for parties' agency in transitions from authoritarian rule elaborated in this study conceives political parties' choices in this phase as the result of pre-existent social divisions, ideological orientation, and power position. The first is the raw materials political parties' leadership have to deal with. The second is the parties' placement in the party system. The third is basically the share of parliamentary seats that parties control. As per our theoretical model then, in game-theoretical terms the failure of the transition can occur when deeply divided societies are not counterbalanced by political parties' interactions or a fair power distribution among the parties involved; when one faction is able to use its parliamentary strength to unilaterally impose its will to consolidate its power advantage; and when political polarization hampers parties' coalescence on a set of self-enforcing democratic norms.

Yet, when coming to the examination of the Tunisian and the Egyptian cases, a workable model parties' agency in transition from authoritarian rule has to account also for the fact that the political parties operating in such processes were present and active even during the previous electoral authoritarian regimes, which is something the model presented in this work allows to do. From this perspective, the choice to focus on political parties proves to be a particularly good one not only for its adherence to the empirics but also for its usefulness in combining into a unified theoretical framework the insights stemming from the paradigms of democratization and post-democratization studies. In this respect, social divisions might be drawn and exacerbated by autocrats' protection-racket policies while parties' transitional power distribution might have its roots in the previous institutional context providing for an unfair playing field for the different opposition movements. In the same vein, parties' ideological orientation, or better, the way political parties' entrepreneurs decide to structure the political debate, might be influenced by authoritarian learning, that is the way they were used to politicking under the previous electoral authoritarianism, which we know to be characterized by the demonization of political adversaries and the concomitant search of dictator's benevolence. Moving from this theoretical framework, the empirical investigation proceeded along the aforementioned determinants of political parties' agency.

The focus on pre-existent social divisions is due to the assumption that parties might be somewhat responsive to the demands of their electorate. In this regard, deeply divided societies are deemed to hinder democratic installations, which largely coincide with the process of constitution-making, in light of the need for a "pre-constitutional societal consensus regarding shared norms and values that underpin the state" (Lerner 2011, 27), or what has been alternatively referred to as the sentiment of national unity (Rustow 1970) or some set of shared beliefs (Elster 1995; Higley and Burton 1989). From this understanding, the analysis of the determinants of voting behavior at the 2011–2 founding elections in Tunisia and Egypt is aimed at looking for possible cleavages, understood as forms of closure of social relationships (Bartolini and Mair 1990, 216). A cleavage so defined is then the result of the overlap of the socio/economic conditions of individuals, their beliefs, and political preferences, but also of the organization through which they socialize. Each of these levels has been then considered both separately and in conjunction with the others through a multinomial model on survey data provided by the Arab Barometer project. This analysis has revealed that the religious divide stemming from the elections in Tunisia and Egypt was not really a genuine cleavage because it was solely confined to the role individuals ascribe to religion in law-making. Interestingly enough, such a normative orientation, and with it vote intention, is correlated also to mosque attendance. This finding suggests that the political division in Tunisia and Egypt was arguably driven by organizational intermediaries, corroborating Masoud's (2014) hypothesis that the strength of Islamist parties is to be found in their capacities of infiltrating pre-existing religious networks, like the mosques and other organizations somewhat linked to the religious milieu. More generally, such a result also consolidates the saliency of intermediation recently developed to account for voting behavior in other parts of the world (Gunther, Montero, and Puhle 2007).

The scrutiny of parties' power positions has revolved around the causes of Islamists' power advantage over leftist and secular parties in both Tunisia and Egypt, notwithstanding the different electoral systems in use. For different reasons, Islamists' parliamentary dominance in Egypt was deemed responsible for the failure of the transition. Yet, the Egyptian scenario differs from the Tunisian one only in its magnitude, but not in the content and conceals an apparent paradox. In demanding dignity, work, and democracy, protesters taking to the streets in late 2010 and early 2011 were motivated by left-inspired issues and spoke a leftist jargon. More than that, on the eve of the founding elections, the primary concern of citizens was the economy. Yet, only a few weeks later the role of religion in the political sphere animated the electoral campaigns and Islamist parties gained impressive victories, thus assuming the control of the processes of transition they did nothing to bring about. At the heart of this puzzling "electoral gap," lies the management of political competition on the part of the previous dictators. The division between legal and illegal oppositions along with the concomitant recourse to violence – engineered with the scope of preventing the unification of oppositions by increasing the costs of cooperation – benefited Islamists while at the same heavily undermining its rivals, in particular the Left. First, the division between legal and illegal oppositions, which largely overlapped with the division between secular and Islamist oppositions, allowed the co-optation of the seculars while leaving Islamists at the margins of the formal structures of political participation, even though in some cases they ran in elections as independents. This had the twofold effect of depicting the Left as part of the system, inducing to the disaffection of its voters and its fragmentation into a myriad of small parties, while rewarding Islamists with reputational benefits. Second, the use of repression proved more effective in jeopardizing leftists' channels of mobilization than Islamists' ones. It was so both because the constituencies of the Left largely overlapped with those the regimes wanted to secure to stay in power, but also because the natural channels of leftist mobilization, such as trade unions, universities, and poorer areas, were much more institutionalized and easily recognizable than those infiltrated by Islamists, like charitable associations, health-care centers, and places of religious proselytism. As a result, during the last thirty years of authoritarian rule, the partisan Left almost disappeared, while Islamists, at times enjoying the benevolence of the regime to counterbalancing the Left, controlled a 'parallel sector'. This double advantage created by the previous authoritarian structures is at the heart of the electoral gap characterizing the 2011 founding elections in both countries. One the one hand, thanks to their embeddedness in religious organizations, Islamist parties outperformed the Left in reaching voters who might have otherwise preferred a leftist option that they actually did not know existed. On the other hand, Islamists' formal state of illegality during the authoritarian era rewarded them with the reputation of the only true alternative to the previous regime. This magnitude of Islamists' power advantage was greater in Egypt than in Tunisia because while in the latter case the Islamists were banned and repressed, in Egypt they were formally banned but allowed to participate in the political sphere as independent candidates or from within the ranks of other parties, thus having the opportunity to develop their political organizations and institutionalize.

Readings pointing to the power advantage of Islamist parties as the cause of the failed Egyptian transitions fail nonetheless to acknowledge that even from the ranks of the Islamist faction no party controlled the absolute majority of seats and a governmental coalition was needed to rule. In this regard, the appraisal of party-system polarization is necessary to investigate whether at the heart of the Egyptian failure and the concomitant Tunisian success lies parties' ideological positioning. Following earlier accounts, we expected to find greater polarization between the Islamists and the other parties in Egypt, whence the FJP coalition with al-Nour and the inability of the fronts to dialogue, than in Tunisia, where indeed we expected to find no significant political distance among the transitional parties. To test these hypotheses, we availed of a scaling method for estimating political parties' positioning in accordance to the party manifestos they produced for the founding elections. Contrary to our expectations, the results showed that political distance was greater between Ennahda and its left/secular counterparts than between the FJP and its competitors. More precisely, the FJP, which occupied the center of the political space, was as distant from the other Salafi parties as it was from the secular ones. From this perspective, what hampered the FJP to push forward an inclusionary and consensual transition of the kind of the Tunisian one was not polarization, but rather the absence of common ground with the other political forces. In this case too, the explanation of this inability to dialogue finds its roots in how competition was structured under the previous dictatorship, and in particular in the content of politics in post-populist authoritarian contexts. Dictators accepting to open up their polities to new contenders, even if only superficially, structured political competition along identity lines. Identity is a formidable tool to drive political conflicts because is a malleable concept and as such can be manipulated to divide the opposition and weaken some political forces depending on the circumstances. At the same time, identity provides a never-ending source of legitimation to incumbents inasmuch as it allows them to be the ultimate broker of dispersed identity conflicts in what Brumberg named the "Arab world's protection-racket politics" (2013). Political parties, like the FJP and many others, operating under the previous authoritarianism continued to play politics around identity issues, as they were used to do under electoral authoritarianism by means of political learning. Hence, it is not surprising that, even if ideologically proximate, Egyptian political parties proved unable to overcome their differences (Resta 2019). In this sense, the case of Egypt corroborates the findings in the literature on the pernicious effects of identity politics over democratization processes (Bâli and Lerner 2017; Rustow 1970). In Tunisia, such a phenomenon was less visible because the majority of the relevant political parties during the transition were those that were banned under the previous regime. Such common destiny of repression can be deemed to be at the roots of fruitful coalition-building against Ben Ali that allowed political parties to solve their mutual problems of credible commitment which, in turn, is at the heart of the Tunisian success. In contrast, attempts at coalition-building under Mubarak were all unsuccessful. First, the parties that participated were all coopted by the regime. Second, the political arm of the MB from which the FJP derives, had no incentive in joining forces with other parties because its informal participation in elections granted by the regime allowed it to share the spoils of power from within the institutions while, at the same time, monopolizing the opposition front. Hence, the difference between the inclusionary and consensual Tunisian transition and the exclusionary and non-consensual Egyptian one is not attributable to the degree of polarization but rather to cross-country differences in previous experiences of coalition-building and political learning. This latter finding necessitates a reappraisal of the inclusion-moderation hypothesis according to which the inclusion of anti-system parties, like the Islamists initially were, in the electoral arena fosters their moderation thus contributing to the democratization of the political system. The inclusion of Islamist parties in the previous electoral authoritarianism in Egypt is arguably at the roots of their moderation in terms of harmonization of their agenda with the one of the other parties, as their positioning indicates. Yet, this is not conducive to a democratizing environment, but, quite on the contrary, it just denotes parties' adaptation to the previous regime through political learning. In this vein, Egyptians parties' positioning along identity issues in occasion of the founding elections (Resta 2019) speaks to the fact that the lesson has been digested, but with noxious effects for the process of transition. In Tunisia, in contrast, political polarization was greater but the parties involved in the process of transition were almost all banned and repressed during the authoritarian period and, probably because of this, enjoyed a track record of coalition-building, which allowed them to overcome their political distance, thus easing the process of pact-making that led to the adoption of a democratic constitution in January 2014.

Adopting a transitology approach, this work has ended up highlighting the importance of the structures underpinning the previous authoritarianism regime. Even though the process of political transition, defined as the interval between one regime and another, has been portrayed as the phase in which "anything can happen" to underline its volatility, the transition processes of Tunisia and Egypt suggest a more path dependent reading. Contrary to the transition processes of the Third Wave that inform the literature on transitology and democratization, like for instance those of Western Europe following the turmoil of the WWII, or those of Latin America after the collapse of military dictatorships, or even those of Eastern Europe moving away from a one-party regime, the processes of transition in Tunisia and Egypt took place against a background of electoral authoritarianisms. The hallmark of such kind of regimes is the presence of nominal democratic institutions, like parliaments, elections, and political pluralism. Hence, contrary to the "*tabula rasa*" assumption informing large part of transitology, political parties are not the result of the liberalization brought about by the transition but are already in place and are the key players of the transition itself.

In this way then, political parties are at once the key players for a new democratic regime to see the light, but also the carriers of the legacy of the authoritarian rule that has just come to an end both through their passive and active role. On the one hand, they transpose the uneven playing field characterizing electoral authoritarianism in the new regime through their unbalanced power relations. Parties' strength at the time of the founding elections is much more the result of decades of the uneven structures of opportunity available to political parties than the real expression of the demand of representation. On the other hand, they inevitably re-enact authoritarian politicking through political (and authoritarian) learning. Simply put, even during the transition from authoritarian rule, political parties' entrepreneurs continue to structure the political debate in the way they used to do in the past for it is the one they have internalized.

Seen in this light, the different outcomes of the transition in Tunisia and Egypt owes in large part to the rate of turnover of political parties (and their leaders, of course) with respect to the previous regime. While in Tunisia the major parties involved in the transition were all banned and repressed by Ben Ali, in Egypt they were in large part imported from Mubarak's times, even though in some cases under a different party label. Hence, they just continued to play the game they had been playing up to the transition. The hallmark of such a game was the predominance of identity issues coupled with the demonization of political adversaries and the cherishing of arbiters' protection. From this perspective, another difference that distinguishes the two processes of transition is the availability of such arbiters. In Tunisia nobody could take control of the transition and/or act as a watchdog and so it was necessary to devolve the designing of the transitional roadmap to a series of collegial bodies – eventually embodied by High Authority for the Achievement of the Revolution objectives, Political Reform, and Democratic Transition – composed of personalities issued from civil society and parties that had opposed Ben Ali. Once the functions of the Authority were exhausted, parties found themselves alone in the management of the transition and were thus obliged to find a solution to the 2013 political crisis within the boundaries of party politics. In Egypt, in contrast, the SCAF could count on its legitimacy to take control of the transition since its inception. In the beginning it decided the transitional roadmap, then it also arrogated itself the power to take initiatives whenever the transition would, in its eyes, stray or undermine Egypt's integrity. This eventually ended with the military coup. Not only, in so doing, the SCAF was almost unchallenged (with the exception, at a later stage, of few political forces, first and foremost the FJP), but its intervention was even encouraged and welcomed. Yet, while the SCAF was the most important arbiter of the Egyptian transition, it was not alone. The judiciary, notably Supreme Constitutional Court, played as well an important role out of parties' incapability to resolve a political matter through political means and, in so doing, opened the door to the inter-institutional conflict that culminated with the SCAF's military coup. Of course, counterfactual analysis is not a viable option, yet one might wonder whether the absence of such arbiters on the Egyptian panorama would have encouraged political parties to search a dialogue.

These theoretical insights build on new data that make up an important part of the empirical contribution of this work. The use of party manifestos to infer parties' policy positions has no precedent in the realm of the study of Arab Politics, even after five years since the dissemination of the first results of this work through seminars, conferences, and journal articles. With the exception of Charles Kurzman's datasets on Islamist parties' manifestos, political parties' electoral programs across the Arab MENA region are just off the radar of comparative politics and Arab Politics altogether. The reasons behind this are manifold. The region in question is the least democratic region in the world and political parties, elsewhere considered the anchors of democracy, are thus deemed too weak and too irrelevant to deserve a literature on their own. Yet, an emerging body of scholarship has shown how political parties, from all political families, are worth investigating even in this region for the functions they perform, which of course might differ from the ones parties perform in consolidated democracies, and for what they can tell us about the features of the regimes wherein they operate and, more broadly, about MENA politics (Aydogan 2020; Cavatorta and Storm 2018). A second set of reasons, related to the poor democratic credentials of the region, pertains to the difficulties of collecting party manifestos across the MENA region. Because of the presence of networks of kinship, patronage, and clientelism, the programmatic party–voter relation is not the central and the idea of the relevance of the electoral program is still to be consolidated in the region. In some cases, party manifestos are available only in a paperback format and research trips are needed; in other cases, they consist of a one-page document inducing researchers to ponder whether the research enterprise is worth it; in some other cases, political parties do not even produce their party manifestos. Another set of reasons why parties' platforms in the Arab region are disregarded has to do with the bias surrounding the region. In fact, in the field of comparative politics, there is the tendency to consider the MENA region as somewhat 'exceptional'. Of course, there is some truth in this awkward distinction: the MENA region turned to religion in a world that seemed to secularize and fortify its undemocratic governance in a democratizing world. Yet, such a bias reflected itself in a methodological gap inasmuch as students of comparative politics and regional experts gave up on appraising the MENA region with the same toolkits for the analysis adopted elsewhere in the world and to insert the study of the MENA region in a more general theoretical framework. Hence, while the Comparative Manifesto Project gained increasing popularity and more refined techniques for expert surveys were implemented, scholars regarded political parties in the Arab region as irrelevant even if elections and multiparty competition are, since the 1970s, the hallmark of a good number of regimes in the region. The only remarkable exception to this tendency is the great attention scholars have devoted to Islamist parties, but which ended up in reinforcing the idea of exceptionalism surrounding the region.

Against this background, this work has shown the merits of working with party manifestos and of producing parties' positions estimates that allow us to better understand the dynamics informing the processes of transitions in Tunisia and Egypt and, also, to reappraise some of the mainstream theoretical frameworks in use to understand democratizations and party politics in post-electoral authoritarian settings. From such a standpoint, the techniques of analysis employed here constitute the first step in bridging the methodological gap that affects the study of Arab Politics with regard to the rest of the world and placing it under the umbrella of comparative politics. To do so, the future research agenda needs to be guided by the necessity of data collection and systematization of our knowledge. If, for instance, we were able to collect data over a reasonable span of time across the electoral authoritarianisms of the region we would be able to appraise for instance how parties belonging to the same political family behave from country to country; how political parties orient their political offer from one election to the other; how party politics is evolving, thus looking for the causes of the changes taking place. We still know too little about political parties in the region and findings are almost exclusively confined to single case studies or comparisons among parties of the same political families in two or small-n countries, thus making it hard to produce midrange theories. As this book goes to press, only another study has ventured in such an enterprise availing itself of expert surveys (Aydogan 2020). Aydogan's study is an important step not only for our understanding of the region (also because, by chance, it serves as external validation to some of the results here presented) but also for the future of the discipline. By opening the 'old toolkit' of political science and, at the same time, recurring to the new methods and techniques of analysis in the field of comparative politics, we can be better able to make the study of Arab politics less parochial and more integrated in mainstream comparative politics. To venture in such a research agenda we need to start approaching Arab politics as just politics.

References

Aydogan, Abdullah. 2020. "Party Systems and Ideological Cleavages in the Middle East and North Africa." *Party Politics*, no. November 2018: 1–13. https://doi.org/10.1177/1354068819894299.

Bâli, Aslı Ü., and Hanna Lerner. 2017. "Design in Constitutions in Religiously Divided Societies." In *Constitution Writing, Religion and Democracy*, edited by Aslı Ü. Bâli and Hanna Lerner, 373–96. Cambridge: Cambridge University Press.

Bartolini, Stefano, and Peter Mair. 1990. *Identity, Competition and Electoral Availability: The Stabilisation of European Electorates 1885-1985*. Cambridge: Cambridge University Press.

Brumberg, Daniel. 2013. "Transforming the Arab World's Protection-Racket Politics." *Journal of Democracy* 24 (3): 88–103. https://doi.org/10.1353/jod.2013.0042.

Cavatorta, Francesco, and Lise Storm. 2018. *Political Parties in the Arabic World: Continuity and Change*. Edited by Francesco Cavatorta and Lise Storm. Edinburgh: Edinburgh University Press.

Hinnebusch, Raymond, Francesco Cavatorta and Lise Storm. 2021. Political parties in the MENA: an Introduction p.1-13. *Routledge Handbook on Political Parties in the Middle East and North Africa*. Edited by Francesco Cavatorta, Lise Storm, and Valeria Resta. Abingdon, Oxon: Routledge.

Elster, Jon. 1995. "Forces and Mechanisms in the Constitution-Making Process." *Duke Law Journal* 45 (2): 364–96.

Gunther, Richard, José Ramón Montero, and Hans-Jürgen Puhle. 2007. *Democracy, Intermediation, and Voting on Four Continents*. Edited by Richard Gunther, José Ramón Montero, and Hans-Jürgen Puhle. Oxford: Oxford University Press.

Higley, John, and Michael G. Burton. 1989. "The Elite Variable in Democratic Transitions and Breakdowns." *American Sociological Review* 54 (1): 17–32. https://repositories.lib.utexas.edu/handle/2152/10296.

Lerner, Hanna. 2011. *Making Constitutions in Deeply Divided Societies*. Cambridge: Cambridge University Press.

Masoud, Tarek. 2014. *Counting Islam: Religion, Class and Elections in Egypt*. New York: Cambridge University Press.

Resta, Valeria. 2019. "The Effect of Electoral Autocracy in Egypt's Failed Transition: A Party Politics Perspective." *Italian Political Science Review/Rivista Italiana Di Scienza Politica* 49 (2): 157–73. https://doi.org/10.1017/ipo.2019.6.

Rustow, Dankwart A. 1970. "Transition to Democracy: Toward a Dynamic Model." *Comparative Politics* 2 (3): 337–63.

Appendix

Table A.1 Variables' construction for the vote choice models

Variable	ABII question	Coding
House income	Q1016: Which of these statements comes closest to describing your household income?	1 = our household income does not cover our expenses and we face significant difficulties in meeting our needs 2 = our household income does not cover our expenses and we face some difficulties in meeting our needs 3 = our household income covers our expenses without notable difficulties 4 = our household income covers our expenses well and we are able to save
Schooling years	Q1003: Level of education	0 = illiterate/no formal education 6 = elementary level 9 = preparatory/basic 13 = secondary level 16 = BA degree 18 = MA and above
Urban/Rural	Q13: Urban/Rural	0 = urban 1 = rural
Marginalized	*Q1: Province/Governorate/State*	*0 = favored areas* Tunisia *Tunis; Ariana; Manouba; Nabeul; Zaghouan; Bizerte; Sousse; Monastir; Mahdia* Egypt *Cairo; Alexandria; Port Said; Suez; Damietta* *1 = marginalized areas* Tunisia *Beja; Jendouba; Kef; Siliana; Kairouan; Kasserine; Sidi Bouzid; Gafsa; Touzeur; Qbli; Qabs; Medenine; Tataouine* Egypt *Dakahlia; East; Qaliubiya; Kafr el-Sheikh; Western; Menoufia; Beheira; Ismailia; Giza; Beni Suef; Fayoum; Minya; Assiut; Sohag; Qena; Aswan*

(*Continued*)

Table A.1 (Continued)

Variable	ABII question	Coding
Self-definition of religiosity	Q609: Generally speaking, would you describe yourself as…?	1 = not religious 2 = somewhat religious 3 = religious
Cultural conservatism	Q60101–Q60116: Questions regarding individual attitude toward gender equality	Continuous variable from 1 to 4 (whereby conservatism increases)
Suitability of democracy	Q512: To what extent do you think democracy is appropriate for your country?	Ordinal variable from 1 to 10 (increasing suitability)
State preference	EG815/T917: Do you prefer that the state be…?	1 = civil state 2 = religious state
Islamic law	Q6052: The government and parliament should enact laws in accordance with Islamic law.	1 = strongly disagree 2 = disagree 3 = agree 4 = strongly agree
Popular will	Q6051: The government and parliament should enact laws in accordance with the people's wishes.	1 = strongly disagree 2 = disagree 3 = agree 4 = strongly agree
Trust in institutions	Q2012: trust in the judiciary Q2014: trust in the police Q2018: trust in the SCAF	1 = absolutely don't trust 2 = trust to a limited extent 3 = trust to a medium extent 4 = trust to a great extent
Mosque attendance	Q6105: Do you attend Friday services?	1 = never 2 = sometimes 3 = most of the time 4 = always
Trade Union Membership	Q5013: Are you a member of a professional association/trade union?	0 = no 1 = yes

Table A.2 Variables' construction for detecting leftist orientations

Variable	ABII question	Coding
Pluralism	Q5181: How suitable is for your country a parliamentary system wherein all parties can contest elections?	1 = not suitable at all 2 = somewhat suitable 3 = suitable 4 = very suitable
Redistribution	Q2061 What is the most important challenge facing your country today?	1 = economic redistribution 2 = fight against corruption 3 = stability and internal democracy 4 = others 5 = don't know
Secularism	Q6052; Q6061–Q6064: Questions related to the source of law and the role of religion in politics	Index from 1 to 4 (as resulting from a factor analysis on a polychoric correlation matrix)
Gender equality	Q6012–Q6014: Questions regarding individual attitudes toward gender equality	Index from 1 to 4 (as resulting from a factor analysis on a polychoric correlation matrix)

Index

14th January Front 14
18 October Coalition 124, 126–27, 129

agency, definition of 45; agency of political parties 41–45; agency within transitions to democracy 36–40, 43, 45, 134
al-Aridha 113; *see also* Aridha Chaabia
Al-Sadat, Anwar 25, 89–91, 92, 97, 99
Aridha Chaabia 113–15
authoritarian legacy 6, 45–49, 87–92, 118–20
authoritarian resilience 9, 13, 30

Belaïd, Chockri 18
Ben Achour Commission *see* Higher Reform Political Commission
Ben Ali, Zine al-Abidine 13–15, 94–97
Ben Jaafar, Mustapha 1, 13, 16, 19
Bourguiba, Habib 59, 93–96
Brahmi, Mohamed 1, 13, 19
Building and Development Party (BD) 24, 61, 113–15

Call for Tunis 124
commitment, problems of credible 127–29
Committee for Coordination among Political Parties and Forces (CCPPF) 126
competition 7, 8, 22, 54–49; structures of – in authoritarian settings 99–102; political-in authoritarian settings 87–92
Congress for Republic (CPR) 15–17, 60, 110
Constituent Assembly: in Egypt 20, 22–27; in Tunisia (ANC) 1, 13–16, 60
coordination 38, 40, 84, 126–20

demand of representation 43–44, 55–75, 80, 138
Democratic Alliance 24, 114
Democratic Constitutional Rally (RCD) 14
Democratic Forum for Labour and Liberties (Ettakatol) 16, 46, 60–61, 79, 113, 115, 128
democratization 4, 46, 58, 90, 100, 110, 120–23, 133–34; paradigm of – 3, 9, 30, 138; process of – 36–37, 42, 109

Egyptian Popular Committee for the Support of the Palestinian Intifada (EPCSPI) 127
electoral system 26, 44–45, 48, 83–84, 101, 108; in Tunisia 85; in Egypt 86, 94
Ennahda 1, 2, 8, 13, 14, 16–19, 60, 61, 67, 69–70, 79, 84, 87, 95, 99, 70–86, 137
Essebsi, Béji Caïd 13, 15–16, 18
Ettajdid 13, 60, 61, 95, 99
Ettakatol *see* Democratic Forum for Labour and Liberties

Free Egyptians Party 22, 24–25, 28, 61, 114
Freedom and Justice Party (FJP) 22, 46, 61, 99, 102, 107, 113–15, 118, 123, 127–29, 136–37, 139

game theoretic model of party agency within installations 41–43
game theoretic modelling of transitions 39–45
General Union of the Tunisian workers (UGTT) 14, 19, 93

Index

Higher Committee for Political Reform 14
Higher Independent Electoral Commission (ISIE) 15–17, 19
Higher Reform Political Commission 12, 86
Hussayn al-Tantawi, Muhammad 20–21

identity issues 7–8, 55, 62, 137–39
inclusion-moderation hypothesis 9–10, 49, 107, 118–22, 137
ISIE *see* Higher Independent Electoral Commission

Jebali, Hamadi 16, 18

Kaïs Saïed 2–3
Kifaya 100, 127

Laarayedh, Ali 18

Moncef Marzouki 13, 14, 16, 19, 113, 123–24
Morsi, Mohamed 1, 20, 26–29, 134
Mubarak, Hosni 10, 20, 21, 26–28, 91–92, 97, 99, 114, 137
Muslim Brotherhood (MB) 7, 19, 21, 23, 89–92, 99, 114, 125, 127, 137
Muslim Brothers *see* Muslim Brotherhood

National Accord Conference 22
National Alliance to Support Legitimacy 29
National Committee for the Defense of Democracy (NCDD) 126, 128
National Consensus Project 126
National Constituency Assembly *see* National Constituent Assembly
National Constituent Assembly, in Tunisia (ANC) 13, 16, 18–19; in Egypt 6, 13
National Council for the Protection of the Revolution 14
National Democratic Party (NDC) 21
National Dialogue 1, 16, 19, 29
National Dialogue Quartet *see* Quartet
National League for the Protection of the Revolution 18
National order of lawyers 1, 19
National Progressive Unionist Party (NPUP) 21–22, 24–25, 37–28, 90–92, 97, 99, 126
National Salvation Front (Egypt) 28–29
National Salvation Front (Tunisia) 19

New Wafd party 21, 24, 29, 113–14
Nidaa Tounes 13, 18–19, 127
Nour Party 6, 24, 61, 99, 114–15, 118, 128, 136

opposition, division between legal and illegal ones 47, 87–89, 96–99; left opposition in Tunisia 92–95, 122–24; left opposition in Egypt 89–92, 125–27; Islamist opposition in Tunisia 92–95, 122–24; Islamist opposition in Egypt 89–92, 125–27

polarization 48, 107–10; polarization among the Tunisian oppositions 115, 123; polarization among the Egyptian oppositions 116, 125; measuring polarization 122–27; polarization and political learning 48, 118–20, 127–28
political offer 43, 101, 140
political polarization *see* polarization
political police 14
power resources 6, 30, 36, 40, 45–46, 48, 80, 95
Progressive Democratic Party (PDP) 13, 15–17, 60–61, 113, 115, 124

Quartet 19

Rachid Gannouchi 14, 60
religious divide 44, 49, 56–57, 75, 107, 119, 135
Revolutionary Youth Coalition 21–23

SCAF *see* Supreme Council of the Armed Forces
Sisi, Abdel Fattah al-1, 27, 29
social democratic party 22, 24, 28, 113–15
social divisions 43; pre-existent – 6, 35, 43–45, 75, 79, 134–35; role of 55
Supreme Constitutional Court (SCC) 21, 25–27, 134, 139
Supreme Council of the Armed Forces (SCAF) 5, 20–23, 26–30, 86, 134, 139, 143

Tagammu *see* National Progressive Unionist Party (NPUP)
Tamarrod 29

transition, definition of 36; and political elite 36–40; and political parties 41–45
Troika government 1, 16–19, 113
Tunisian General Labour Union (UGTT) 14, 19, 93
Tunisian League for the Defense of Human Rights (LTDH) 1, 19
Tunisian Union for the Industry, Commerce and Craftsmanship (UTICA) 1, 19

Tunisian Workers' Communist Party (PCOT) 14–15, 17, 60–61, 99
Tunisian Workers Party (PTT) 60

upgraded autocracy 45, 47

Virtue Party 61

Wasat 24, 46, 61, 115, 127–28